Base Ball 12

Base Ball 12

*New Research
on the Early Game*

EDITED BY DON JENSEN

McFarland & Company, Inc., Publishers

Jefferson, North Carolina

ISSN 1934-2802

ISBN (print) 978-1-4766-7473-5
ISBN (ebook) 978-1-4766-4112-6

softcover : acid free paper ∞

Back issue requests to McFarland by mail
at Box 611, Jefferson NC 28640, by phone at 800-253-2187,
by fax at 336-246-5018, or online at www.mcfarlandpub.com.

Front cover: The 1902 Oliver Typewriter baseball
team practicing at Woodstock Fairgrounds

Printed in the United States of America

McFarland & Company, Inc., Publishers
Box 611, Jefferson, North Carolina 28640
www.mcfarlandpub.com

Table of Contents

Table of Contents

Editor's Note

NOT LONG AGO I ASKED A QUESTION of a friend whose work has graced these pages, whether he thought baseball historians were running out of Deadball Era topics to cover. "No," he quickly replied, giving the obvious answer. There would always be new information coming to light and new angles to be pursued, as in any other historical endeavor. In retrospect, the question of whether the chance for further expansion of work on that era had been exhausted was my problem, not one reflecting the state of the field. As a schoolboy, I had discovered two dusty old books in my father's closet that he had purchased during World War II. The first, Harry's Grayson's *They Played the Game*, was a hagiographic, statistically inaccurate but riveting collection of profiles of mostly Deadball players. The second, John P. Carmichael's *My Greatest Day in Baseball*, was a compilation of reminiscences by the players themselves, many of whom played in that era. I read and reread them both. A few years later, I bumped into Ritter's *The Glory of Their Times*, and I was further hooked. But eventually I became dissatisfied. The world of Cobb, Speaker, Mathewson, and Lajoie, which I thought I had mastered, was not enough. I started to look further backward, to the exploits of King Kelly, Johnnie Ward, and Amos Rusie (was he faster than Walter Johnson?), and the *Sporting Life* in the Gilded Age that nourished these heroes.

As this volume of *Base Ball* demonstrates, the question to my friend was silly. There is much new that can be done to understand both eras. We begin the volume with profiles of individuals generally ignored in the current research. Veteran historian Art Ahrens leads off with an examination of Deadball pitcher Harry Coveleski, older brother of the far better-known Hall of Famer, Stanley. Both siblings were among the first Polish-American major leaguers, but Harry, an excellent pitcher at his peak, was remembered for little more than his alleged mastery over McGraw's men. Ahrens sets the record straight. Regular contributor Thomas W. Gilbert then profiles little-known Thomas Fitzgerald, a pioneer in early Philadelphia baseball and advocate of social justice. It is a remarkable story and should have been told much earlier.

Editor's Note

The estimable David Nemec recounts the career of Bill Joyce, who patrolled the infields of several clubs in the 1890s. He asks whether Joyce's fine career warrants a plaque in Cooperstown. Let the reader be the judge.

Next, we turn to our attention to four influential people off the field. Bill Lamb profiles James J. Coogan and his heiress wife, the former Harriet Gardiner Lynch, a 19th-century power couple. Coogan was a significant actor in the political and sporting life of New York City for decades, but Lamb gives Harriet her due: as titleholder of the property on which sat the Polo Grounds, Mrs. Coogan may have had even more influence over events in Giants history than her husband. David Kathman's profile of John T. Brush during the Brotherhood War shows a man far more admired than is appreciated today. Jack Bales's recounting of William Hulbert's dismantling of the Chicago Base Ball Association a generation earlier relies on important new research.

The second half of this volume includes wide ranging work that should suit any taste. Baseball in Brooklyn is the focus of articles by Brock E. Helander and Bill Scheeren. Brock looks at baseball there outside the confines of the National League after the Mutuals were expelled in 1876. Scheeren analyzes the rise of the Pirate dynasty a century ago and the simultaneous decline of the Superbas (a subject that warms the heart of this Giants fan). John Thorn, next up, offers the fascinating story of the hitherto obscure William Wood, the sportsman in New York City two centuries ago who set the stage for the rise of baseball in that city. The racist imagery of Gilded Age artist Thomas B. Worth is the subject of James E. Brunson III's provocative article. Craig G. Greenham goes north of the border to look at the state of the pastime in Canada during the Great War, while Peter Weil shows how the combination of typewriter companies and baseball was a part of the more extensive creation of an American culture in which the game became a vital part of the lives of workers. Finally, *Base Ball* regular Eric Miklich transports us back to the August 3, 1863, showdown between the Mutual Club of New York and the Atlantic Club of Brooklyn with its memorable cast of characters.

The book review section in *Base Ball* is becoming a lively place for the exchange of ideas, as I had hoped when I became editor three years ago. Stalwarts Peter Mancuso, Andrew Milner, John Rall, Bill Scheeren (again), and Chuck Wharton have mixed opinions about the latest crop of books on the early game, but who could resist a debate about McGraw or Cobb?

It is a pleasure to work with such a talented group of experts. I look forward to the next volume, already in the works.

Don Jensen

Harry Coveleski

The Life and Legend of the "Giant Killer"

ART AHRENS

At the tail end of the 1908 season, a 22-year-old Polish-American pitcher from the heart of Pennsylvania's coal mining region hurled three complete game victories over the New York Giants to all but ruin their bid for the National League flag. His name was Harry Coveleski, and his feat bestowed upon him the lifelong nickname of "Giant Killer." A disappointing 1909 season, however, resulted in his spending most of 1910 and all of the following three years back in the minor leagues. Returning to the big time in 1914 with the Detroit Tigers, Coveleski reeled off three successive 20-plus-win seasons in which he was one of the American League's most dominant pitchers, finishing in the top five in multiple categories each year. Unfortunately, the heavy workload took its toll. By late 1918, Harry was again out of the majors, this time for good. Since players of Slavic extraction were an anomaly in baseball at the time, Coveleski was the butt of much ethnicity-related ridicule during his early years in the game. Moreover, the numerous stories about his alleged phobias appear to have been, like Mark Twain's famous joke concerning the rumors of his death, "greatly exaggerated."

LEFT-HANDED PITCHER HARRY COVELESKI is generally remembered for two things: he was the older brother of Hall of Famer Stan Coveleski, and he beat the New York Giants three times in five days in late 1908 to help ruin their pennant bid. Largely forgotten is the fact that the elder Coveleski was among the most dominant hurlers in the American League for three succes-

Base Ball 12, pp. 1–26
ISSN 1934-2802 (Print) / ISSN 1934-3167 (Online)
978-1-4766-7473-5 (Print) / 978-1-4766-4112-6 (ebook)

sive years before succumbing to arm problems. He also was arguably the first Polish-American baseball star, even if somewhat briefly.

Coal Miner's Son

The fourth of five children of Polish immigrants Anthony and Ann Kowalewski, Harry Frank Kowalewski (later "Americanized" to Coveleski), was born April 23, 1886, at Shamokin, Pennsylvania, a coal-mining town about halfway between Scranton and Harrisburg. By the time he was 12 years old, Coveleski was a slate picker in the mines for $3.75 a week and was called "donkey boy" because he also drove the mine mules.[1] During his spare time, Harry pitched in sandlot ball, developing skills that would eventually liberate him from the filth, arduous labor, black lung, and possible early grave of the coal mines.

In 1907 Coveleski joined the Kane, Pennsylvania, Mountaineers of the Tri-State League for his initiation into professional baseball. He put together a 4–7 record before the financially unstable Mountaineers folded on July 16 after 17 wins and 26 losses. One of his teammates was Jake Daubert, who would become the National League batting champion in 1913 and 1914.[2] For the remainder of the year, Harry pitched for an independent team in Wildwood, New Jersey, where he made a good impression on the Philadelphia Phillies, who signed him for $250 per month on September 3, 1907.[3]

Giant Killer

Seven days later, Coveleski faced major league hitting for the first time. Facing Brooklyn at home, Harry was the second pitcher used in relief of starter and loser Lew Moren. On the mound for the last five innings, he held the Superbas to two hits and no runs in a 5–3 Phillies loss.[4] Two more bullpen appearances without a decision followed.

Coveleski finally got his first major league win in the morning game of a doubleheader against the Giants on October 5, the last day of the regular season. Again relieving Lew Moren on his home grounds, Harry took the slab to start the third inning after Moren had given up three runs the previous inning. Coveleski shut New York out for the rest of the game, scattering four hits and fanning two as the Phillies enjoyed a 7–3 comeback victory. To quote the *New York Times*, "The Giants started out like winners in the second inning, when they hit Moren hard and tallied three runs but manager (Billy) Murray took the latter out and put in the big Pole from Shamokin, Cobaleski (*sic*) and he held the Giants guessing the rest of the game. He allowed four hits in seven innings and permitted the Phillies to romp home winners."[5] For good measure, the Quakers also won the afternoon game, 3–2, George McQuillan over Christy Mathewson. Since the contests were meaningless efforts between two lame duck teams, Coveleski's performance was otherwise unnoticed. However, the misspelling of his surname would be a problem for years to come.

Harry was back with the Phillies as the 1908 season unfolded, but not for long. At Philadelphia on April 17, the visiting Giants were not very cordial to their hosts as they mopped up the floor with starter Moren, Coveleski, and Charles "Buster" Brown in a 14–2 slaughter.[6] Although all three hurlers were equally ineffective, it was a no-decision for Coveleski and Moren was charged with the loss. One horrendous outing was enough to give Coveleski a ticket back to the Tri-State League as the Phillies optioned him to Lancaster, where he switched his pitching motion from sidearm to overhand. Around the same time, Shamokin of the Atlantic League signed brother Stan, reportedly on Harry's recommendation. (Two other siblings, Frank and John also played minor league ball but would never make it to the majors.)

Harry's 22–15 showing at Lancaster earned him another trial in the City of Brotherly Love as the season was winding down. At Philadelphia on September 23, 1908, Coveleski and Jack Rowan of the Reds held each other scoreless for eight innings before Cincinnati squeezed a run across in the top of the ninth to win, 1–0.[7] On the same day at New York's Polo Grounds, Giants rookie Fred Merkle failed to touch second base as Moose McCormick scored the apparent winning run in a crucial game with the Cubs. Under an obscure and previously unenforced rule, Merkle was declared out, thereby nullifying the run. Because fans had already swarmed the field, it was impossible to resume play, and the contest was called a 1–1 tie. A few days later, National League President Harry Pulliam upheld umpire Hank O'Day's decision, adding that the game would be replayed if necessary to determine the league championship. Although no one could have foreseen it at the time, the event would become a factor in a roundabout way the legacy of young Harry Coveleski.

On September 26, Coveleski notched his first major league shutout, edging the Cardinals 1–0 at Philadelphia during the second game of a twin bill that was called due to darkness after five innings. (It had taken St. Louis 14 innings to eke out a 3–2 win in the first match.)[8] Two days later, the Giants began an eight-game series versus the Phillies, with the first four to be played at the Polo Grounds. Since the Giants had already won 11 of 14 contests with the Quakers, John McGraw's troops were licking their chops. Long since eliminated from the race, the fourth-place Phillies could look forward only to playing the role of spoilers.

When the Giants' Joe McGinnity outlasted Philadelphia, 7–6, on the 28th, followed by Christy Mathewson's 6–2 triumph in game one of a double-header the next day, it appeared to be business as usual. Then Coveleski entered the picture in what some consider the defining moment of his entire life: he slammed the door on the men of Gotham in the nightcap, 7–0. Scattering a half-dozen hits, Harry boosted his cause when his triple to lead off the sixth inning opened the door for a five-run rally to put the game out of reach. *New York Times* writer W.W. Aulick attempted to turn the loss into an ethnic slur against Coveleski's ancestry:

> More in anger than in sorrow, it has to be reported that Philadelphia sprung something yesterday. It was unpronounceable and spelled C-O-V-A-L-E-S-K-I (*sic*). It pitched and that's why we're in second place.
>
> Coveleski comes from the Warsaw team of the Polander Leaguesky.... Bar a couple of strikeouts in the course of the afternoon, this gentleman was all pitchovitch....
>
> Doggone these foreigners anyway. Why don't they confine themselves to skat or ski-balling or whatever their national game is, and leave America for the Americans?

In a parting cheap shot, the caption above the box score read, "dangers of unrestricted immigration."[9] While the long-forgotten reporter's words were likely only a crude attempt to make humor over the loss, his phraseology would be unacceptable today. For John McGraw, it was no laughing matter, as every defeat was now another nail in his team's coffin. However, when Leon Ames outdueled the Phillies' Earl Moore, 2–1, on the 30th, the Giants could breathe a bit easier. They relaxed on the train to Philadelphia.

October 1 witnessed another doubleheader, as the teams squared off at Baker Bowl, with Mathewson winning his second game of the pivotal series, 4–2, over Frank Corridon in the morning affair. Then Coveleski, pitching on one day's rest, took New York by a 6–2 margin in the afternoon. The Giants managed but four hits. Their two runs came in the sixth when Mike Donlin doubled home Buck Herzog and Moose McCormick. Even the unbylined correspondent of the *New York Times* had to admit that "Coveleski pitched superbly, holding New York to four hits, and two of these, scratches by Fred Tenney, were of the luckiest kind."[10] Once again, Harry had kept the Giants from pulling into the lead. The morning standings of October 2 showed the Giants in a virtual tie with the Cubs and the Pirates for first place. New York had a record of 94–54, while Chicago and Pittsburgh posted 95–55 each.

The Giants kept abreast with the Cubs by taking the Phillies, 7–2, October 2, but fell half a game behind the Pirates, who took the lead by beating the Cardinals twice. On October 3, the Giants took the field, only to face the now dreaded Coveleski yet a third time. Philadelphia skipper Billy Murray promised Harry a $50 bonus to pitch while McGraw countered with his undisputed ace, Mathewson.

In a well-pitched match-up on both sides, the coal miner's son outlasted New York's workhorse, 3–2, allowing six hits and driving in a run with a fifth inning single. Finally showing the effects of hurling three complete games in five days, Coveleski was just barely able to survive a shaky ninth inning. The tying run was on third base when Art Devlin fanned for the final out.[11] Harry's third victory shoved the Giants into third place. On the same day, the Pirates kept the league lead by snipping the Cardinals, 3–2, while the Cubs retained the number two spot with a 16–2 romp over the Reds.

In the meantime, Coveleski had become a hero in Chicago. The *Chicago Tribune* plastered his picture on the front page of its Sunday sports section, noting that "[i]f the Cubs should finally win that coveted piece of bunting, it will be as much due to the efforts of this youngster as to the Herculean efforts of Chance, Brown and the other local heroes."[12] Under the headline, "COVELESKI IDOL OF CHICAGO FANS," the *Chicago Daily News* crowed, "Whenever the history of the greatest fight for a baseball championship ever known is told, the name Coveleski will be heard," and that "Coveleski, for the brilliant part he has taken in the fight, will be handsomely rewarded by the Chicago players financially."[13] The paper also quoted Floyd Kroh, a freshman hurler whom the Cubs had recently purchased from Johnstown, Pennsylvania, of the Tri-State League and someone who knew Coveleski well, who said that Harry "has plenty of speed, all that a pitcher wants, and has a great curveball. His fastball has a jump on it, and his greatest asset all season at Lancaster was his control."[14] Finally, the *Daily News* added that "Coveleski never turned a hair when McGraw attempted to rattle him."[15] This statement needs to be kept in mind when evaluating later claims and events.

On Sunday, October 4, the Cubs knocked Pittsburgh out of the race with 5–2 victory over the Bucs before a then city record crowd of 30,247 at Chicago's West Side Grounds. The win guaranteed the Cubs at least a tie for first while eliminating the Pirates. The standings now read, Cubs, 98–55; Pirates, 98–56; and Giants, 95–55.

The regular season was now over for Chicago and Pittsburgh, but New York still had three games remaining against the Boston Nationals, then briefly known as the Doves. They played like doves also, as the Giants swept the series to force a replay of the disputed September 23 game. The Cubs won it, 4–2, at the Polo Grounds October 8 to reduce the Giants to also-rans. Had the Giants taken just one of the games that Coveleski pitched, the pennant would have been theirs. There would have been no replay, and "Merkle's Boner" would have been, at most, a footnote in history with Fred Merkle remembered as the fine ballplayer he was instead of by the cruel misnomer, "Bonehead." As Stan Coveleski emphasized in his interview with Lawrence Ritter for *The Glory of Their Times*, "Most people think it was Merkle (who) lost the 1908 pennant for the Giants. Well, they're wrong. It was Harry Coveleski."[16]

The Giants-Phillies series had its dark undertones as well. According to Fred Lieb and Stan Baumgartner in *The Philadelphia Phillies*, John McGraw complained, "What has Billy against me? Nobody in a tight race has a right to play favorites. It was a lousy trick of Murray pitching that young lefthander out of turn to beat us out of the pennant." Murray is said to have retorted, "He

Supplement to the NATIONAL POLICE GAZETTE, No. 1664, Saturday, July 3, 1909.

PITCHER COVALESKI.
The Crack Twirler of the Philadelphia National League Team Whose Work
in the Box Last Season Cost the Giants the Championship.

"The Giant Killer," Harry Coveleski.

won five of the games, what's he kicking about? When I found I had one man who could beat him, naturally, I used Coveleski as much as possible."[17]

If this exchange of words—cited 45 years later—was accurate, one gets the impression that McGraw expected his friends to lay down for him when their teams happened to be out of the race. In 1920, during the investigation of the Black Sox scandal, Charles "Red" Dooin, the Phillies' regular catcher in 1908, stated that several Phillies players were offered $40,000 during that series and that "the money was placed in my lap by a noted catcher of the New York Giants." According to Dooin, the men approached were Michael "Mickey" Doolan, Bill "Kitty" Bransfield, Otto Knabe, Sherry Magee, and himself.[18] Coveleski's name was not mentioned. However, Doug Myers in *Essential Cubs* (1999) claimed that Coveleski *was* propositioned, but unfortunately he did not provide any documentation supporting the accusation.[19] Even if Coveleski had been offered a bribe, it obviously did not have its desired effect. His teammates apparently all remained honest as well. Not wanting to have a second scandal on its hands, organized ball swept the Phillies-Giants controversy under the rug while concentrating solely on the Black Sox.

As soon as the Cubs defeated the Detroit Tigers in the World Series on October 14, talk began floating around that Coveleski might be pitching for Chicago in an exhibition contest to be held with Detroit at Chicago's West Side Grounds the following Sunday. This was claimed by both the *Chicago Tribune* and the *Chicago Journal*.[20] However, the *Chicago Daily News* stated: "Tigers and Cubs ball players deny that pitcher Coveleski was asked to pitch here Sunday in the game for the benefit of the World Series players."[21] While the Cubs did play three exhibitions following the World Series—two with the Tigers and another with a semipro team in Kenosha, Wisconsin, Coveleski appeared in none of them, either as a Cub or a member of the opposition. Thus, the rumor proved to be groundless. It would have been an appropriate epilogue to the season if he had put on a Cub jersey.

Even so, Coveleski was not yet out of the news. On October 20, a dispatch to the *Chicago Inter-Ocean* commented: "Shamokin, Pa., October 19—Harry Covelaski ... received a letter and a check for $50 from President William Shettsline of the Phillies today, the writer informing him that a Cub admirer of the big southpaw had handed him a check to send to Covelaski on account of showing up so well in the recent New York-Philadelphia series." Could this have been his payoff from the Cubs, by way of an intermediary? The piece went on to say that Harry had taken a job as a blacksmith's helper "in order to keep in training."[22] Even the drudgery of the blacksmith's shop was preferable to that of the coal mine.

Easily Rattled?

Sadly for Coveleski, his days as a Giant killer were numbered. However, there are conflicting stories as to how this came about, so it is difficult to separate the truth from the spurious. According to Christy Mathewson, "The club was tipped off to a certain unfortunate circumstance in the twirler's early life, which left a lasting impression on his mind. The (Giant) players never let him forget this when he was in a game and it was like constantly hitting him on a boil."[23] As Mathewson told the tale, after the 1908 season ended, a scout for the Reds named Eddie "Tacks" Ashenbach informed McGraw that Coveleski could be rattled by players imitating snare drums. It seemed that Harry had once had a crush on a girl who told him that if he wanted to keep seeing her, he would have to learn how to play a musical instrument. He tried the snare drum, failed miserably, and lost his fickle lady love. Mathewson continued:

> When Coveleski looked at McGraw coaching third base, the manager made as if to beat a snare drum and as he glanced at (coach) Latham stationed at first. "Arlie" would reply with the rat-a-tat-tat.
>
> The team on the bench sounded like a fife and drum corp. without the fifes and Coveleski got no peace ... we all knew that we had found Coveleski's "groove" with that "rat-a-tat-tat" chorus. The man who had beaten the New York club out of a pennant never won another game against the Giants.[24]

Interestingly. Matty's teammate Fred Snodgrass, interviewed decades later by Lawrence Ritter, came up with a different account of how the Giants allegedly drove Harry to distraction:

McGraw was told by a friend of his who had managed Coveleski in the minor leagues before he came up to Philadelphia, that Coveleski always carried some bologna in his back pocket and always chewed on that bologna throughout the game—and that he did this more or less secretly, maybe somewhat ashamed of his habit. It was sort of an obsession with him.

So this manager told McGraw and McGraw saw to it that some of his players would always meet Coveleski as he was going to and from the pitcher's box whenever he pitched against us. We'd stop him and say "Hey, give us some of that bologna, will you?" Well, this so upset this fellow that he couldn't pitch against us to save his life. He never beat us again, word got around the league and the other clubs started doing the same thing, and it chased him right back to the minors—*or at least that's what we Giants always claimed*[25] (emphasis mine).

Stan Coveleski vehemently denied the Snodgrass assertion, saying that:

> They say McGraw never forgave Harry for that (the three wins in 1908). A lot of nonsense. They also say that the Giants ran him out of the league the next season. Some-

thing about harmonicas or bologna or something. Supposed to have gotten Harry's goat. What a lot of bull that story. Nobody ever ran Harry out of any league. What happened is that he got hurt the next season.[26]

Obviously, both sides had an axe to grind.

Now is the time to examine what happened. Coveleski's first outing versus New York in 1909 came on May 3 at Philadelphia. Mathewson claimed that during "the first game Coveleski started against the Giants the next season there was a chorus of 'rat-a-tat-tat' from the bench," "the Giants made three runs off him (in the first inning)," and "In the fourth inning, after the game had been hopelessly lost by the Philadelphia club, Coveleski was taken out."[27]

This story is incorrect on at least two counts and probably three. Rather than surrendering three runs in the first inning and getting yanked in the fourth, Harry slapped Leon Ames, 5–1, pitching a complete game. Coveleski fanned five while the only New York hits were a double by Fred Taney and singles by George Schlei and Fred Merkle. If McGraw and his underlings were already employing the bologna tactic and/or the snare drum routine, it must not have registered on Harry. As the *New York Times* observed, "Coveleski was steady and effective in his delivery, permitting no batsmen to reach first on base on balls, although he hit one, and but three men hit safely. The Giants were practically helpless before the magnificent pitching of this Polish wonder."[28] At least they finally spelled his name correctly, at least for the time being. It thus appears that Mathewson's memory (or that of his ghostwriter) was playing tricks on him. Although it would be Coveleski's last victory over the Giants, it does diminish the criticism in some quarters that he never beat them again after 1908.

On May 17, 1909, Coveleski made his first visit to Chicago's West Side Grounds. If he hoped that the Cubs would go easy on him, he was in for a rude awakening. As Ring Lardner expounded in the *Chicago Tribune*:

> The Cubs this afternoon formally expressed their thanks to Harry Coveleski for helping them win the pennant last year by batting him off the mound in less than six innings. The champs probably were trying to show the tall Pole that he did the right thing in beating New York out of the flag by proving the Giants had absolutely no right to it, for they played with more pepper and dash than they previously had this season and trampled on the Phillies, 8 to 1.... Frank Schulte took all the pepper out of the Pole when he drove in the second run in the third inning with a long triple to left center. This tally was enough to win, but six more served the purpose of delaying the game. Another triple by Joe Tinker in the sixth was the cause of Coveleskie's retirement.[29]

The payback for 1908 was now officially over. Gratitude as always had its limitations.

Exactly one week after the loss in Chicago, the Phillies were back home facing the team whose scout had supposedly tipped John McGraw off regarding Coveleski's Achilles heel. Instead of falling apart, Coveleski held the Reds to one run and three hits in seven innings before being lifted for a pinch-hitter with the score tied. George McQuillan replaced him. Unfortunately, McQuillan yielded four runs in the ninth inning and was tagged with a 5–1 loss and Harry's excellent performance was wasted. At Cincinnati on June 19, Coveleski was even stronger, scattering three safeties and striking out six in a 2–0 complete game victory.

If Reds' scout Ashenbach possessed any "inside dope" on Coveleski's quirks, it was far from evident during these two outings. It is also highly unlikely that "Tacks" would have shared his foolproof secret with McGraw while withholding it from the club that was issuing his paychecks. By the time Mathewson's narrative was published in 1912, Ashenbach was conveniently dead.

Between his two appearances versus the Reds, Coveleski finally lost to the Giants, 3–0, at the Polo Grounds May 28 in a game that was called halfway through the seventh inning by way of darkness and looming rain. Harry's showing was credible except for the fifth inning, when he allowed all three runs on four hits and a walk. The *New York Sun* noted that "Mathewson and the Pole had a stiff duel for pitching honors except in the one inning in which McGraw's men laid the Covaleskie spectre. Each had fine control, splitting the plate in twain time and time again with hairline accuracy when three balls had been called against them."[30] The *New York World* conceded that the Giants only "poked the Pole's shoots a few times before the break came that gave them the game."[31]

The Philadelphia scribes blamed the loss more on bad luck and defensive lapses by the Phillies rather than any fault of Coveleski. According to the *Philadelphia Inquirer*:

> The hard proposition from the soft coal regions was holding his own with Matty up to this time (the fifth inning). He began the inning badly by trudging Devlin. Bridwell suicided and Arthur perched on second. He would not have reached the plate on Schlei's rap to left, which (Eddie) Grant partially blocked, but did because Magee fumbled the ball and then kicked it around. The Admiral took second while Sherwood Nottingham was abusing the sphere. Matty doubled him home and reached third on Herzog's well-trained bunt, which refused to go where Grant wanted it to—on foul territory. With the infield pulled in Doyle lined past Knabe and Matty pulled up at the plate.[32]

The *Philadelphia Record* remarked that "there might have been a different tale to tell if Harry had been properly supported,"[33] while the *Philadelphia Evening Bulletin* griped, "'Cove' was poorly supported whereas Big Six

(Mathewson) had everything."[34] Both also confirmed that "Magee began kicking the ball about the field."[35]

All the while, Mathewson had the Phillies eating out of his hand, scattering three safeties before the weather intervened. None of the above-cited dailies, nor any of the others covering the game, reported anything concerning snare drums, bologna or any other form of badgering directed at Coveleski.

With the Phillies still in New York, Coveleski next faced the Giants in the afternoon game of a May 31 doubleheader before a crowd of 35,000. Entering at the start of the fifth inning in relief of Earl Moore with the Giants ahead 3–2, Harry forced Buck Herzog to ground out to Eddie Grant at third, after which Jack Murray tripled. Art Devlin then laid down a squeeze bunt, which Coveleski fielded cleanly but heaved past catcher Red Dooin as Murray scored. Harry held the Giants scoreless after that but was not the pitcher of record. After the Phillies tied it up at four apiece in the top of the seventh, Lew Moren replaced Coveleski on the mound. With two gone in the bottom of the eighth, Christy Mathewson's home run off Moren deep into the crowd in left field put New York ahead for keeps, 5–4. According to the *New York Times*, when Matty connected for the game-winning blast, "The band at once struck up 'Dixie' and 'Marching Through Georgia.'"[36] Once again, there was no mention in the newspapers of any unusual behavior from the Giants, either while Coveleski was pitching or any other time.

Coveleski and the Giants did not meet again until July 5 at Philadelphia during the morning contest of a belated Independence Day twin bill because July 4 came on a Sunday that year. While George "Hooks" Wiltse held the Quakers to three singles, Coveleski was shaky the entire game, yielding 10 hits and four walks in a 3–0 defeat, with all the scoring coming in the fifth inning. This contest also witnessed the first documented sign that McGraw had found a sensitive nerve in Coveleski's makeup. As the *Philadelphia Inquirer* related:

> McGraw, who was coaching at third base during the (second) inning, must have hurled a few choice remarks at Coveleskie, for the latter, as soon as the inning was over, went right at McGraw in a threatening manner. Some of the Phillies, however, quickly interfered and trouble for the time being, as well as saving McGraw a licking, was averted for the moment.[37]

The confrontation was verified by the *New York Sun*, which noted that "[t]here came near to being a war between McGraw and Coveleskie in the second inning,"[38] and the *New York World*, which stated that "McGraw and Coveleskie had a run-in after the second inning.... The inning started with Murray and (Bill) O'Hara singling, but the next three men died easy deaths, which caused McGraw to say things to Coveleskie."[39] Arlie Latham,

McGraw's alleged cohort in the snare drum scheme, was not named in any of the newspaper accounts, nor was there any mention of the Giants' bench being involved. Based on available information, therefore, it appears that the tirade was instigated by McGraw alone.

Two days later, the Phillies started Harry against the visiting Giants again. It was during this game that Giants appear to have first used psychological warfare *as a team*. As the *New York Times* gleefully elaborated:

> Coveleski seemed especially nervous when facing the very men whom last year he beat out of the championship. McGraw s hitters plainly had no fear of their one-time almost invincible opponent. They grinned on him in a procession, and in processional form they went to first by the easy route....
>
> The forced runs started when a man was down in the sixth. Tenney scowled at Coveleski and the scowl had its effect, for Fred got a ticket o'leave (a walk). Next Doyle turned his gentle visage Coveleskiward. The pitcher whose name sounds as if he ought to be President of the Russian Road to Anthracite also lost his nerve to Larry and a walk resulted. McCormick adopted the same tactic, whereupon Handsome Harry also got a gift. Murray's trot pushed Tenney under the wire.
>
> That was enough for the home manager. He prescribed the rest cure for Coveleski and put Corridon in. But O'Hara and Devlin had as much patience as the big fellows, and the trudges they drew meant two more lots for their side.[40]

The six walks proved to be all the New Yorkers needed in a 3–1 victory that was handed to them. They made only three hits. The *New York Press* revealed that when the gift inning started, "From the coaching lines Manager McGraw wigwagged the signal to Fred Tenney to be patient and make Coveleski put the ball over. This Harry couldn't do."[41] The *New York Sun* described Coveleski as "wild and unsteady from the start"[42] while the *New York Tribune* noted that "the Giants were laughing in their sleeves."[43]

Even if they were reluctant to do so, the Philadelphia chroniclers were obliged to agree. Perhaps trying to soften the blow, James Isaminger in the *Philadelphia North American* spoke only in generic terms of Coveleski's "uncommon exhibition of hysteria."[44] The *Philadelphia Record* also alluded to Harry's nervousness, reporting, "Captain Doolan came in from his position more than once to give Coveleskie an opportunity to steady himself...."It also noted that the Giants "played a waiting, winning game."[45] The *Philadelphia Evening Bulletin* pulled no punches in sighing, "Coveleskie, whose work last season knocked the New Yorkers out of a pennant, has no more fear for the Giants. 'Cove the Giant Killer,' like the story relating to our friend Jack of the nursery rhyme days, is now but a dream of the past."[46] Still, it appears that the Giants got to Harry by staring him down and laughing at him rather than by imitating snare drums or talking about a certain sausage. Also, if McGraw had been cued in during the previous winter on how to make Coveleski implode on the mound, as Mathewson claimed in *Pitching in Pinch*, why did he apparently wait until midseason before putting this vital information to use? It simply does not add up.

Coveleski's next—and final—try at the Giants that season came August 18 in the morning match of a double bill at Philadelphia. Entering in the third inning in relief of Frank Corridon, Harry lasted one and two-thirds innings, giving up three hits, two walks, and a run. Since the Giants were already ahead 3–0 when Coveleski came in, he did not get the decision, as McGraw's warriors bludgeoned their way to a 14–1 win. Although the *Tribune* stated that "Coveleski came in amid cheers from the Giants," there was no other mention of harassment in the coverage of the contest. In this instance, New York did not need to engage in any shenanigans, as Coveleski had nothing on the ball to begin with.[47]

Arm Problems

Against the rest of the league, Coveleski's pitching was a mixed bag. He finished at 6–10, although his ERA (2.74) was only slightly higher than the league average (2.59). At this point it should be noted that following a 6–4 relief loss to the Cardinals on July 14, Harry made only three more appearances for the season—the game mentioned above in August, a no-decision start versus the Reds on September 3 which the Phillies eventually won, 6–5, in 13 innings, and a 5–3, complete-game win over the Doves on September 8. This would tend to support Stan Coveleski's claim that his brother had sustained an injury. Furthermore, in Harry's three unsuccessful starts against the Giants in 1909, the Phillies were shut out twice and scored only once on the other occasion. Backed up by that kind of offense, even Cy Young would have had difficulty accumulating victories.

Coveleski and Philadelphia soon parted company. On January 20, 1910, Harry and Frank Corridon were traded to Cincinnati for pitchers Bob Ewing and Ad Brennan. Reds manager Clark Griffith reportedly sought Coveleski because he needed a southpaw. However, following four appearances without a decision in which Harry walked twice as many batters as he struck out, Coveleski was optioned to Birmingham of the Southern Association on May 17. His 21–10 with the Barons earned Harry a recall to the Reds after the Southern Association season ended. Coveleski made his return a triumphant one as he fireballed his way to a career-high 12 strikeouts while limiting the Superbas to six hits in a 7–3 Reds victory at Brooklyn September 16. Five days later, he started against his old teammates at Philadelphia but was belted for five hits, three walks, and six runs in three and two-thirds innings before being sent to the showers. Luckily, he was not the losing pitcher, since the lead switched back and forth before the Phillies finally pulled ahead to a 13–11 win. Although he had gotten off the hook this time, Coveleski would not be so fortunate a week later.

The Reds and the Giants met at the Polo Grounds on September 28, 1910, as a still bitter and vindictive John McGraw thirsted for more vengeance. According to the *New York Herald*, "As Coveleskie stepped into the box, McGraw shouted, 'Come on, boys. Let's get this fellow. We owe him a few.'"[48] Whether McGraw uttered these exact words is immaterial. He might as well have done so considering the outcome.

A portent of impending doom could be sensed when Harry opened the bottom of the first inning by issuing seven straight balls. Surprisingly, Clark Griffith, usually not opposed to removing a pitcher when he was wild, "kept the left-handed wonder right in the game, forcing him to take his medicine inning after inning and he took it like a baby taking castor oil."[49] By the time the nightmare had ended, Coveleski had been hammered for 14 hits, 11 free passes, two hit batsmen and a wild pitch in a 16–4 bloodbath. The Giants stole seven bases and pitcher Otis "Doc" Crandall slammed one of Coveleski's offerings for a home run in the eighth inning for the ultimate insult.

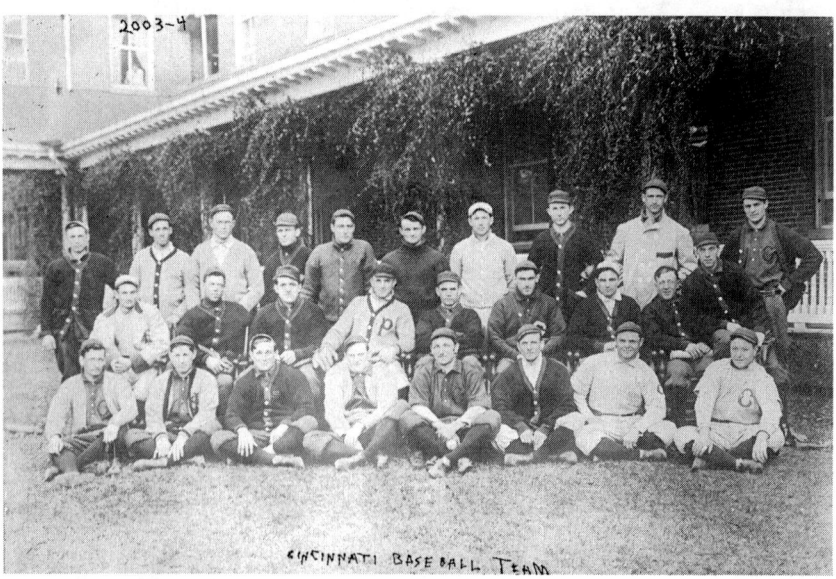

Cincinnati Reds 1910 team photograph. Harry Coveleski is at center, in a Philadelphia sweater.

All the papers concurred that the vitriol heaped upon Coveleski was immense, and a few of them added some of their own. According to the *New York Times*: "Besides the harsh baseball treatment to which he was subjected the Red twirler had to stand for considerable roasting from the Giants, who evidently have not forgotten the part 'Covie' played two years ago."[50] William F. Kirk in the *New York American* added, "The home boys laughed at Clark Griffith and kidded the life out of Coveleski. Among those present at the kidding was Jawn McGraw. He said some things to Mr. Coveleski, did Jawn Mc-Graw."[51] The *New York Sun* noted that "[t]he Reds had two men on bases (*sic*) with two out in the sixth when Coveleskie struck out for the second time and got a great laugh from McGraw."[52] The *New York Herald* account was replete with unflattering but colorful, sneering analogies. "The Pole's appearance in the pitching box was about as soothing to the Giants as a red flag is to a peevish bull.... The old enemy was as effective as a Canadian cent in a slot machine.... He was wild and besides had as little on the ball as a Salome dancer has on her feet."[53]

The reports in the Cincinnati press were equally devastating. The *Cincinnati Tribune* observed, "The big southpaw was the butt of all kinds of remarks during the afternoon, and the fans took keen enjoy(ment) in the beating he received."[54] W.A. Phelon in the *Cincinnati Times-Star*, while ignoring the Giants heckling, let loose full blast in dragging ethnic invective to a new low. Aside from verbal lampoons at "the Hurling Hun," the "Plunging Pole," and "the pitchski Kid with the steelski nerves," Phelon delivered the clincher in cackling "The pitching (?) done by Coveleski at New York Wednesday was a cross between the ravings of an intoxicated Pottawatomie and an explosion in a cheese factory."[55]

In the *Cincinnati Enquirer*, Jack Ryder penned the most thorough description of all concerning the vituperation aimed at Coveleski, either in this game or any other:

> The heartless Giants got a belated revenge on poor Harry Coveleskie.... Using every known means to rattle the big fellow, they had his goat before the game was well underway and he was a sight for a specialist on nervousness before he got through. McGraw and his men attacked him right from the jump, commencing before the game.... McGraw was always out there on the third base line informing Cove in no uncertain terms that he was a gone gosling and that every Giant would knock the cover off the ball if he would kindly get it near enough to the plate. Cove was worked up to the point where he had neither speed, curves nor control....
>
> He passed the first two men up in the opening round and that was the signal to McGraw that he could be reached by conversation. From that moment the talk never ceased for an instant. The Giant leader was foxy enough to keep fairly well within the bounds of decency, so that he could not be chased off the field.... His line of gab

was not as raw as he has sometimes handed out. It consisted of constant references to the fact that Cove could not get it over, and it would be hit into the stands if he did, together with threats as to what would happen to him if he hit any of the sacred Giant batsmen with his wide shoots…. Cove could not stand for this stuff and was a loser from the get-away. He was nervous, excited and erratic.[56]

Yet for all his meticulous attention to detail, Ryder spoke nary a syllable regarding lunch meat or musical instruments, nor did any other pundit who was on the scene.

In *Pitching in a Pinch*, Mathewson gave a reasonably accurate account of the September 28 game. However, Matty then added that "[e]ach game he started against us (with Cincinnati) he got the old 'rat-a-tat-tat.' Griffith protested to the umpires, but it is impossible to stop a thing of that sort even though the judges of play did try."[57] The use of the words "each game" implies that Coveleski had faced the Giants on multiple occasions in 1910. The September 28 debacle was the only time Coveleski pitched against New York while he was with the Reds, as well as the sole occurrence in which they humiliated him. His other six appearances were against the Cubs (April 15 and 21), the Cardinals (April 25 and May 4), the Superbas (September 16), and the Phillies (September 21).

While it is clear that the Giants did something to get under Coveleski's skin, just what that elusive something was is a bit murky. From what can be gleaned from the newspaper reports, McGraw's crew pulled such relatively pedestrian tricks as staring, laughing, disparaging Coveleski's pitching, and just waiting him out. The last could easily have been the result of detecting flaws in Harry's delivery. Although it is still possible that they engaged in snare drum mimicry as part of their repertoire, the absence of any first-hand, game day references to it cannot help but lend itself to skepticism about the claim, especially since accounts mention other forms of taunting. Fred Snodgrass's bologna tale of more than half a century later—to which Snodgrass himself attached a caveat—is probably just that. Nevertheless, such anecdotes make for juicier copy (and more book sales) than do stories of standard bench jockeying.

Truth versus mythology notwithstanding, Harry's last outing soured the Reds on him once and for all. He was demoted to the Southern Association, this time with Chattanooga. He was about to begin a purgatorial exile of three years.

As a member of the Chattanooga Lookouts in 1911, Coveleski looked like a 25-year-old has-been whose career was on the verge of extinction. He struggled to an 11–22 ledger. Apparently regaining his confidence, Harry improved to 13–15 the following year before blossoming in 1913 with a 28–9 record, seven shutouts, and a 1.44 ERA. Desperate for pitching, the Detroit Tigers purchased his contract for the next season on August 12, 1913.

Led on the diamond by the mercurial Hughie Jennings, the Tigers had gradually deteriorated after winning three straight pennants from 1907 through 1909. Although the Bengals were still competitive during the following two seasons, they sank to sixth place in 1912 and remained there the next season. In 1913 they served up the worst pitching in the American League, allowed the most runs (716), had the highest ERA (3.41), and gained the fewest shutouts (four in the league). Their record, 66–87, was the club's poorest showing since 1904. Detroit management probably felt that, if nothing else, Coveleski could not do any worse.

Comeback

If there were any naysayers around, Harry quickly made them eat their words. In his American League debut on April 17, 1914, at Detroit's Navin Field, Coveleski pitched well enough to win, but Earl Hamilton of the St. Louis Browns was a bit better, edging the Tigers, 2–1. Four days later, the Cleveland Naps (Indians) were in town, knocking Tigers rookie John Wil-

Coveleski, a Detroit mainstay, in 1914.

liams out of the box with a four-run first inning. Taking the slab to start the second frame, Coveleski dispersed six hits in holding Cleveland scoreless while Detroit rallied to win, 7–4, for Harry's first victory in the junior circuit.

By May 12, Coveleski had returned to the Polo Grounds for the first time since that fateful encounter in late 1910. This time, however, he was facing the Yankees, who were tenants of the Giants from 1913 until the opening of Yankee Stadium a decade later. Ironically, their manager was Frank Chance, who led the Cubs when Coveleski helped them win the flag six years earlier. If Harry had any misgivings about being back in New York, they soon evaporated. He handcuffed the Yankees in a four-hit 4–0 complete game triumph. The *New York Times* commented that "with the Tigers' hitting and Coveleski's pitching, the Yankees occupied precisely the same position as the rejected suitor at a wedding."[58] In the *Chicago Tribune*, Ring Lardner jested, "Harry Coveleskie shut out the Yanks and we'll bet that Frank Chance was so forgetful of past favors as to cuss him for it."[59] The victory also put the Tigers in first place with a 17–7 record. Although they would not retain the lead for long, it was a sign that their situation was already improving.

In the morning contest of a Memorial Day doubleheader at Sportsman's Park in St. Louis, Coveleski came the closest he would ever get to a no-hit game in the majors when he held the Browns to one hit in a 2–1 win. Clarence "Tilly" Walker doubled in the fifth inning, then scored on John Leary's sacrifice and third baseman George Moriarty's error on Ivan Howard's grounder as the Browns took a 1–0 lead in their sole display of offense. The Tigers took command in a two-run eighth, with Coveleski winning his own game when his Texas League single just over second base sent Moriarty across with the deciding run. The *Detroit Free Press* remarked that Harry "deserved a shutout and but for a lapse in the Detroit defense in the fifth, would have owned one … the solitary swat, though netting Clarence Walker two bases, hugged the line and one foot further to the left would have resulted in a foul ball."[60] Coveleski had missed a no-hitter by literally a matter of inches.

Coveleski's greatest sustained achievement was soon to come. After holding the Philadelphia Athletics scoreless during the final three innings of a 4–1 triumph at his home park June 7, Harry wove three consecutive shutout victories, all of which went the full nine innings as he dispatched the Red Sox 1–0 on June 12, the Yankees 3–0 on June 16, and the Senators 1–0 on June 20. He was almost as parsimonious with hits as he was with runs, granting two to Boston, four to New York, and another four to Washington. In addition, Coveleski registered one and two-thirds innings of scoreless relief in a 3–2 win over Washington on the 19th. All the games were at Detroit, so the home field advantage probably helped. Following the June 20 contest, Stanley T. Milliken of the *Washington Post* expressed grudging admiration of Harry's steadiness in pressure situations. He acknowledged that

> Coveleskie … was most effective, especially with men on base. (Eddie) Foster's triple in the opening frame with two out gave the Nationals an opportunity for a run. In every inning thereafter with the possible exception of two, the Griffmen threatened, but the punch that would turn the trick was not forthcoming…. There were two Nationals on base in the ninth when (Ray) Morgan ended the game (with a roller to Donie Bush at shortstop).[61]

Harry's string of goose eggs checked in at 31 and two-thirds with his third whitewash. It would eventually reach 34 innings before the White Sox broke the string on June 24 with one out in the third inning during a 5–2 Chicago win at Comiskey Park.

Although Coveleski would never again scale these heights, he continued to pitch solidly for the rest of the season, finishing at 22–12. He was second in the league in innings pitched (303), and complete games (23), and tied for fifth in shutouts (five). The Tigers climbed to fourth place with an 80–73 log. Had Comeback if the Year awards been around in 1914, Coveleski would have been a prime candidate for the honors. Now that Harry had established himself as a pitcher to be reckoned with, the jabs concerning his ancestry mostly came to an end.

The stories regarding his alleged phobias did not. In an apparent spinoff of his questionable aversion to snare drums, the *Washington Post* on December 13, 1914, featured an unsigned article which claimed that the Yankees had discovered they could upset Coveleski by singing "Silver Threads Among the Gold." The piece asserted:

> Just before the season closed … when the Tigers made their final appearance in New York, Coveleskie took up the pitching chores. For a few innings he performed in great style. And then (all) of a sudden there came from the Yankee bench: "Darling, I am growing old/Silver threads among the gold." Coveleskie stopped in his duties, and searched the bench with his eyes…. While Coveleskie looked, the singing ceased. When he took up pitching again it resumed. Sometimes the strains came in solo order. Then it was a duet. Now it rolled out as a chorus. The Yanks on the coaching line began to whistle it. The air became filled with music—and Coveleskie was through for the day. He went so high that Jennings feared for a time he'd never be able to recover his star hurler without the aid of an aerial scout.[62]

In his last appearance versus New York on August 29, Coveleski had indeed lost, 6–5, after having beaten the Yankees in three of four previous decisions. However, he was rocked in the early innings—one run in the first, one in the second, three in the third, and one in the fourth—not well into the game as the *Post* writeup indicated. From the fifth inning onward, Harry settled down and went the distance, but a three-run Detroit rally in the eighth fell short.

If there was any truth at all to the "Silver Threads" yarn, its efficacy was of short duration. In 1915 Coveleski reeled off five consecutive complete-game victories over the Yankees, conquering them 3–1 on May 19 at Detroit, 3–2 on June 7 at New York, 3–2 on July 13 at Detroit, 7–3 on July 27 at New York, and 6–2 on August 28 at Detroit. For an encore at the last Detroit–New York meeting of the year, September 15 at the Polo Grounds, Harry came through with a relief job that would have earned him a save today. Working the final three innings, Coveleski shut out the Yankees on two hits to preserve a 4–2 victory. As the *New York Times* mused, "(Bernie) Boland was on the verge of toppling in the seventh, but Harry Coveleskie came to the rescue and so put a damper on the Yankee enthusiasm."[63] For the season, the Tigers took 17 of 22 from the Yankees. Coveleski did not pitch in any of the losses. The silver threads had come with golden needles, and Harry was doing all the sewing.

Yet Coveleski's most memorable performance that season might have been one that he lost. At Boston's Fenway Park, September 18, Harry and Ernie Shore of the Red Sox battled to a 0–0 tie for 11½ innings before a Saturday throng of 37,528, reportedly the largest ever at the Hub up to that time. In the top of the 12th, the Tigers loaded the bases with no outs, but Shore was able to wriggle free from the jam. When the Red Sox came to bat, Duffy Lewis singled, after which Larry Gardner beat out a drag bunt. Jack Barry then moved them up with a sacrifice. Coveleski walked Forrest "Hick" Cady intentionally, hoping for an inning-ending double play. Manager Bill Carrigan, batting for Shore, knocked a bouncer to Donie Bush at shortstop, so it looked as if Detroit's strategy would pay off. However, Cady slid hard into the keystone sack, causing second baseman Ralph Young to muff Bush's relay as Lewis raced home for a 1–0 victory. Giving credit where it was due, the *Detroit Free Press* stated, "Both men worked well enough to have richly deserved victory. It was by far the most impressive performance of Coveleskie's career as a Tiger, while any man who can shut the Detroit club out for 12 innings, as Shore did today, has earned a niche in the Hall of Fame" and "When Coveleskie came to bat in the 11th inning, he was given a fine round of applause."[64]

Closing out the season at 22–13, Coveleski finished tied for the league lead in pitching appearances (50), second in games started (38) and innings pitched (313), third in wins, and fourth in strikeouts (150). Pumped up even further by George Dauss's 24 wins, Ty Cobb's ninth-straight batting title (.369) and 96 stolen bases, plus Sam Crawford's and Bobby Veach's league-high 112 RBIs apiece, the Bengals were once again a powerhouse. The team topped the American League in batting (.268), slugging (.358), runs scored (778), doubles (207), and stolen bases (241). While the Tigers gave the Red Sox stiff competition in the pennant hunt, the Bostonians ultimately won out thanks to greater pitching depth and superior defense, copping the flag with a 101–50 ledger. Detroit finished in second place at 100–54, two and one-half games behind. In so doing, the bridesmaid Tigers became the first American League team to attain 100 wins without capturing the pennant. For Hughie Jennings, it was the winningest aggregation he would ever manage, as the best showing of his champion clubs had been 98–54 in 1909.

Over the offseason, the seventh-place Indians obtained the rights to Harry's brother Stan, who had been hurling minor league ball on the West Coast with mixed success, first with Spokane of the Northwestern League (1913–14), then with Portland of the Pacific Coast League in 1915. Stan had been given a trial with the Athletics in 1912, but since Connie Mack then had pitching to spare, Stan was an unneeded commodity and was released. Like the Tigers two years before, the pitching-thin Indians had nothing to lose by hiring one of the Coveleskis.

The Tigers opened the 1916 season at Chicago April 12, with Harry Coveleski holding the White Sox to three singles en route to a 4–0 complete game win in which the Sox were "on their knees begging for their lives most of the time" and "like woolly lambs in the hands of Coveleskie," according to I.E. Sanborn of the *Chicago Tribune*.[65] Although not a heavy-hitting pitcher (Harry's lifetime average was .189), he enjoyed a perfect day at the plate, going four-for-four with two singles, a double, a triple, and a run scored. The *Detroit News* beamed, "It seldom has happened that the Tigers have shown as much satisfaction over winning an opener."[66]

By April 17, the Tigers had moved on to Cleveland, where Jennings and Indians manager Lee Fohl had scheduled Harry and Stan Coveleski to face each other in anticipation of a sellout crowd at League Park. But a complication arose when Harry refused to take the mound. In the elder Coveleski's words, "No, I won't go in. I've made good in the big league and the kid has his piece to make. I know I would be holding back if I went against him. I couldn't put my heart into an effort that might send him back to the bushes."[67]

Catering to the civic pride of his hometown readers, Henry P. Edwards of the *Cleveland Plain Dealer* put a cheerleading spin on the non-event in saying, "Brother Stan had a chip on his shoulder and dared brother Harry of the Tigers to knock it off, but brother Harry begged off, claiming he would be unable to do himself justice against a brother who was attempting to earn his baseball spurs."[68]

Jennings hurriedly pressed rookie George Cunningham into service. The freshman responded surprisingly well as he and the younger Coveleski crossed swords to a 1–1 draw for 11 innings. Stanley finally weakened in the top of the 12th as Detroit bunched five hits and two runs for a 3–1 win. When Stan struck out Ty Cobb in the first inning, he received congratulations from Harry after the side had been retired. (Cobb was not liked by most of his teammates, and it appears that Coveleski was no exception.) Ed Bang of the *Cleveland News* would prove to be prescient in forecasting, "Stanley Coveleskie, spitballer de luxe … is destined to win additional fame for the name of Coveleskie in the major leagues. He should emulate the example of Brother Harry of the Detroit Tigers and be a consistent winner."[69] Despite pressure to do so, the brothers would never pitch directly against each other.

Harry's team sputtered during the early stages of the season, but that could not be blamed on him. On May 19, Harry labored through the longest marathon of his career, a 2–2 standoff with the Yankees in New York that was halted by darkness at the end of 16 innings. After the Yankees had tied the game at two apiece in the last of the ninth, he held them hitless for the final seven rounds. Bob Shawkey of New York, who had replaced Nick Cullop after the eighth inning, was almost as stingy, limiting Detroit to three hits the rest of the way. Along with his durability. Coveleski had also become the stopper of the Tigers pitching corps. His 2–1 win over the Browns at Detroit May 7 snapped a five-game losing streak, while his 3–1 triumph against the same team at the same place May 27 put an end to an eight-game skid. Following the latter win, the Tigers found themselves in sixth place with a 14–20 log.

The Bengals ran hot and cold during the next two months before becoming ferocious at the start of August, going 35–20 for the rest of the season. In the morning game of a Labor Day doubleheader at Navin Field, September 4, 1916, fans at last got to see both Coveleskis, albeit not in the manner they would have preferred. Stan started for the Indians but was bombed out after two-thirds of an inning, surrendering five runs on four hits and two walks. In the top of the eighth, brother Harry replaced Bill James, who had relieved Tigers starter Bernie Boland the previous inning. Like his younger brother, Harry lasted only two-thirds of an inning, when a line drive off the bat of Billy Wambsganss hit him in the stomach to force an early exit. He was carried off on a stretcher. Jean Dubuc finished up as the Tigers held on to win, 7–5, then took the nightcap by an 11–8 margin. Without debating the merits of Harry and Stan, the *Cleveland Plain Dealer* merely commented, "Pitching on both sides was horrible."[70] This was the closest the brothers would ever come to an actual face-off. In mid–September, the Tigers ever so briefly grabbed the number one spot, but a three-game sweep by Boston at Detroit on September 19–21 dealt the Bengals a crippling blow. They slipped to third place, while the Red Sox again took the flag.

Winding up the campaign at 21–11. Coveleski was again one of the league's premier hurlers. He finished second in innings pitched (324), and fewest walks per nine innings (1.75), third in winning percentage (.656), fourth in ERA (1.97) and wins, and fifth in complete games (22). Continuing his dominance over the Yankees, he went 4–1 against them—the one-time Giant killer had evolved into a Yankee slayer.

Final Decline

Harry's pitching arm was burned out by the strenuous workload. During his first three years with the Tigers, Coveleski had endured a grueling 940 innings. In 1916 alone, six of his complete games had been extra-inning affairs. Sore-armed and used only intermittently, Harry tailed off to a 4–6 record in 1917 as the Tigers fell to a distant fourth despite another batting title and a 35-game hitting streak by Ty Cobb. For Coveleski, the high point of the campaign came June 29, when he savored the easiest victory of his career. Scattering four hits, he laughed his way to a 19–1 pulverizing of the Browns at St. Louis in a lark featuring home runs by Harry Heilmann and Bobby Veach, as well as five stolen bases by the Tigers. Even the light-hitting Donie Bush contributed three singles, a double, and four runs scored to the massacre. Coveleski chipped in with two singles himself and scored both times. It was his second and last complete game of the year.

In 1918 the situation became bleaker as Harry made only three appearances the entire summer. At Detroit on June 23, he took part in both ends of a doubleheader for the first time since he was with Phillies. After working the ninth inning in relief of loser Bernie Boland, Coveleski was the starter in the second game of a doubleheader. Although he managed to finish the outing, St. Louis was again victorious, 4–2.[71] This proved to be Harry's swan song. He was given his release on August 2.

Retirement

Harry Coveleski left behind a major league ledger of 81–55 with a 2.39 ERA and 13 shutouts. As he was fading from the scene, brother Stan was hitting his stride, eventually compiling 215 wins by the time he retired in 1928. Before the advent of the Perrys and the Niekros, the Coveleskis' combined 296 victories set the record for two brothers in the major leagues under the present-day pitching distance. (Unless the Mathewson brothers are included:

Christy won 373 games while brother Henry, to whom the Giants gave a brief look-see in 1906–07, won zero.) One can only speculate on the career Harry might have had with the benefits of today's sports medicine.

Following several failed comeback attempts in the lower minor leagues, Harry Coveleski worked at various times as a night watchman, policeman, and bartender in a Prohibition-era speakeasy. In 1937, four years after the repeal of Prohibition, he opened a tavern in Shamokin, regaling his customers with stories of his baseball days as he tended bar. Appropriately, the popular watering hole was named "The Giant Killer Cafe."

A diabetic for the last 10 years of his life, Coveleski suffered a cerebral hemorrhage on August 1, 1950, from which he died three days later. Survived by his wife, son, and brother Stan, he was buried at St. Stanislaus Cemetery in his hometown, His death certificate listed lists his occupation as "bartender."[72]

During a 1947 interview, Harry said that once he became successful in baseball, "I made up my mind never to look at another mine mule."[73] In keeping his promise to himself, Coveleski helped blaze the trail for later Polish-Americans in baseball, from his brother Stan, to Joe and Phil Niekro, to Carl Yastrzemski—whether or not the Giants drummed him out of the National League.

NOTES

1. Unidentified newspaper obituary in Coveleski's file, Giamatti Research Center, National Baseball Hall of Fame.

2. Ed Rose, "Pop Kelchner, Gentleman Jake, The Giant Killer and the Kane Mountaineers," SABR, *Baseball Research Journal 2012*, 47–49.

3. Rose, 47–49.

4. *New York Times*, September 11, 1907.

5. *New York Times*, October 6, 1907.

6. *New York Times*, April 18, 1908.

7. *New York Times*, September 24, 1908.

8. *New York Times*, September 27, 1908.

9. *New York Times*, September 30, 1908.

10. *New York Times*, October 2, 1908.

11. *Chicago Inter-Ocean*, October 4, 1908.

12. *Chicago Tribune*, October 4, 1908.

13. *Chicago Daily News*, October 5, 1908.

14. *Chicago Daily News*, October 5, 1908.

15. *Chicago Daily News*, October 5, 1908.

16. Lawrence Ritter, *The Glory of Their Times: The Story of the Early Days of Baseball Told by the Men Who Played It* (New York: Macmillan, 1966), 104.

17. Fred Lieb and Stan Baumgartner, *The Philadelphia Phillies* (New York: Putnam's, 1953), 80–81.

18. *New York Herald*, October 1, 1920.

19. Doug Myers, *Essential Cubs* (Contemporary Books: 1999), 248. The author fittingly called Coveleski, "An Honorary Cub."
20. *Chicago Tribune*, October 15, 1908; *Chicago Journal*, October 15, 1908.
21. *Chicago Daily News*, October 15, 1908.
22. *Chicago Inter-Ocean*, October 20, 1908.
23. Christy Mathewson, *Pitching in a Pinch* (New York: Penguin Books Reprint, 2006), 46.
24. Mathewson, 47.
25. Ritter, 101.
26. Ritter, 110.
27. Mathewson, 46–47.
28. *New York Times*, May 4, 1909.
29. *Chicago Tribune*, May 18, 1909.
30. *New York World*, May 29, 1909.
31. *Philadelphia Inquirer*, May 29, 1909.
32. *Philadelphia Inquirer*, May 29, 1909.
33. *Philadelphia Record*, May 29, 1909.
34. *Philadelphia Evening Bulletin*, May 29, 1909.
35. *Philadelphia Inquirer*, June 1, 1909.
36. *New York Times*, June 1, 1909.
37. *Philadelphia Inquirer*, July 6, 1909.
38. *New York Sun*, July 6. 1909.
39. *New York World*, July 8, 1909.
40. *New York Times*, July 8, 1909.
41. *New York Press*, July 8, 1909.
42. *New York Sun*, July 8, 1909.
43. *New York Tribune*, July 8, 1909.
44. *Philadelphia North American*, July 8, 1909.
45. *Philadelphia Record*, July 8, 1909.
46. *Philadelphia Evening Bulletin*, July 8, 1909.
47. *New York Tribune*, August 19, 1909. However, an interesting sidelight occurred in the top of the ninth inning when Arlie Latham was sent in to pinch run for the injured Bill O'Hara, who had been hit by a pitch. In the words of Harry Schumacher in the *New York Evening Mail* on August 18, 1909: "Latham took a long lead off first to draw a throw from (Phillies pitcher Bill) Foxen, and when he did (Art) Shafer scooted for home and scored, Latham reached second." The 49-year-old Latham thus became the oldest player to steal a base in the majors, and remains so as of this writing.
48. *New York Herald*, September 29, 1910.
49. *New York American*, September 29, 1910.
50. *New York Times*, September 29, 1910.
51. *New York American*, September 29, 1910.
52. *New York Sun*, September 29, 1910.
53. *New York Herald*, September 29, 1910.
54. *Cincinnati Commercial Tribune*, September 29, 1910.
55. *Cincinnati Times-Star*, September 29, 1910. Phelon was an old hand at ethnic baiting, having in earlier years zeroes in on players of French and German ancestry,
56. *Cincinnati Enquirer*, September 29, 1910.
57. Mathewson, 49.
58. *New York Times*, May 13, 1914.
59. *Chicago Tribune*, May 14, 1914.
60. *Detroit Free Press*, May 31, 1914.
61. *Washington Post*, June 21, 1914.
62. *Washington Post*, December 13, 1914.
63. *New York Times*, September 16, 1915.

64. *Detroit Free Press*, September 19, 1915.

65. *Chicago Tribune*, April 13, 1916.

66. *Detroit News*, April 13, 1916. In addition to seeing the opposing hurler leading the charge in the enemy's offense, many White Sox fans took home another unexpected keepsake, courtesy of upper management. A filler item in the *Chicago Tribune* on April 13, 1916 stated: "That handsome new coat of green and white in which Comiskey Park was clad for yesterday's opening proved expensive. Not enough time was allowed for the color schemists to dry all the paint. As a result, many a male suit and female gown carried away souvenirs of the occasion in spots of green picked up from the refurbished furniture. This raised the estimate of the original cost by considerable (*sic*). The worst of it was that the undried paint concealed itself foxily under the slate of the chairs or on the under side of railings where its presence was unsuspected until too late." Whether or not the club reimbursed the painted patrons for their ruined clothing is unknown.

67. *Chicago Tribune*, April 13, 1916.

68. *Cleveland Plain Dealer*, April 18, 1919.

69. *Cleveland News*, April 18, 1916.

70. *Cleveland Plain Dealer*, September 5, 1916.

71. *Chicago Tribune,* June 24, 1918. Coveleski had previously made relief appearances in both games of a doubleheader versus Boston, July 3, 1909. Philadelphia won the first game, 7–6. But lost the second, 4–0. Coveleki earned a relief win in the morning contest and did not get the decision in the nightcap.

72. Unidentified newspaper obituary in Coveleski's file, Giamatti Research Center, National Baseball Hall of Fame.

73. *Washington Post*, January 6, 1947.

Editor's Note: At places in the article where contemporaneous reportage is quoted, our subject's surname is spelled *Coveleskie*. This spelling was commonplace during the playing careers of both Harry and Stan Coveleski.

Colonel Fitzgerald of Philadelphia

Baseball Apostle and Closet New Yorker

Thomas W. Gilbert

*Baseball, of course, began as the "New York game," one of several re-
gional American bat-and-ball folk games. The reason that baseball went
national and eclipsed the homegrown pastimes of Boston, Philadelphia
and elsewhere had nothing to do with any inherent superiority of the
game as played. What distinguished baseball was the ambition of those
who played the game to establish it as America's first national sport. In
the 1850s and 1860s, the baseball men of New York realized that ambition by exporting and marketing their game to the rest of the country.
Philadelphia, the home of town ball, was the first major urban domino
to fall, thanks in part to transplanted New Yorker Thomas Fitzgerald.
This paper discusses the underrated role played by Fitzgerald in Philadelphia's conversion from town ball to baseball, and Fitzgerald's central
role in the racial and ethical controversies that roiled the amateur game
in the post–Civil War years. It also offers new research into Fitzgerald's
life story, particularly his little-known childhood and youth—and its rel-
evance to this key chapter in the story of the spread of baseball.*

THE GRAND THEME OF BASEBALL's Amateur Era is how baseball, an ancient
folk game played only in New York, metastasized into America's first national
sport, ultimately driving cricket and other bat and ball games into extinction.

Baseball's victory was sudden and decisive. When the first general meeting of baseball clubs was held in 1857, all the sixteen attendees were from in or
around New York City and Brooklyn. Only ten years later, there were thriving
baseball clubs in thousands of American cities and towns, and calling base-

Base Ball 12, pp. 27–51
ISSN 1934-2802 (Print) / ISSN 1934-3167 (Online)
978-1-4766-7473-5 (Print) / 978-1-4766-4112-6 (ebook)

BASE-BALL MATCH BETWEEN THE "ATHLETICS", OF PHILADELPHIA, PA., AND THE "ATLANTICS," OF

Above and facing page: The October 30, 1865, game at Philadelphia's Camac's Woods between the Atlantics of Brooklyn and the Athletics of Philadelphia. Brooklyn won, 21–15. The Atlantics clinched the national championship with a 27–24 victory over the Athletics in November. Note the fistfight between spectators in the foreground (Library of Congress).

ball the "National Pastime" was a cliché. The game travelled outward from New York by different routes and in different ways, but the most common way was with New Yorkers themselves. Dozens of the earliest clubs in New Jersey, upstate New York, Connecticut, Washington, D.C., and Massachusetts were founded by amateur baseball players from New York City or Brooklyn who had gone there to do business, serve in the military, attend school or for other non-baseball reasons.

The Athletics Switch Sides

Philadelphia was a necessary conquest. Baseball aimed to be a national sport, but America's second-largest city had a bat and ball game of its own, town ball, that was a potential rival to New York's baseball. (Both cities had cricket clubs, but that sport's foreign origins disqualified it as a national

BROOKLYN, N. Y., PLAYED AT PHILADELPHIA, October 30, 1865.—Sketched by J. B. Beale.—[See Page 730.]

sport in nativist 19th-century America). In 1860, the Philadelphia Athletics dropped town ball in favor of the New York game. They were not the first or only Philadelphia club to make the switch, but they were the most important. The Athletics became baseball's most valuable ally in Philadelphia because of their social influence and because they quickly achieved competitive parity with the top New York and Brooklyn clubs.

Why did the Athletics so readily convert to baseball? There is a clue in their leadership. The Athletics' most important member was Colonel Thomas Fitzgerald. (He was given the honorary rank for non-military contributions to the Unionist cause in the Civil War.) Fitzgerald was not a front-line player. Well past his athletic prime in the 1860s, he was the club's chief executive and president from 1861 to 1866, the period when, under his guiding hand, the club grew into a national baseball power.

Thomas Fitzgerald was not a native Philadelphian. He came to Philadelphia as an adult, and likely brought with him some knowledge and experience of the game. Fitzgerald said remarkably little about his life before 1844, when he came to Philadelphia in his mid–20s. Some baseball histories mention that he was born in New York City in 1819, but few connect this fact to baseball's conquest of Philadelphia. And none gives a full account of Fitzgerald's background and early life.

The Self-Invented Thomas Fitzgerald

A successful newspaperman who had married into a respectable Philadelphia family, Thomas Fitzgerald was the kind of influential figure that baseball enthusiasts were looking for in order to promote the game. Baseball's movers and shakers warmly welcomed the Athletics' delegates to the 1860 baseball convention in New York City. In late 1862, they elected Thomas Fitzgerald president of the NABBP, baseball's *soi-disant* national governing body. A former town ball player living well outside the New York metropolitan area might seem a strange pick for baseball's top job at that early date. But it is doubtful that Fitzgerald was either a baseball novice or a stranger to the New York baseball scene. Colonel Fitzgerald's career with the Athletics is full of hints of his New York City upbringing and pre-existing personal connections to the Brooklyn and the New York City baseball clubs. Like so many other early New York ballplayers, Fitzgerald served in a militia unit; he probably also belonged to a volunteer fire company. On a trip to Washington in the 1860s, he mentioned that he had visited that city years earlier as a member of a New York City militia. In Philadelphia in 1859, although he held no public office in the fire department or anywhere else, he was one of the dignitaries who personally welcomed the visiting "Constitution" Engine Company No. 7 of Brooklyn. During the early 1860s, it was Fitzgerald who arranged for New Jersey and New York baseball clubs to exchange visits with Philadelphia clubs in order to spread and teach the game.

The *New York Clipper's* coverage of an 1862 visit to Philadelphia by the Eckfords of Greenpoint conveys the warm relations that Fitzgerald had with clubs from Brooklyn, in particular those in the Eastern District, now called Williamsburg and Greenpoint.

> On Tuesday morning the Eckfords and their friends were escorted to the Navy Yard by the Philadelphians…. At night they accepted the invitation of Mrs. John [Louisa Lane] Drew to visit the Arch Street Theatre, where seats were reserved for them. On Wednesday they were taken to the Exhibition of Fine Arts, and in the evening went to the Walnut Street Theatre … the performances of [popular English actress] Miss Charlotte Thompson especially pleasing the Eckfords. On Thursday morning the party went out to Girard College, and in the evening were hospitably entertained at the residence of Col. Fitzgerald. After supper at the hotel that evening, they marched round to the colonel's residence, where he was awaiting them, and after enjoying some delightful piano playing at the hands of Mr. [Riter] Fitzgerald [Thomas Fitzgerald's son].[1]

Incidentally, stories like this help us make sense of the odd fact that the Athletic club grew out of a classical music organization, Philadelphia's Haydn and Handel Musical Society.[2] Many founding and early members of the club were involved in music, singing, or the theater. This included star player DeWitt Clinton Moore, who was superintendent of Philadelphia's Sunday schools and a church choir director. Hicks Hayhurst and Joseph Megary were amateur actors who belonged to the Boothenian Dramatic Association, which was named after John Wilkes Booth's pro–Union older brother Edwin Booth. Fitzgerald himself was an amateur vocalist, a drama critic, and a frequent lecturer on classical music.

Like Dr. Joseph Jones of the Brooklyn Excelsiors of the late 1850s, Fitzgerald aggressively improved the Athletics by merging with other clubs, by recruiting established players from other clubs, and by casting a wide net for young talent. A key part of the Athletics' crash development plan was to play as many games as possible against the superior New York-area clubs. In mid-summer of 1862, the A's issued a challenge to the baseball clubs of Newark, New Jersey, New York City, and Brooklyn, "if not to win the ball," said Moore, then "merely to learn their way of 'doing the thing.'"[3] Thomas Fitzgerald's idea, this was the first-ever multi-club intercity tournament. In front of large crowds, a composite team representing Philadelphia surprised no one by losing to a team of players from Newark and Brooklyn, but it upset a New York team made up of Eagles, Empires, Knickerbockers, and Gothams, (including future major-league manager and Hall of Famer Harry Wright and William Van Cott, the first president of the NABBP), 46–23.

Sucker Punch

This victory gained the Philadelphia clubs some credibility, but nobody would have bet on any of them against a good Brooklyn club with a good night's sleep. In June, players from four Brooklyn clubs (Atlantic, Enterprise, Star, and Exercise) made a return trip to Philadelphia and got hustled. Both cities were asked to divide their players into an "A" team and a "B" team. The Brooklynites assumed that they were supposed to put their best players on the "A" team. The four teams then played a four-game round robin. Henry Chadwick explained what happened.

The Brooklyn players left New York on Monday, June 30, at 2 p.m., and arrived at Philadelphia at 6:30, where they were met by a numerous delegation of the Philadelphia players, and duly escorted to the Washington House, Chestnut Street, a first class hotel…. On their arrival, they were taken into the parlor, where two splendid bowls of claret [red Bordeaux wine] punch were placed, and as fast as they were emptied by the thirsty travelers, they were replenished…. The players of the Brooklyn party should have retired early after their trip, in view of the work they had before them, but their friends in the city of Philadelphia would not think of such a thing, so parties were made up for rambles around the town, and they did not get "home until morning": the consequence was that the majority were totally unfit to play...[4]

Beside getting them drunk, the Philadelphians hoodwinked the Brooklynites by putting some of their best players on the "B" team. So, after the Philadelphia "A" team beat a hung-over Brooklyn "A" team 16–10, Philadelphia "B" easily defeated Brooklyn "B," 22–9. In the end, Brooklyn won only one of the four games in the tournament, by the close score of 18–15. As the *New York Clipper* tells it, there were no hard feelings at the post-tournament dinner, which ended awash in brandy and wartime patriotism. Thomas Fitzgerald raised a glass to the baseball players of Brooklyn, "which was received with all the honors. From this time to the close, a delightful social time was had, songs, sentiments and speeches ruling the hour for the time being, in which Col.s Fitzgerald and Moore ... took a prominent part.... At 12 o'clock the party broke up, the last song being *The Star Spangled Banner*, which was given with a will."[5]

In 1865, Colonel Fitzgerald finally had a contender for baseball's national championship. The finishing touch was importing 25-year-old slugging sec-

Colonel Thomas Fitzgerald, publisher, playwright, politician, and advocate for racial integration in baseball (Library of Congress).

ond baseman Al Reach from Reach's hometown Greenpoint Eckfords. The 1865 Athletics went 15–3, winning two from the solid Unions of Morrisania and losing two close games to the champion Brooklyn Atlantics. The 1866 club was even better, winning 23 and losing only two. That A's club defeated the Unions, the Nationals of Washington, D.C., and the Atlantics; their two losses came against the Unions and Atlantics. The *Clipper* praised Colonel Fitzgerald as "the prime mover of everything calculated to advance the interests or extend the popularity of baseball in [Philadelphia]."[6] Fitzgerald took the field with the Athletics only once that we know of, in an intramural game, but he knew too much about baseball and baseball players not to have grown up playing the game. Because he was born in 1819, however, Fitzgerald's playing days—his teens and twenties—came during baseball's Dark Ages. We know that baseball was played in the 1830s, but we have almost no names, box scores or game accounts. Of course, in order to have played baseball at that time, Thomas Fitzgerald would also have to have lived in or around New York City. Fitzgerald was in fact a New Yorker, born and raised.

Out of the 4th Ward

You may have met people who, when asked about their childhood, recite the same impersonal facts, things like the exact time, date, and place of their birth, and little more. Usually, there is a reason. Sometimes it is trauma or unhappiness that they want to forget; sometimes they were orphaned or adopted and that is all they know. When Thomas Fitzgerald was asked about his childhood, he said that he was born in New York City on December 22, 1819, at the future site of the Harper Brothers publishing house. He sometimes added that he was working as a printer at a young age, when other children were in school.[7] Other than suggesting that he was related to Irish nobility, the titled Hiberno-Norman Fitzgerald family known as the Geraldines, that was the whole story.

Family was important to Thomas Fitzgerald when he was an adult. In middle age, he made annual summer visits to Ireland, where he met and hobnobbed with aristocratic Fitzgeralds like the Duke of Leinster and the Marquis of Kildare, who he allowed people to believe were relatives. He was very close to his daughter and his five sons, who helped him run his newspaper, the *City Item*. All of Fitzgerald's sons played for Philadelphia baseball clubs, including the Minervas, the *City Item*'s own team and—significantly—a junior club named after the Eckfords of Greenpoint, Brooklyn. Yet Thomas Fitzgerald never, as far as we know, uttered a single word about his mother, father, or siblings, not even their names. Searching for Thomas Fitzgerald's origins, I could not locate a birth or baptismal record that matches his own account of his birth, which given the state of records from that time is not surprising. But the specificity of Fitzgerald's statement that he was born on the site of the Harper Brothers printing house is a clue that leads to a particular part of lower Manhattan.

In the nineteenth century the Harper Brothers publishing house was located on Franklin Square in the Fourth Ward, a rough neighborhood that in the early nineteenth century was shared by printers, sailors, poor Irish immigrants, African Americans, and New York's earliest Chinese community. No one was living at that exact address in 1819. But just to the east of the Harper Brothers buildings was tiny Hague Street, which intersected Franklin Square. Hague Street, located near the present intersection of Pearl and Dover Streets, is no longer there; it was obliterated to construct an off-ramp for the Brooklyn Bridge. Around 1820, a publisher named William Colyer had a printing

A 19th-century view of the Harper Brothers publishing house on Franklin Square in lower Manhattan's Fourth Ward (New York Public Library).

plant at number 5 Hague Street.[8] Colyer was a cousin and business partner of the Harper brothers.

Longworth's New York City directories for the early decades of the nineteenth century contain only a handful of people named Fitzgerald. Many of them lived in the Fourth Ward of Manhattan, particularly in several households on tiny Hague Street and nearby Oak Street. These families were most likely related. The 1827 directory contains only 11 people named Fitzgerald; one is listed as "Fitzgerald, widow of Edmund, grocer." She lived at 8 Hague. Born in Ireland in 1774, her name was Ellen Fitzgerald. Her husband Edmund Fitzgerald, also born in Ireland, had died in 1823, leaving no money or possessions. Censuses from 1840 and earlier list only heads of households by name; for everyone else they give only numbers broken down by sex, race, age range, and, for African Americans, if they were free or slaves. Comparing all the Fitzgerald families in New York City listed in the 1820 and 1830 censuses, there are two who fit most of what Thomas Fitzgerald said about his early background, and who had a male child born around 1819 who could have been Thomas Fitzgerald.

One is the family of Edmund and Ellen Fitzgerald. They lived within literal spitting distance of a printing house owned by a member of the Harper family. They emigrated to the U.S. in 1799. The date suggests that Edmund and Ellen Fitzgerald were among New York's many refugees from the Irish Rebellion of 1798. Perhaps Thomas Fitzgerald inherited his parents' Irish Republicanism; as an adult, he was active in organizations that supported Irish independence and opposed American slavery. New York City in 1823 was a rough place for a widowed unskilled immigrant. Some in Ellen Fitzgerald's position abandoned their children or resorted to prostitution. She had three children: Edmund, Jr., who was 15 or 16 years old; Ellen, who was 7 or 8; and a younger son, presumably three-year-old Thomas. We do not know how Mrs. Fitzgerald survived the next six or seven years. According to a city directory, in 1827 Edmund, Jr., was working as a grocer, as his father had. But it would have been difficult for an unskilled laborer in his teens to support an entire family. The likelihood is that they were desperately poor.

The other likely candidates for Thomas Fitzgerald's parents are Garrit Fitzgerald and his wife Catherine Fitzgerald, who lived on Oak Street in the Fourth Ward and who may well have been related to Edmund and Ellen. Their story is even bleaker. Catherine Fitzgerald died in childbirth in 1826; and a Garrit Fitzgerald of Oak Street died in the cholera epidemic of 1832, when Thomas Fitzgerald would have been between 11 and 13 years old. A couple named Garrit and Catherine Fitzgerald baptized a son named Thomas at St. Peter's Roman Catholic Church in New York City in late December of 1818, which is tantalizing because it is almost one year earlier to the day than the date of birth given by the adult Thomas Fitzgerald. Could Thomas Fitzgerald actually have been born not on December 22, 1819, but on December 22, *1818*? Perhaps, but it is hard to imagine how, throughout his life, Thomas Fitzgerald could have consistently thought that he was exactly one year younger than his actual age. One of the less far-fetched possible explanations would be that he was cared for by an orphanage or other strangers in infancy and that they mis-recorded or misunderstood his birth year. Another is that two different Thomas Fitzgeralds were born about a year apart. Given names, of course, run in families; some or all of the 4th Ward Fitzgerald families may have been related, and Thomas is not an uncommon name.

Printer's Devil

Whichever of these families Thomas Fitzgerald was born into, his childhood appears to have been Dickensian. Widowers in 1826 did not normally raise children. If he was the son of Garrit Fitzgerald, Thomas would have been sent to relatives, an orphanage, into an apprenticeship—or first one of these and then another. According to Thomas Fitzgerald himself, he worked as a printer at a very young age. If he was the son of Ellen Fitzgerald, she might have decided to apprentice her youngest son to a printer as soon as he was old enough in order to have one fewer mouth to feed. Irish immigrant families of the time were known to sacrifice one child's education for the sake of the others. (Apprenticeships normally lasted for four to seven years and were legally binding. Apprentices worked for free or for very little.) We do not know how young Thomas Fitzgerald was when he was in effect sold into temporary slavery. Eleven or younger was unusual but not unheard of. Apprentices often lived at their employer's home or shop. Many were exploited by their employers and hazed by older apprentices. We can only wonder what kind of misery lies behind Thomas Fitzgerald's statement that he was working "at an age when other children were in school."

There is reason to think that the printer that Thomas Fitzgerald went to work for was the family's neighbor on Hague Street, Harper Brothers cousin William Colyer. This gets a bit complicated. Colyer worked in Manhattan, but lived across the East River in Williamsburg, where in 1840 he hired fresh-off-the-boat political radical Thomas Ainge Devyr, who had escaped prosecution in the U.K. to edit a Democratic Party newspaper that he was launching in Brooklyn. In his eccentric and entertaining autobiography, Devyr says that Colyer paid him through an associate named Fitzgerald.[9] Devyr's son

Thomas Devyr, Jr., born in Brooklyn in 1844, was an outstanding athlete who played baseball for the Marions, Eckfords, and Mutuals. He was caught up in baseball's first game-fixing scandal in 1865 and banned from the sport, but he was reinstated after one year thanks to lobbying by Henry Chadwick, a fellow Brooklynite who also had a father who had left England as a political refugee. The Devyrs and Chadwicks probably knew each other—it would be surprising if they didn't—but there is no question that Tom Devyr the ballplayer knew Thomas Fitzgerald. In 1896, after Thomas Devyr, Jr., died at 51, a reporter visited his bare Greenpoint apartment and reflected on the former baseball star's faded glory. "Of all the many prizes he received," he wrote, "none remained in his possession at the time of his death, save a book of poems, bestowed on him by Colonel Thomas Fitzgerald, president of the Athletic Club of Philadelphia."[10] It is at least possible that Thomas Fitzgerald knew Devyr and other baseball figures in Brooklyn as a boy or young man, before he moved to Philadelphia. All we know about Thomas Fitzgerald's life immediately before his arrival in Philadelphia in the mid–1840s are the names of the newspapers he worked for, as he moved up from printer to journalist to editor. Beside the New York *Commercial Advertiser*, the list includes the New Brunswick, New Jersey *Fredonian*, the Philadelphia *Bulletin* and the Tallahassee *Floridian*. He had no known family in any of these places. In his teens and early twenties, Thomas Fitzgerald seems to have been, like Walt Whitman, a rootless printer and journalist, single and living alone. Did he resent being apprenticed as a boy? Did he simply want to put an unhappy childhood behind him? Whatever the reason, Thomas Fitzgerald moved to Philadelphia and decided to become someone else.

City Items

Thomas Fitzgerald founded the *City Item* as a weekly in 1847. He had three partners, friends from his days as a printer and journalist in New York; one of them was George G. Foster, who had invented the "City Items" column for the New York *Tribune*. The original "City Items" was a potpourri of gossip items, comments on musical concerts or plays, politics, crime, and city life, all delivered with Foster's urbane wit. "His special contribution," writes historian George Rogers Taylor:

> arises from his focusing his attention so largely on common people, not only beggars and prostitutes but on the great numbers of working men and women, the dandies and the bill posters, the [Bowery] b'hoys and g'hals, the women arriving by carriage to shop at Stewart's [the elegant New York department store] and the seamstresses

working in garrets.... Foster described in realistic detail those whom Walt Whitman sketched poetically in the 15th section of "Song of Myself."[11]

The idea of Fitzgerald and his partners was to turn this journalistic innovation from New York City into a business plan for an entire newspaper in Philadelphia. It worked. In the 1850s Fitzgerald bought out Foster and the others, and eventually made the *Item* a daily newspaper. Thomas Fitzgerald married Sarah Levering Riter of Germantown in 1844. We do not know what his wife and family knew about his early life, but the face that Thomas Fitzgerald showed to Philadelphia and the world after he became a successful publisher was largely a work of fiction. Fitzgerald gave talks on Mozart and wrote about opera, classical instrumental music, and the theater. He published articles and poetry for the Philadelphia-based national magazines, *Graham's Magazine* and *Godey's Ladies Book,* and composed popular songs. An eloquent public speaker, he was active in local Democratic politics (the only kind there was in Philadelphia) and advocated successfully for musical education in the public schools. He had several plays produced, his greatest success being the 1868 "Light at Last," starring Louisa Lane Drew, the great-great-grandmother of actress Drew Barrymore.

In the 1860s, Thomas Fitzgerald joined the Republican Party. A fervent Abolitionist, he had campaigned across Pennsylvania for Abraham Lincoln as a War Democrat; they became friends. Another part of Fitzgerald's self-reinvention was changing religions. In 1870 Fitzgerald and three of his sons were confirmed in the Congregational Church; church records note that Thomas Fitzgerald had been baptized Roman Catholic.[12] Finally, in the 1880s and 1890s he began making regular trips to Europe, where he visited Maynooth Castle and Carton House in Ireland, owned by the Duke of Leinster, whose surname was Fitzgerald. American newspapers carried stories about Thomas Fitzgerald's visits to his illustrious relatives in the old country. But in 1888, New York's *Irish American Weekly* pointed out that the Catholic-born Thomas Fitzgerald of Philadelphia could not have been related to the Duke of Leinster or anyone else in the family in the 1880s.

> The New York *Herald* must have been betrayed into a curious historical jumble, when ... it referred to Colonel Thomas Fitzgerald of Philadelphia as a possible Presidential candidate in the following terms: "Fitzgerald ... has been put in nomination as the lineal descendant of a dynasty of Irish kings and the oldest American representative of the Duke of Leinster's family." [It is] absurd ... to connect the present Duke of Leinster with the Geraldines. He is neither a Geraldine nor an Irishman; and every true Fitzgerald repudiates him and his claims.[13]

Not to detour into the thickets of an aristocratic succession controversy, Thomas Fitzgerald was probably no more closely related to the Duke of

Leinster or the original Geraldines than F. Scott, Ella, or any other of the thousands of people in the world named Fitzgerald. Significantly, Thomas Fitzgerald himself never explicitly claimed to be related to the aristocratic Fitzgeralds. Perhaps the Duke of Leinster socialized with Thomas Fitzgerald simply because he enjoyed the company of a gregarious American million-aire. He would not have been the first European aristocrat to do so.

What explains Thomas Fitzgerald's transformation from unschooled child of the slums into erudite man of the world? His wife had a good educa-tion and may have educated him about classical music. But a more plausible answer is that Fitzgerald educated himself. In the early nineteenth century, a well-travelled path led from apprentice to printer to journalist to writer; printers' and typographers' unions offered free night classes, access to librar-ies, and other forms of education. Many 19th-century American literary men rose from equally humble origins. This includes other members of Thomas Fitzgerald's New York City social and professional milieu, such as Rufus Gris-wold (Edgar Allan Poe's literary executor), George Wilkes, and George G. Fos-ter. Rumored to have been illegitimate and raised in a brothel, George Wilkes did not have an expensive education, but he went on to publish a scholarly work on the plays of Shakespeare and the national sports weekly, *Wilkes' Spirit of the Times*. The child of a Vermont shoemaker, Griswold left home at 15 and educated himself while working as printer. He became a published poet and literary critic. Fellow Vermonter Foster was another self-made man of letters.

Thomas Fitzgerald's writing style tells us where he came from. It is well seasoned with Bowery B'hoy self-assertion and the joy in puncturing smug-ness and hypocrisy that characterizes Mike Walsh or the George Wilkes of the *Subterranean* and *National Police Gazette* days. For a time, Fitzgerald's *City Item* used the advertising slogan, "Independent in Everything," an allusion to the *Subterranean*'s famous motto, "Independent in Everything—Neutral in Nothing."

Meanwhile, back in New York City's Fourth Ward, Edmund Fitzgerald, Jr.—our prime candidate for Thomas Fitzgerald's older brother—was moving up the Tammany Hall food chain. In 1841 he appears on a Democratic com-mittee with publisher William Colyer. In 1845 he is a poll inspector and mem-ber of the party ward committee. Later that year he was named police captain of the Fourth Ward; he and his mother Ellen moved into an apartment above the police station at 9 Oak Street, less than half a block from Hague Street. In 1847 Edmund Fitzgerald ran successfully for New York City Alderman, a lucrative position. The Fitzgerald family fortunes were looking up, but in 1852 the single and unmarried Edmund died, leaving his entire estate to his mother, Ellen Fitzgerald. She died five years later at the age of 83. There is one final interesting detail about Ellen Fitzgerald. She is buried in the crypt under old St. Patrick's Cathedral on New York City's Mulberry Street. The inelegant inscription on the vault's marble door—"Ellen Fitzgerald's Family Vault 1852"—conveys the vanity of a simple woman who, after a long and hard life, managed to afford an expensive exit.

It is not hard to imagine why Thomas Fitzgerald never discussed his early life. He lost one or both parents as a boy. He was sent to work instead of school. Even if he had no hard feelings toward the rest of his family, the sophisticated, successful, Protestant, and Abolitionist pillar of Philadelphia society, friend of aristocrats, and political ally of Presidents that he became did not need or want any connection to the Fitzgeralds of the Fourth Ward.

Hired Men

Thomas Fitzgerald the Philadelphian was a shrewd baseball man who was determined to build the Athletics into a top club. But there were things that he was not willing to do to win baseball games. Several times during the 1860s, a dispute within the Athletics would cause Fitzgerald to put his foot down and resign as club president. Each time the dispute was settled, and the club asked him to come back. We do not know what these disputes were about, but a good guess would be club actions that, in Fitzgerald's mind, violated baseball's amateur ethic. The 1866 dispute was so bitter that Fitzgerald's resignation was accepted. It is clear from the public relations war that broke out afterward that Fitzgerald had resigned over the Athletics, in Fitzgerald's view, paying players illegally and lowering their admission standards in order to improve the club on the field. Because baseball amateurism was essentially a form of social exclusion, these two issues overlapped. Because clubs throughout baseball were facing the same issues and conflicts, the dispute between Fitzgerald and the Athletics went national.

In early March of 1866, the Athletics had unanimously re-elected Fitzgerald as president for the fifth time. They were at a high point, with the largest membership of any baseball club in the country—over 400 members who paid dues of $20 per year—a fat bank account, and some of the nation's best players. The Athletics were about to come within one, un-played game of becoming the first club from outside baseball's Holy Land, the New York City metropolitan area, to win a national baseball championship.

But in May, newspapers reported the shocking news that Fitzgerald had resigned to take over as president of the Equity club (which immediately began to improve). Fitzgerald's *City Item* then ran a series of stories accusing

DeWitt Clinton Moore and Hicks Hayhurst of the Athletics of using "hired men," mercenaries who were paid $20 a week, in violation of NABBP rules on amateurism.[14] The *Item* gave Fitzgerald's old friend, successor as club president, and choir director DeWitt Clinton Moore, the derisive nickname of "the psalm-singing hypocrite" or "P.S.H." for short. That had to hurt.[15] The paper asked, rhetorically, "Now in the case of a close game—a game, say, between the Atlantics, Excelsiors, Mutuals and Eurekas—would you trust some of these 'hired men' should they receive liberal offers from the outside betting fraternity? Don't you think an offer of $500 would have its effect? Can you trust a fellow who sells his services to the highest bidder?"[16] In July, the *City Item* reprinted the following want ad from the *New York Clipper*, with commentary added by Fitzgerald.

> WANTED—A FIRST-CLASS BASE BALL PITCHER, *for a series of match games to come off this season. By addressing to A. Sneider, P.O. Box 141, Sunbury, [PA], you can learn particulars.*
>
> We call the attention of pitchers, who desire to hire themselves out by the day, week, month, or year, to the above advertisement.... How much can Sneider give? Can he pay $20 per week? What security does he offer? Has he any poor relations? Will cold victuals be thrown in?[17]

Fitzgerald's *jihad* against professionalism on his old club made enemies. Some of them retaliated by falsely accusing him of offering cash to entice players to join his new club, the Equity. Fitzgerald was publicly expelled from the Athletics, the club that he had co-founded. But many in baseball took his side. When Fitzgerald ran a comic caricature of one of the "hired men," and said of them, "They generally come from New York, with only one or two exceptions (hint, hint), and are about the hardest set [i.e., the roughest characters] we ever saw," he received a fan letter from Brooklyn. "Dear Sir," it read, "Will you have the kindness to mail me three or four copies of your paper containing the portrait of the 'Hired Man?' I called at the 'Excelsior' Club Room the other evening, and was much amused, *as were many others*, by hearing Dr. Jones read several extracts from last week's paper. Hoping 'Our National Game' may continue to prosper as it has done, and that the 'Hired Men' may soon become extinct...."[18]

Fitzgerald's newspaper specified that the Athletics had four players who were paid, directly or "constructively." He did not name names, but he offered enough information, including publishing a list of starting Athletics players who were *not* paid, that we can identify the filthy four with some confidence. Three of the players were: Patsy Dockney from Hoboken; Lipman Pike from Brooklyn; and Al Reach, also from Brooklyn. The other one is almost certainly star pitcher Dick McBride, a native Philadelphian.

Dockney and Pike are a good fit for the category of "the hardest set we ever saw." Both were far more at home in a saloon than in a concert hall. As Fitzgerald wrote, "The officers of the Athletic Club have done much to bring the game into contempt by employing men to play in their nine who have been repeatedly arrested and confined in the station house ... on the charge of drunkenness and rioting. There was a time when a player would have been expelled from the club for drunkenness and rioting, but that day seems to have passed." Dockney's brilliant career as a catcher was derailed by a barroom brawl in which his chest was sliced open by a meat cleaver. He later filleted fish in New York City's Washington Market and served a prison stretch for theft.

A speedy left-handed power hitter who once won a foot race around the bases against a thoroughbred horse, Pike had a long career in amateur and pro baseball. Modern baseball historians like to portray Pike, baseball's first Jewish star, as a victim of persistent anti–Semitism, but the evidence for this is non-existent. Amateur Era baseball and mid–19th-century America, particularly New York City, were refreshingly free of anti–Semitism. In 1881 Lipman Pike was put on a temporary blacklist by the National League for being "dissipated [i.e., drunk] and insubordinate [i.e., he annoyed a club owner]." If there was an ulterior reason, we do not know it; none of the other eight players on the list was Jewish. Al Reach was no low life, but rumor had it that in 1866 the Athletics paid him by giving him a house. Both Dockney and Pike left Philadelphia soon after the *City Item* stories, in late 1866.

It is often claimed that in 1865 the ostensibly amateur Reach was paid $25 per week by Fitzgerald and the A's to

The above beautiful cut, which has been prepared by us at a great expense, represents a Hired Man in our Great National Game of Base Ball. Many correspondents have desired us to state where all these Hired Men come from. In reply we may say that they generally come from New York, with only one or two exceptions, and are about the hardest set we ever saw. It is unfortunate that one of our best clubs has been infested by these nuisances. Our readers by this time must know that it is against the rules of the convention to have players who are paid salaries, yet this state of things actually exists. The officers of the Club when asked, "Have you any Hired Men?" reply "No!" thus uttering an untruth.

A caricature of the infamous Amateur Era baseball "hired man" from Fitzgerald's *City Item* newspaper.

leave the Eckfords and play for Philadelphia, and that this makes Thomas Fitzgerald a hypocrite. Today, Reach and James Creighton are at the top of modern lists of Amateur Era secret professionals, players who were paid "under the table." But this misreads the times and the baseball world in which Reach and Creighton lived.

Until the 1869 season the letter of the NABBP rules prohibited clubs from paying or compensating players in any form, but as applied the prohibition was more subtle. No one in baseball in 1865 considered Reach's relationship with his club to be improper; the same is true of Creighton pre–1862. The fact that we are confused today about the distinction between amateurism and professionalism in 1860s baseball—or that the NABBP did not want to police it—does not mean that the distinction did not exist.

Philadelphia native and star pitcher for the Athletics Dick McBride (New York Public Library).

Two things are clear. Some forms of player compensation were generally regarded as honest and others were not; and this depended on the player's relationship with his club. Virtually all the outrage about so-called professionalism in the Amateur Era, for example, was about players jumping, or "revolving" from one club to another. The central issue in these cases was loyalty, not payment *per se*. The same Excelsiors who applauded Thomas Fitzgerald's campaign against "hired men" had helped James Creighton and his father buy a house and obtain no-show patronage posts in the New York City Customs House. They also secured star second baseman and police telegrapher George Flanley, who came from a poor family, a better job in the Brooklyn Police Department. These were not seen as violations of the amateur ethic but as mutual assistance by club members. Even the moralistic Henry Chadwick himself drew a distinction between "hired men" and "those whose loss of time and necessary expenses are very properly paid." "All clubs," he wrote:

who have first class players in their nines whose positions in life are not surrounded with pecuniary advantages, or who are not, in fact, well off in the world, of course take care that their players are not sufferers from sacrificing their time to sustain the playing reputation of the club of which they are prominent players. But this style of thing is ... very different from "hiring men," or paying them so much a week for their services, just as "professional" cricketers are paid.[19]

The Excelsiors may have aided James Creighton financially in order to allow him to play, but the Excelsiors did not lie about it and they did not need to. Interestingly, they did finesse the issue of when Creighton had come to Brooklyn, saying that he had moved there as a young boy, instead of in 1858, when he was 17 years old. (Baseball references today repeat this falsehood.) The reason they did so was to suggest that Creighton legitimately belonged to the community that had produced his teammates. In any case, Creighton remained with the Excelsiors for the rest of his (albeit brief) life.

So did Al Reach, who lived to 87. In 1865, Reach was playing for the Athletics but still living in his hometown of Brooklyn, while he considered moving his entire family—father, brothers, and fiancée—to Philadelphia. A likely explanation for the $25 per week the club gave him is that it was reimbursement for expenses, the two or three round trips a week that he had to make by train between New York and Philadelphia during the summer and fall of 1865 in order to play with the Athletics. Based on advertised contemporary train fares, the amount is about right. After Reach brought his family to Philadelphia in 1866, Thomas Fitzgerald helped him and his brother establish a cigar shop, but this was already Reach's brother's business. The important fact is that, in 1865 at least, no one saw Reach as in any sense a mercenary. He came to Philadelphia with his entire family, intending to put down roots, and he did. It is revealing that in 1866 Thomas Fitzgerald's baseball enemies did not attack him for having paid Al Reach. Instead they used made-up charges that he had was dangling money in front of other players to get them to jump to his Equity club. Al Reach played the rest of his career in Philadelphia, where he started the sporting goods business that made him rich and where, in 1883, he co-founded the National League Philadelphia Phillies. Dick McBride also played virtually his entire amateur and professional career in Philadelphia, his hometown. Like Reach, McBride was one of the Athletics' most valuable players.

There are two possible reasons why these non-hired men might have been paid by the club in 1866. One is fairness; equal or lesser players brought from outside were getting paid. The other is that in the late 1860s, baseball clubs throughout the country were raiding each other's rosters in a kind of feeding frenzy; the A's may have paid Reach and McBride so they would not be tempted to leave. One look at their career stats, on the other hand, will tell you that Patsy Dockney and Lipman Pike were out and out mercenaries. Dockney played for the Gothams in 1864 and 1865; the Athletics in 1866; the Eurekas of Newark, New Jersey, in 1867; and both the Cincinnati Buckeyes and the New York Mutuals in 1868. Lipman Pike came up through Brooklyn junior clubs under the control of the Atlantics, where he was playing when he jumped to the Philadelphia A's for the 1866 season. He went on to play in New York, Baltimore, Hartford, St. Louis, Cincinnati, and Providence.

The controversy over Fitzgerald and the four hired men blew over without anybody being disciplined or suspended. It was just one more bit of unpleasantness in a chaotic and quarrelsome baseball season. In 1866 baseball was caught between two eras. Home clubs still treated visiting clubs to banquets and outings, as if they were personal guests, but when it came to money issues like scheduling championship games or divvying up gate receipts, clubs played hardball. In 1866, a war-weary America embraced baseball as entertainment and the money poured in.

Not all the men who ran the top clubs, however, were up to handling the change. As with other Amateur Era traditions, baseball was outgrowing the traditional way of determining a national champion, a three-game series negotiated by the interested parties themselves. A scheduling disagreement marred the championship series between the Athletics and the Atlantics in 1865. There were left-over hard feelings, but the A's were looking forward to another shot at the Atlantics in the three-game championship series they hoped to play in 1866. They would be disappointed.

Election Day

However reluctantly, every 19th-century American institution had to take a stand on race. Amateur baseball's time came in the fall of 1867, when an African American club, the Pythians of Philadelphia, applied for admission to the NABBP via the Pennsylvania state baseball association. This touched off another bitter baseball controversy with national repercussions that Thomas Fitzgerald jumped into with both feet. The difference this time was that the "hired men" controversy had cost Fitzgerald his position as president of the Athletics, the most important baseball club in Philadelphia. In 1867, when baseball urgently needed an effective advocate for racial inclusion, Fitzgerald's influence in the baseball world was at a low point. Of course, he still had one weapon—the bully pulpit of his popular newspaper, the *City Item*.

To understand the story of the Pythians and organized baseball, a little background is necessary. It is difficult to say which American city had the worst race relations in the mid-nineteenth century, but Philadelphia was certainly a contender. The city had bloody race riots—that is, white people rioting—in 1834, 1838, and 1842. Instead of segregating its streetcars, until 1867 Philadelphia banned African Americans entirely. No exceptions were made for wives and children who, late in the war, were visiting hospitalized Civil War veterans. Frederick Douglass, whose son Frederick Douglass, Jr., played baseball for the African American Alert club in Washington, D.C., called Philadelphia the "up-South."

Thanks to racially progressive Quakers and the Underground Railroad, however, the city also had a large African American community anchored by institutions like the Institute for Colored Youth. A school for higher education founded in 1837 by a wealthy Quaker, originally located at 7th and Lombard Streets, the Institute ultimately moved in 1902 to Delaware County, where it continues today under the name Cheyney University. Like other Philadelphians, African Americans in the city had long played cricket and town ball. In 1866 a group of African American business and professional men founded a baseball club. They named it the Pythians, either after the fraternal organization Knights of Pythias, or after the unselfish friendship of Damon and Pythias in Greek legend. Their on-field leader was Octavius Catto, a teacher at the Institute for Colored Youth and a civil rights activist who led campaigns for African Americans to fight in the Civil War and to use the Philadelphia streetcar system.

The years 1870 and 1871 were racially troubled ones in America. In February of 1870, Congress passed the 15th Amendment to the Constitution, which guaranteed American men voting rights "regardless of race, color, or previous servitude." In Philadelphia, the ruling Democratic Party lashed back with a campaign of intimidation and threats aimed at stopping African Americans, who overwhelmingly supported Republicans, from voting. On Election Day of 1871, African Americans in public places around the city were harassed, assaulted, and fired upon by roving white gangs deployed by city politicians. Octavius Catto was on his way home near the intersection of South Street and 9th, when a Moyamensing volunteer fireman and part-time Democratic Party goon named Frank Kelly walked up and shot him dead. Catto was given full military honors and Philadelphia's largest funeral since the ceremonies for Abraham Lincoln in 1865. Kelly was arrested—six years later—but acquitted of murder. No one in Philadelphia was surprised. (In 2017, a statue of Octavius Catto with his arms out and palms turned up in a questioning gesture, as eyewitnesses said they were when he died, was set up outside Philadelphia City Hall.)

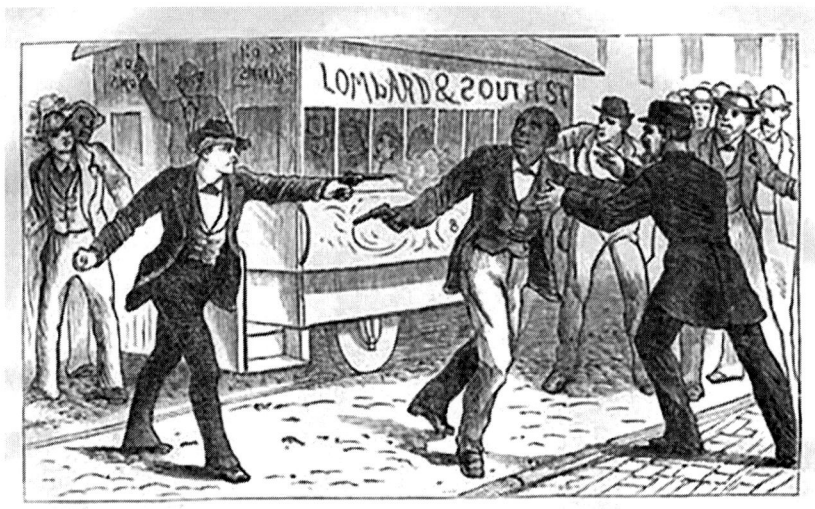

SCENE OF THE SHOOTING OF OCTAVIUS V. CATTO, ON OCTOBER 10, 1871.

The murder of Philadelphia civil rights activist, soldier, teacher, and baseball man Octavius Catto on Election Day, 1871 (Historical Society of Philadelphia).

A Well-Behaved Set of Gentlemen

In 1867, their first full season, Octavius Catto's Pythians had defeated local rivals including the Excelsiors and L'Ouvertures, and established themselves as the consensus African American champions of Philadelphia. They went to Washington, D.C., where they beat the Alerts and Mutuals. The Pythians' success inspired civic pride in some quarters of the mainstream press. When the Philadelphia Excelsiors defeated an African American club from New York in October of 1867, the Philadelphia *Sunday Mercury* wrote:

> [The New York papers] apply the title of Champions to the Excelsiors, and then abuse and ridicule them, after the fashion of New York. The Pythians, also of this city, are the recognized champions among colored organizations, and should they ever conclude to visit New York, an opportunity will be afforded Philadelphia defamers to see a well-behaved set of gentlemen.[20]

Amateur baseball was always looking for a few "well-behaved gentlemen." So far, all of them had been white, but the NABBP had no actual rule banning African Americans. None of the African American clubs in New York City or Brooklyn had ever tried to join.

In October of 1867, the clubs of the Pennsylvania State baseball association, a member organization of the NABBP, were holding their annual convention in Harrisburg. The president of the association happened to be Philadelphia Athletics delegate Hicks Hayhurst, a Quaker and racial liberal who had umpired Pythian games. The Pythians were a credible African American baseball club equal or superior to many NABBP clubs in education and social class. They decided that the time was right to test amateur baseball's principles. They sent Raymond Burr, the son of Abolitionist newspaper editor John Pierre Burr (rumored to be the unacknowledged child of Vice President Aaron Burr and a Haitian servant) to Harrisburg to apply for admission to the NABBP. Burr was treated politely, but after voting to approve 265 out of 266 applications for membership, the nominations committee postponed consideration of the Pythians until the following day. That night, no doubt asked to head off a divisive conflict, Hayhurst convinced Burr to withdraw the Pythians' application by telling him that it had no chance of winning in a public vote.[21]

The nightmare of white discomfort was averted, but men of influence in baseball decided to make sure the issue never came up again. At the NABBP national convention, held soon after in Philadelphia, a committee including respected Knickerbocker James Whyte Davis authored a resolution that barred African Americans. When it passed, baseball's first color line was drawn. A Wall Street stockbroker, Davis had two nicknames, "The Fiend" because of his intensity and "Too Late," because he tended to show up in the middle of the first inning. Like other early Knickerbockers, Davis belonged to volunteer fire company Oceana Hose No. 36. Elected several times to the Knickerbocker club presidency, he served on the three-man committee that put on the 1858 Fashion Course series between New York City and Brooklyn. He was also a good enough outfielder at age 32 to play center field in the second game of the series. Confirming the eternal truth of modern hitting coach Rick Down's mantra, "If you can't dance, you can't hit," Davis won the dance contest at the New York Stock Exchange Christmas Party in 1880, the year that he retired from baseball at the age of 54.

We do not know enough to assess Davis's exact degree of responsibility for organized baseball's first formal act of racial exclusion, but it probably lies somewhere between main actor and guilty bystander. Historians would later call early baseball's color line an informal "gentlemen's agreement," but neither one of these words applies. In 1867 the NABBP wrote it down in black and white. The delegates passed a rule barring from membership any club "composed of persons of color, or any portion of them."[22] This grammatically clumsy resolution was written by the Nominating Committee, which had three members. One was William E. Sinn, owner of Philadelphia's New Chestnut Street Theater and president of its employee baseball club. Sinn had been arrested in 1861 while trying to join the Confederate army and may well have held racist views, but the sole reason that he was on the committee was because he let the convention use his theater; he needed to know who would be attending for logistical reasons. Sinn had zero power or influence in baseball. The other two members were prominent veteran baseball men Dr. William H. Bell, a former member of the NABBP Rules Committee and co-founder of the Eckfords and several other clubs; and James Whyte Davis, one of the two Knickerbocker delegates to the 1867 convention.

The Knickerbockers were orthodox amateurs who dissented from the creeping professionalism of the late Amateur Era. They refused to accept a penny from any ticket sales to their games. Ironically, however, some of them later asserted parental rights over professional baseball. In 1893 James Whyte Davis asked Edward Talcott, one of the owners of the New York Giants, to launch a fund to pay for Davis's grave monument, which he wanted inscribed as follows: "Wrapped in the original flag of the Knickerbocker Base Ball Club of N.Y., here lies the body of James Whyte Davis, a member for thirty years. He was not 'Too Late,' reaching the 'Home Plate.'" Davis thought that this should be paid for by the National League players, who, in Davis's mind, owed their livelihood to him and the Knickerbockers. Neither the fund nor the monument materialized. It is doubtful that anyone then playing major league baseball had ever heard of him. When he died in 1899, James Whyte Davis was dressed in his old uniform, wrapped in the club flag which he had designed in 1855, and buried in Brooklyn's Green-Wood Cemetery in an unmarked grave. One hundred seventeen years later, the Society for American Baseball Research raised the funds to give James Whyte Davis his gravestone, inscribed as he had asked.

In 1868 the Pythians returned to playing other African American clubs, but they still had some friends in white baseball. Colonel Thomas Fitzgerald was a prominent example, but after his 1866 breakup with the Athletics, all he could do was to complain in the pages of his newspaper. He criticized the state convention for rejecting the Pythians in 1867, but to no avail. In 1869, however, seeing that the Pythians had improved to the point that they could hold their own against a mid-level white club, Fitzgerald started to beat the drum for a kind of incremental baseball integration. His tactic was to encourage or, if necessary, embarrass prominent white clubs into playing against the Pythians.

Thomas Fitzgerald's racial attitudes seem shockingly out of their time, but the fact that he published them in a newspaper with a large circulation suggests that there were more people with views like his than we might think. Fitzgerald despised blackface entertainment, calling it low and vulgar. He mocked fellow Athletics co-founder DeWitt Clinton Moore for telling racist jokes in a lame African American accent. In May of 1869, Fitzgerald trolled racists with a news item that read, "There are two baseball clubs in Wilmington, North Carolina, composed of colored men, but they allow white men to play with them occasionally." In July he wrote, "The Pythians Club (colored) have beaten all the colored clubs, and would like to play a match with some of their white brethren. What say you, Athletics, Olympics, Keystones, Intrepids, etc." This was followed by, "Why is it that the Athletics will not play the colored baseball club the Pythians? Are they afraid of them? As I hear the Pythians are very strong, I think it quite possible that *apprehension of being beaten by them* is the real cause."[23]

Calling the white clubs out got results, although not from the Athletics. In September of 1869, Philadelphia's venerable white Olympic club took the field against the Pythians, with Thomas Fitzgerald umpiring. The Olympics won the first baseball game ever played between a NABBP club and an African American club, 44–23. Afterward, the door opened a crack. Isolated interracial games were played in 1869 in Boston and Washington, D.C. The Pythians found a few other willing white opponents, including the *City Item* employees' team, with three of Fitzgerald's sons in the lineup, at the Athletics' grounds. The Pythians won that game, 27–17, in front of a large crowd. "The *City Item*," wrote the Philadelphia *Morning Post*, "is especially to be commended for having the manliness to grapple with our great social question in a practical way. So far from losing anything by this defeat, the *City Item* must gain immensely in the estimation of all people whose opinion is worth the having. The moral effect of these interchanges of good feeling between the classes must be great, and the evidences of it upon the ground were unmistakable."[24] On this note of hope, the story of the Pythians ends. After Catto's assassination, the Pythians announced that "in the death of Octavius V. Catto our organization has lost its most active and valued member."[25] They promised that they would carry on his struggle for "truth, justice and equality." But they would not do it through baseball.

The Amateur Era ended on St. Patrick's Day of 1871, when the National Association, or NA, America's first national professional baseball league, was formed. The NA was all white and hired men were welcome. The same was true for the National League, which replaced the NA in 1876. It was a rough transition to professionalism for most of the top Amateur Era clubs, including those in Philadelphia. The A's handled it better than most. They joined the NA, won its first pennant in 1871, and remained competitive through 1875. They played one season in the new National League in 1876. (The name Athletics was revived in 1901 by an unrelated American League franchise. It is the ancestor of the present Oakland A's.)

Like most of the other great men of the Amateur Era, Colonel Fitzgerald was not involved with baseball at the top competitive levels in the Professional Era. But he continued to sponsor youth and amateur baseball and he remained an important figure in journalism, politics, and Philadelphia society. The *City Item* prospered and made him rich. In 1888 he was spoken of as a possible Presidential candidate. In 1890 he retired, turning over his newspaper to his sons. He died the following year while on his annual trip to Europe. He is buried in West Philadelphia's now vandalized and overgrown Mt. Moriah Cemetery—a place as impoverished and neglected as the inner-city neighborhood that he was born in.

In life, Fitzgerald was a happy warrior. In the 1860s, he waged two high-stakes public battles, one against baseball's racism, the other for the amateur ideal and the young sport's credibility with the Protestant bourgeoisie. In both cases, he fought and ultimately lost the good fight. But Thomas Fitzgerald won the most important fight of his life, the fight to establish baseball in Philadelphia. He co-founded and helped build the Athletics, Philadelphia's first nationally competitive baseball club. He deserves a share of the credit for the victory of the baseball movement itself—a victory that gave us our first national sport, the first professional leagues, and today's vast and varied American sports industry.

NOTES

1. *New York Clipper,* November 8, 1862.
2. *New York Clipper,* October 5, 1861.
3. Brooklyn *Daily Eagle,* June 3, 1862.
4. *New York Clipper,* July 12, 1862.
5. *New York Clipper,* July 12, 1862.
6. New York *Herald,* August 30, 1865.
7. Reading *Times,* June 26, 1891.
8. New York *Evening Post,* August 25, 1843, 2; and July 3, 1845.
9. Thomas A. Devyr, *The Odd Book of the 19th Century,* 26.
10. Brooklyn *Daily Eagle,* February 2, 1896, 36.
11. George Rogers Taylor, *New York History* vol. 58, no. 3 (July 1977), 297–298.
12. St. Paul's Congregational Church Philadelphia Confirmation Record, 1870, 221.
13. New York *Irish American Weekly,* April 7, 1888.
14. Philadelphia *City Item,* August 18, 1866.
15. Philadelphia *City Item,* July 21, 1866.
16. Philadelphia *City Item,* August 25, 1866.
17. Philadelphia *City Item,* July 21, 1866.
18. Philadelphia *City Item,* September 1, 1866.
19. Philadelphia *City Item,* August 18, 1866.
20. Philadelphia *Sunday Mercury,* October 6, 1867.
21. J. Casway, *Octavius Catto and the Pythians of Philadelphia,* Pennsylvania Legacies, May 2007, 5.
22. Philadelphia *Sunday Mercury,* December 15, 1867.
23. Philadelphia *City Item,* July 31, 1869.
24. Philadelphia *Morning Post* quoted in Philadelphia *City Item,* September 25, 1869.
25. *New National Era,* October 19, 1871.

The Hidden Hall of Famer

David Nemec

When the Players League formed in 1890 as a rival to the two extant major leagues—the National League and the American Association— one of its strongest teams was expected to be the Brooklyn Ward's Wonders led by player-manager John M. Ward, the founder and driving force behind the rebel loop. But just before the teams went to spring training camp third baseman Jerry Denny reneged on his pledge to join Ward's team and elected to remain loyal to the National League. Stuck for a replacement, Ward hired a heretofore little-known minor league third baseman named Bill Joyce. The raw rookie proved to be a huge surprise. This article examines Joyce's rise from obscurity to major league stardom and raises the issue of whether he should be deemed eligible for the Hall of Fame.

IN THE DECEMBER 12, 1897, issue of *The Sporting News*, Chicago pitcher Clark Griffith recounted that Bill Joyce had used a bat with a distinctive blue band painted around the end of it ever since he had homered with it in a Texas League game, but noted that by 1897 Joyce no longer used such a bat. The speculation that perhaps it had at long last broken and Joyce's hitting may have suffered for its loss was borne out to a degree. Joyce's bat work did begin to decline in 1897, but he also turned 30 that season—an old 30 due to his many leg injuries and the intensity he brought to every game. Griffith also said in his evaluation of the third sacker, "He hugs the plate," which accounted for him collecting so many walks and why no one could sneak a pitch on the outside corner past him. In addition, Joyce was an excruciatingly patient hitter, an excellent bunter, a good baserunner and hit often by pitches.

Base Ball 12, pp. 52–65
ISSN 1934-2802 (Print) / ISSN 1934-3167 (Online)
978-1-4766-7473-5 (Print) / 978-1-4766-4112-6 (ebook)

In all, he possessed the ideal qualities for a leadoff hitter except for this: He hit with such tremendous power that he was wasted there. During his final five seasons in the National League, Joyce was the best infielder at combining power, average, and an ability to get on base and was arguably the most dangerous offensive threat in the game, period. In that five-year span, 1894–98, his 60 home runs led the entire major league field.

William Michael Joyce was born on September 22, 1867, in Carondelet, Missouri, a small independent city along the Mississippi River that was annexed by St. Louis three years later. The son of Irish immigrants, he played amateur and sandlot ball in his youth with a number of former and future big league players, most prominently the Tebeau brothers, Pat and George, while working in the rolling mills of the many iron and zinc furnaces that dotted the Carondelet riverfront in the late nineteenth century.

Owing to his powerful arm, no doubt enhanced by his heavy labor in the mills, Joyce began as a pitcher but had gravitated to catcher by the summer of 1886 when he joined Abilene, his first professional team, in the independent Texas League. Except for a brief seven-game sojourn with Leavenworth in the Western League in 1887, followed by stretches with several independent teams, as per *The Sporting News's* July 6, 1887, issue (and then a three-game stint with Kansas City of the WA when Leavenworth sold him to Hastings and he refused to abide by the sale), he remained in Lone Star loops through most of the 1889 season when he led the Texas League (by then affiliated with the National Agreement) in homers with 18 but batted just .235 while captaining first-place Houston. Now a third baseman, he headed north after the TL collapsed on August 12 to finish the campaign with Toledo of the International Association, where he hit a meager .164 in 30 games while playing with a badly sprained leg, the first of many such documented injuries he would incur.

Other than displaying tremendous power at the plate and a gritty style of play that buttressed the nickname of "Scrappy" he had first earned in the Carondelet mills, Joyce as yet seemed too unpolished to have any realistic expectations of ever playing major league ball. But after the 1889 season he returned to Texas that fall to play for a Lone Star all-star team against barnstorming major league clubs. St. Louis Browns player-manager Charlie Comiskey, who had already committed to joining the rebel Players League the following year, was so impressed with Joyce's game that he recommended him to PL founder John M. Ward once Ward was compelled to scramble around for a third baseman after National League veteran Jerry Denny reneged on his pledge to join Ward's Brooklyn PL team.

The only rookie in Brooklyn's Opening Day lineup on April 19, 1890,

Joyce occupied third base for Ward's Wonders in every inning of every Brotherhood game, scored 121 runs and led the circuit with 123 walks, a frosh record that remained his alone until it was tied in 2017 by the Yankees' Aaron Judge. Yet he garnered just 123 hits and compiled a .252 batting average, 22 points below the league mark of .274 and evidence that while he already had a firm sense of the strike zone, he still had some maturing to do as a hitter.

When the PL collapsed all players not under contract to another team prior to joining the rebel loop became free agents. Consequently, Ward, who became player-manager of the Brooklyn National League club after his Brotherhood brainchild went up in flames, could have taken Joyce with him but stuck with the Bridegrooms third base incumbent, aging George Pinkney. Joyce instead joined the powerhouse Boston Reds, winners of the PL pennant, who allied with the American Association in 1891 accompanied by almost their full 1890 cast. With a year of facing top-flight pitching under his belt, Joyce not only won the Reds' third base post handily but collected a phenomenal 63 walks in the first 64 games of the season and was hitting a solid .313 with an OPS just a shade below 1.000.

But in the third inning of the 64th game, a 12–4 Boston win against Washington's Frank Foreman, after reaching base via a walk, Joyce broke his ankle sliding into second on an attempted steal. He remained out of action until October 3 when he begged to play in the Reds' celebratory final home game of the season after they had already clinched the AA pennant even though his ankle was still not fully mended. In that game, a 6–2 win over Washington's Kid Carsey, Joyce played first base, batted last and went 0-for-3. When the Reds then traveled to Philadelphia for a season-ending doubleheader on October 5, Joyce did not accompany them. For fully half a century no one noted that Joyce had reached base safely with either a hit or a walk in all of his 64 games before he was injured and in so doing had set a record until it was broken by Joe DiMaggio in 1941 with 74 games. (Ted Williams subsequently broke DiMaggio's record in 1949 with 84 games.)

If Joyce had not insisted on playing in the Reds' final home game, he would have ended 1891 with a perfect season, reaching base in every contest he played. Actually, if such streaks were carried over from one season to the next, had Joyce not played in that October 3, 1891, game, he would now rank second only to Williams on the all-time list of most consecutive games reaching base safely, with 79—Joyce reached base safely in his last five games in 1890 and his first 10 in 1892 before being stopped by Louisville's Alex Jones on April 29 when he went 0-for-4. Joyce also enjoyed two other lengthy on-base-safely streaks—54 games in 1894 and 56 in 1896, putting him in Williams's company as the only two players to own three different streaks of reaching base safely in 50 or more straight games.

Joyce batted left and threw right, stood 5'11" and rattled the scales at a rock-hard 180 pounds. He was the ideal build and temperament for a third baseman in every way but one. He was abominable on ground balls. In the February 17, 1900, issue of *The Sporting News*, after Joyce had been out of the game for more than a year, former major league outfielder Tom Brown claimed that Joyce would still be active and an unequivocal star if he had just followed Brown's advice of some four years earlier when the two were Washington teammates and converted to the outfield. But Joyce had stubbornly insisted he "wanted to smell the smoke of the base ball powder and remain in the inner circle." Staying in the inner circle cost him dearly. In his rookie year he logged 107 errors and an .811 fielding average, the first a record high and the latter a record low by a qualifier at third base since 1889 when the game was set forever at four balls and three strikes. The irony is that Joyce was a wonder at handling sizzling line drives and wind-blown pop flies. Outfielder Tommy Dowd once commented in the October 2, 1896, *St. Louis Post-Dispatch*, "Scrappy Joyce may be an uncertain quantity on grounds balls but when it comes to flies he never had a superior. He's death to a fly ball."

As it happened, when the American Association dissolved after the 1891 season and four of its teams (the champion Boston Reds were not among them) were absorbed into the eight-team National League to form an unwieldy 12-club circuit, Joyce was reunited with Brooklyn player-manager John M. Ward, which proved to be a bad fit. Now an established major leaguer, Joyce was no longer as tolerant of Ward's authoritarian and at times abrasive style of managing as he had been in his rookie season. The two clashed often, their differences commencing even before the season started when Joyce obstinately trained on his own in Hot Springs, Arkansas, and refused to join Ward's team in spring training until April 1 because his contract did not officially begin until then. Soon thereafter, the May 28, 1892, *Sporting Life* flatly labeled Joyce a dirty player, often cited for intentional interference by umpires as both a baserunner and a third baseman. To compound his difficulties, Ward tried to turn him into a left fielder late in the season, but the experiment lasted just three contentious games before Joyce all but quit the team. And again, his season was marred by a serious leg injury in a game against New York on July 30, as per the August 2, 1892, *Washington Post*, that knocked him out of action for all of August and most of September.

The net result was the worst season of Joyce's big league career, a .245 batting average and participation in less than two-thirds of Brooklyn's games. At the behest of first baseman Dave Foutz, who joined Ward in dissing Joyce, in February 1893, Brooklyn owner Charlie Byrne sent his rebellious third baseman along with $1,800 to Washington for infielder Danny Richardson. Few were surprised when Joyce, already recognized for being his own man, was made the first high-caliber player to fall victim of a new rule introduced in 1892 that no longer permitted a player to rescind a trade simply by refusing to report to his new team. Joyce (who had already crossed swords with baseball's powers that be in 1887 when he refused to be sold against his will by Leavenworth) had good reason for his opposition. Not only was Washington a weak club but it purportedly offered him only $1,800 for 1893, a thousand-dollar drop from his salary in 1892. Rather than report to the D.C. club in the spring of 1893, he remained at his home in St. Louis.

When his intransigence failed to convince Washington owner J. Earle Wagner to move him elsewhere even though several teams made Wagner appealing offers, Joyce sat out the entire 1893 season, allegedly betting on horse races in the afternoon after spending his mornings staying in peak condition playing handball. Even when he finally recanted and reported on March 5, 1894, to the Nationals new bench manager Gus Schmelz, it was only grudgingly. As a sop to Joyce, Schmelz named him captain, meaning that he ran the team on the field. The extra responsibility almost immediately revived him. Despite being in Schmelz's doghouse off and on all season for his excessive kicking to umpires (resulting on one occasion, May 1, 1894, in a game being forfeited to Brooklyn due to his antics), Joyce put together the best season of any third baseman in the nineteenth century. Popular almost instantly with Washington teammates, spectators and sportswriters alike, he relished the first of several career games in Washington garb on August 20 at Washington when he went 4-for-5 in an 8–7 Nationals win over Louisville. In the contest he hammered three home runs off the Colonels Phil Knell, marking the first occasion in major league history that a left-handed hitter had taken a southpaw pitcher deep three times in a game.

In all, Joyce compiled a 1.146 OPS but it was just 99 games before yet another grim mishap prematurely ended his season. On September 29, 1894, the *Washington Post* ran a special item forwarded from St. Louis stating that the previous day. "Joyce, of the Senators, had a dangerous operation performed on him this morning at the Hospital of the Alexian Brothers on South Broadway [in St. Louis]. Drs. Hy Marks and Miller cut the inner side of his left hip open and refastened some ligaments which had torn loose from the hip joint and removed several lumps of clotted blood." The news came as a complete shock to the entire Washington club, all of whom had thought that Joyce, at worst, was nursing a slight injury since he had played without incident in the Nationals' last game prior to his surgery. On October 6, 1894, *The Sporting*

News assured its readers that Joyce was on the mend, but given the grisly description of the surgery Washington fans could be excused for not quite believing it until … well, the February 9, 1895, edition of *The Sporting News* announced that Joyce was threatening to hold out yet again when the first contract offer he received was for the same amount he had been paid in 1894.

Joyce's latest holdout lasted until early April 1895. Any worries about his left leg were allayed when he was in Washington's Opening Day lineup on Friday, April 20, at Boston, occupying his usual spots—third base and second in the batting order—and doubled against the Beaneaters' Jack Stivetts on his first trip to the plate. Once more he was named captain by Schmelz, and he responded by again leading the Nation-

Bill Joyce, accompanied by his legendary blue-tipped bat. His 1.143 OPS in 1894 with Washington still ranks as the best ever by a third baseman batting title qualifier. Among his 126 hits that season, 56 were for extra bases (Library of Congress).

als in almost every major batting department. That summer he nearly caught a break when Cleveland, battling for the pennant, made a lavish offer for him in hopes of replacing Chippy McGarr, among the weakest third basemen in the league. But J. Earle Wagner, even knowing his club had no chance for a decent finish—it came in tenth in the 12-team circuit—chose that juncture to refuse to sell any of his top players, no matter the size of the offer, according to *The Sporting News*'s October 26, 1895, issue.

Wagner was also aware that Joyce was far and away his most valuable asset, worshipped for his never-say-die spirit and deemed "the real funny man of the base ball world" in the November 30, 1895, *Sporting Life*. As a sample, a Boston paper that season quoted his quip about his hair graying even though he was only 28: "Because I am gray the public believe I must be at least 38 or 40 years old. I have heard it said that I am as old as [Cap] Anson, and Anse, you know, listened to Washington's farewell address way back in 1782."

But if Joyce drew the attention of all from the first pitch to the last on the ball field and then again with his repartee in the postgame dressing room, his personal life, other than his close friendships with several fellow players who were St. Louis natives, remained almost completely veiled. Unlike George Davis, another great third baseman in the mid–1890s whose off-the-field dalliances were the constant stuff of headlines in sporting papers, not until 1897 did *The Sporting News* reveal the offhanded tidbit that Joyce was the only bachelor among the present crew of National League managers.

In the fall of 1895, Washington owner J. Earle Wagner and his brother George, who also had stock in the club, optioned a stage production called "The Texas Steer Show," a comedy about an illiterate cowboy who through a series of misunderstandings becomes a congressman, and hired their manager, Gus Schmelz, who also had experience in running stage shows, to oversee it. Little was expected at first of the production, but when it had a record-breaking run in early January, the Wagners extended it indefinitely. Consequently, the Nationals started spring training in 1896 with Schmelz still on the road. In his absence, Wagner appointed himself the titular manager of the club but turned over full charge of the team to Joyce, making him responsible for its movements both on and off the field. Even after Schmelz returned to the team on May 10, except for arranging hotel stays in advance when the club was on the road, a chore left to Schmelz, Joyce remained in complete charge of the team until he was traded to New York on July 31. At the time of his departure the Nationals were 34–46, but despite compelling evidence to the contrary offered by Kerin and Kevin Flynn in their blog on Washington Baseball History, the games he managed are still credited to Schmelz by MLB.

Earlier in the 1896 season on April 22, Joyce had been clobbered by a pitch from Brooklyn's George Harper. His nose was so badly broken that he was expected to miss at least a week or two, maybe more, but he was back in the lineup after only a one-game absence. Some five weeks later, in the first game of a Memorial Day doubleheader at Pittsburgh, Joyce hit for the cycle in a 17–13 loss to the Pirates' Frank Killen, who that season became the National League's last southpaw 30-game winner. As late as July 6, Joyce had his Nationals over .500 at 30–29, but when the club won only four more games that month, Schmelz began to quibble about the captain's handling of the team, gaining more traction with each defeat. Finally, after a 5–4 loss to Baltimore on July 31, Schmelz was promoted again to manager by Wagner and Joyce was dealt to New York for catcher Duke Farrell, pitcher Carney

Flynn and $2,500. The August 9 *Washington Post* said the $2,500 "would be spent for any player that strikes Mr. Wagner's fancy, providing that player can be purchased." The same *Post* edition said that Wagner had made Louisville "a liberal offer for [outfielder Tom] McCreery." But the Colonels declined it and the best Wagner could do to replace Joyce at third base was hire medical student Harvey Smith.

Upon his arrival in the Gotham, Joyce was soon named player-manager, replacing Arthur Irwin on August 8. On his first morning at the Giants' helm, the team was 36–53. In its final 42 games of the season, under Joyce's leadership the club won two-thirds of them (28–14) and rose from near the bottom of the league to just outside the six-team first division, finishing in seventh place. The man most responsible for the abrupt change in fortune was none other than the new manager himself, who hit a torrid .370 that year in his 49 games in Giants attire, rapped five home runs that combined with his eight for Washington to tie him with Ed Delahanty for the 1896 league four-bagger crown with 13, and registered a 1.042 OPS.

To say that Joyce was ecstatic over being traded to New York would be a vast understatement. At least initially.

Joyce and the Giants eyed the upcoming 1897 season with high hopes. His presence at third base enabled George Davis to move from third to shortstop, where he quickly emerged as the best in the league at his new position. The Giants had acquired Bill Gleason and Jake Beckley the previous year to man second and first base, respectively, and now featured arguably the best infield in the league. The outfield was solid, Jack Warner was among the better catchers. The pitching rotation was headed by Amos Rusie, the strikeout king in the 1890s who had sat out the 1896 season in a contract dispute. It included Jouett Meekin, another perennial 20-game winner, and sophomore southpaw Cy Seymour on tap to support him.

In 1897 Rusie and Meekin both won 20 games, Seymour led all pitchers in strikeouts and Davis set a retrospective RBI record for shortstops that lasted until 1948. But Joyce sustained several injuries that kept him out of the lineup for sizeable stretches and prompted the Giants to claim third baseman Jim Donnelly on waivers and finish the season with rookie Charlie Gettig occupying Joyce's customary spot when Donnelly hit just .188 in 23 games. What's more, Joyce's BA slipped to .303 and he collected just three home runs.

Beckley, whose reckless style clashed with both Joyce and Giants owner Andrew Freedman, was an additional loss. During spring training, he was suspended temporarily for bad behavior and soon thereafter, on May 17, was rudely yanked by Joyce at Pittsburgh, his original home in the NL, and pinch hit for by pitcher Meekin. Beckley reacted to the embarrassment by cursing out Joyce and the entire Giants organization and was summarily released on May 22. Five days later he signed with Cincinnati, but the bad blood between him and Joyce only thickened until Joyce left the game behind.

For all that, the Giants owned a 75–40 record as late as September 10 and even though they could do no better than split their last 16 games, their .634 winning percentage was their best since Freedman had bought the team in January 1895. Their home attendance of 390,340 led the league. That Joyce's men could finish no higher than third place was only because Boston (.705) and Baltimore (.692) played at an extraordinarily blistering pace. Joyce, in addition, could point to his last record-setting day on May 18 at Pittsburgh when he became only the second batter in history to hit four triples in a game while going 4-for-5 against the Pirates Pink Hawley and Jim Gardner. There have been none since.

In the spring of 1898, numerous sporting papers broadcast Joyce's pledge that "without a doubt" his Giants would take the flag that season. But Joyce had not reckoned on the Giants' front office and, in particular, its owner. Andrew Freedman is favorably remembered outside the baseball world as an extremely successful financier and for organizing the construction of the IRT, New York City's first subway line. But as a man used to operating behind the scenes, he was ill prepared for the highly public environment baseball thrust on him, especially since his Gotham club delivered the game its largest market.

Considered by many historians to have been the most toxic owner in nineteenth century baseball, Freedman has been depicted by Bill James as "George Steinbrenner on quaaludes." But unlike Steinbrenner, Freedman loathed publicity and rather than courting New York baseball writers, tried everything in his power to keep them out of the Polo Grounds, the Giants' home park, for fear of what new criticism they would level at him. He had first drawn their wrath in 1896, barely a year after taking control of the club, when he had tried to cut the salary paid in 1895 to Rusie after he first suspended his ace pitcher for drinking, and drove Rusie into sitting out the entire 1896 season. That alone should have been fair warning to Joyce, who had also lost a full year out of his career to a recalcitrant owner.

Contrary to Joyce's predictions, New York looked like anything but a pennant winner once the 1898 season began. After their first six games the Giants were 1–5 and did not reach .500 for the first time until May 10 when Rusie's 5–0 shutout against Brooklyn brought their record to 8–8. Less than a month later, the June 4 *Sporting Life* called the Giants "listless" in their play and pushing Joyce into constantly "nagging at his own men" with "complaints and tirades." Joyce was in turn being harassed daily by Freedman, who had become an unstoppable font of orders on how to run the team even though he knew little about baseball. A key incident occurred just before the June 4 *Sporting Life* hit the newsstands. On June 3, in the course of a wild 16–10 home win over Cincinnati, with Joyce playing first base, Reds first sacker Jake Beckley, a left-handed hitter, dragged a bunt down the first-base line. There was hard contact between them as Joyce fielded the ball. Whether or not Beckley's bunt was a deliberate effort to stage a collision is unknown, but the bad blood between them instantly blew the lid off Joyce. He fired the ball at Beckley's head, striking him behind the ear. The *Cincinnati Enquirer* led the almost universal condemnation of Joyce, culminating in its June 7 edition which grumbled that while Joyce had issued an apology, it was insincere in that he maintained Beckley had it coming to him.

After their June 3 victory over Cincinnati, the Giants were 22–15, seven games over .500, but by the end of the month they were below .500 again and nineteenth century immortal, Cap Anson, had replaced Joyce as manager on July 11, operating from the bench and looking to have Joyce traded when he realized the clubhouse was divided between him and Joyce. When Anson could tolerate working under Freedman and a divided clubhouse for a mere 22 games, Joyce was restored at the helm on July 7. The club immediately perked up and had won 12 of their first 15 games in his second stint in 1898 as their skipper as of July 23 when Seymour shut out Baltimore 8–0 at New York.

But two days later at the Polo Grounds, the wheels came off completely. In a rematch against Baltimore, Orioles outfielder Ducky Holmes, a former Giant who loathed Freedman, fanned in the top of fourth inning. As he slunk back to the Baltimore bench, a Giants fan hollered, "Holmes, you're a lobster. That's what you left here for." Holmes retorted, "It's a good thing I'm not working for a Sheeny now." Between innings, Freedman charged onto the field and ordered umpire Tom Lynch to remove Holmes from the game for besmirching his ethnicity. Lynch said he hadn't heard Holmes say anything insulting, and Freedman then secured the police and refused to let the game continue until Holmes was removed from the park. After a futile attempt to pacify Freedman, Lynch threw up his hands and forfeited the game to Baltimore, whereupon the crowd demanded its money be refunded and threatened violence until Freedman grudgingly assented. During the furor, Holmes was given a protective escort from the grounds. The forfeit dropped the Giants' record to 44–38. After that they played below .500 and finished in seventh place. No sooner had the season ended on October 15, than Joyce angrily declared to all who would listen that he was not at fault for the Giants' dismal showing and blamed Freedman for not spending money to acquire better players or appreciating the good ones he already had.

Predictably, Freedman chose not to bring Joyce back as manager for the 1899 season but nonetheless reserved him and refused to grant his wish to be traded or sold to another team. So the two came to a stalemate that lasted into the early 1900s, when Joyce finally accepted that his major league finale had come at age 31 in a doubleheader on October 12, 1898, in Baltimore when he went 1-for-3 in each game, raising his average a point to an uninspiring .258. Against that, he could boast that he had finished second in the league in walks and tied for second with Jimmy Collins in home runs with 10.

On December 17, 1898, *The Sporting News* summed up the Giants' season by pointing to the team's overall low morale and a correspondingly huge plunge in attendance from nearly 400,000 to 206,700. As for 1899, the St. Louis-based paper noted there was now talk of Joyce coming to his hometown and taking over at first base from his companion since boyhood, Pat Tebeau, who was nearing the end of as a player and would stay on as a bench manager. The February 9, 1899, *Sporting Life* affirmed that Joyce's sojourn with the Giants was likely over.

> It begins to look as if Scrappy Bill Joyce will not wear a New York uniform this season. Manager [John] Day is quoted as saying positively that Bill will not accompany the New Yorks to Charleston [for spring training].... In view of the circumstances there is nothing strange in the passing of Joyce now that he is no longer manager of the team. Joyce has by no means outlived his usefulness, as is shown by his high standing among long-hitters of the League. Impartial base ball men will never say that the failure of the New York Club last year was due to Bill Joyce.

All that winter he tried in vain to engineer escape from baseball hell under Freedman. Then, at the last minute, Joyce decided to stay home in St. Louis and work out with the cream of the 1898 Cleveland team, which had been transferred to the Mound City when the two clubs fell under syndicate ownership and the Robison brothers, the dual owners, decided St. Louis would prove the more lucrative of the two cities. Stymied, Freedman pondered the Robisons' offer of Cleveland outfielder Tommy Dowd for Joyce, but the deal fell through when Joyce wanted too much money from the decimated Spiders' organization. "You'll never find Bill Joyce among the cheap men," said Joyce at his home in St. Louis to a correspondent from *The Sporting News* in its April 15, 1899, issue. Stubborn and proud to the end, he maintained the same regimen for the entire 1899 season, morning workouts with the Spiders contingent, masquerading as the St. Louis Perfectos, and afternoons at the racetrack, where he usually won, as reported by the July 29, 1899, *The Sporting News*. Late in the season there were rumors he might replace Tebeau as St. Louis's manager and first baseman, but nothing ever came of them. In December he announced his retirement from the game at age 32.

Nonetheless, the February 17, 1900, *Sporting Life* reported "Scrappy Bill" Joyce has received his 1900 contract from the New York Club. The gray-topped player smiled as he showed it, and said:

> Just as soon as Andrew Freedman pays me what he owes me on my 1898 contract I will talk business, but not before. There is an indebtedness amounting to a cool $1000 according to the specific terms of that contract, and he's got to make that good before I will notice him. Joyce is so fixed at present that he is not required to return to diamond duty in order to gain a living. His new enterprise has proven a big success, and the former great third baseman is able to give his former employer the laugh.

The new enterprise referred to had been reported the previous month in the January 20, 1900, *Sporting Life*. "Bill Joyce and Patsey [*sic*] Tebeau opened their new saloon, 215 North Sixth Street, St. Louis, with a grand flourish on last Saturday evening. The place was thronged with the hundreds of friends of the proprietors, who were over whelmed [*sic*] with good wishes."

Scarcely two years later, in its February 21, 1903, issue, *Sporting Life* reported that on February 10 the partnership between the two ended abruptly and with it, as events would later reveal, their longtime friendship.

> "Scrappy" Bill Joyce and "Patsy" Oliver Tebeau, erstwhile stars on the ball field, but of late dispensers of high balls to a thirsty public, dissolved partnership to-day as the result of a mixup [*sic*] recently. According to reports, a wellknown [*sic*] local railroad magnate was in Joyce & Tebeau's celebrating an extension of the system with which he is connected and attempted to make a rough house, when "Scrappy" Bill called him down. This Tebeau resented and there was an inevitable mix-up, as a result of which the partners decided to separate. Each turned in a sealed bid to a disinterested third party [with the top bidder to become sole owner] … Joyce proved to be the highest bidder.

Though Joyce remained a close follower of the game, he seemed content otherwise to operate his saloon, stay in shape and schmooze with longstanding friends and customers. In 1908, at age 41, he finally abandoned bachelorhood and married 29-year-old Irish-born Adele Brockel (nee Walters). Whether the couple had children is unknown. Also unknown is the fate of Joyce's saloon, but one might suspect that with Tebeau's cordiality no longer around to temper his own somewhat arrogant and officious manner its popularity soon diminished. Whatever the case, Joyce trusted that his enduring reputation as a dedicated no-nonsense player along with his penchant for keeping in peak condition even into his forties would serve him if he ever decided to get back into the game.

But he misunderstood how much the climate had changed since he was last in uniform.

At age 43 in 1911, Joyce took a flier at becoming part owner and manager of the Missoula Scrappers of the newly formed Class D Union Association. The circuit featured six clubs in Montana, one in Idaho and one in Utah, with the Great Falls Electrics the runaway pennant winner and Missoula bringing up the rear. The respect Joyce had commanded as a player-manager of major league veterans in the 1890s did not translate well in the lower minors among much younger men some 15 years later. Nor did his fierce kicking to umpires at every decision against his Scrappers. Whether Joyce attempted at his advanced age to play for the Scrappers is not certain, but the suspicion is that he did. In any event, by July Missoula fans were clamoring for him to trash his uniform and keep away from the park. Joyce eventually took the resounding hint, selling his share of the club and turning the managerial reins over to pitcher Charlie McCafferty.

The humiliating experience no doubt sobered Joyce, as did the disappointing dearth of invitations to participate in post–1900 Old Timers' games and similar events staged by the two St. Louis major league clubs, the American League Browns and the National League Cardinals, in part because, despite being a St. Louis native, he had never worn the uniform of a local team. Joyce did serve as a scout for the St. Louis Terriers of the Federal League in 1914–15 and subsequently for the Browns in 1916, but there is no record that any players he helped sign played for either club. Neither do we ever learn if Joyce and Tebeau patched up their differences prior to Tebeau's sudden suicide in 1918. By 1920 Joyce was not only out of baseball but also out of the saloon business, perhaps for some while, and was working as a watchman for an oil company in St. Louis. Ten years later U.S. census records show him as a Mound City smoke inspector.

On May 8, 1941, Joyce died at St. Louis City Hospital at the age of 73 of hypertrophy of the prostate and bilateral pyelonephritis. At the time he was living at 4400 Bircher Boulevard. His wife Adele died 13 years later. The two are buried side by side in the Mound City's Bellefontaine Cemetery in her family plot.

During the 10 seasons (1890–99) Bill Joyce was under reserve to major league teams he ranks third in on-base percentage and seventh in OPS among all players with a minimum of 2,000 plate appearances in that span. Although he did not compete in the required ten seasons for eligibility, an exception was made in the instance of Addie Joss. Too, Joyce played eight full seasons, more than some like Dizzy Dean. If he were credited, as arguably he should be, with the two full seasons he was a helpless holdout, a case can easily be made that his overall body of work is far superior to numerous players now enshrined in Cooperstown and that he too belongs.

Sources

The author relied on the following primary sources in assembling his biography of Bill Joyce: *The Sporting News*; *Sporting Life*; the *Boston Globe*; the *Washington Post*; the *New York Times*; the *Brooklyn Eagle*; the *St. Louis Post-Dispatch*; the *Chicago Tribune*; a copy of Joyce's death certificate; and Baseball-Reference.com (https://www.baseball-reference.com/players/j/joycebi01.shtml). Key passages are attributed in the article's text to the precise date and issue of their source.

Manhattan Politics, Newport Society, and the Polo Grounds

The Turn-of-the-Century Haunts of James and Harriet Coogan

BILL LAMB

*The Bobby Thomson home run that won the New York Giants the 1951
National League pennant was celebrated as "The Miracle of Coogan's
Bluff." This article recalls the bluff's namesake James J. Coogan and his
heiress wife, the former Harriet Gardiner Lynch. Now long-forgotten,
James Coogan was a significant actor in the political and sporting life of
New York City for decades. As titleholder of the real property on which
the Polo Grounds sat, the tough-minded but intensely private Harriet
Coogan may have had even more influence over events in Giants history than her husband. And Harriet's long-running feud with the social
elite of posh Newport, Rhode Island, went from newspaper gossip column fodder to the stuff of enduring local legend.*

FROM EARLY JULY 1889 until the removal of the franchise to the West
Coast following the 1957 season, the New York Giants played often exciting,
and sometimes championship, baseball at the northern Manhattan ballpark
known as the Polo Grounds. Inexorably over the decades, Giants players,
managers, club owners, front office personnel, sportswriters, and team rooters
came and went. Even the Polo Grounds itself changed identity several times.
Through the years, however, one thing remained constant: The Giants' de-
pendence upon the family from whom it leased the real property on which its

Base Ball 12, pp. 66–85
ISSN 1934-2802 (Print) / ISSN 1934-3167 (Online)
978-1-4766-7473-5 (Print) / 978-1-4766-4112-6 (ebook)

ballparks sat—the Coogans, or more particularly, the Gardiner-Lynch-Coogan family. The text below profiles the clan's two most prominent members: James J. Coogan, the furniture dealer-turned-Manhattan politico who managed the family's vast real estate holdings, and his heiress wife, the former Harriet Gardiner Lynch, a business-savvy but private woman who, after her husband's death in 1915, assumed oversight of the family property portfolio and dealt with the Giants for the ensuing 30 years.

James J. Coogan and Harriet Gardiner Lynch: A Union of Social Unequals

The Coogans were something of an odd couple, separated by considerable difference in age, affluence, and social station. Throughout his life, James Jay Coogan was evasive about the year and place of his birth. But in all probability, he was born on January 16, 1845, in County Carlow, Ireland. James was the oldest of the six children[1] known to have been born to Patrick Peter Coogan (1821–1905) and his wife Alice (nee McGinty, 1825–1898). About 1852, the Irish Catholic Coogans emigrated to America and settled in New York City.[2] Once on their feet, Patrick Coogan and his brother James established a furniture-making business in lower Manhattan. Although he would obtain a law degree from New York University, son James was intended for the family business and trained in upholstery. Over time, he and younger brothers Edward and Thomas assumed control of the operation, soon headquartered in the Bowery and styled Coogan Brothers Furniture. Catering to the Irish and German immigrants who had moved into the area and willing to do business via installment payments from its generally cash-strapped clientele, the business thrived, eventually opening outlets elsewhere in Manhattan. By the early 1880s, the Coogan brothers were prosperous city businessmen. But in the end, James J. Coogan made his fortune in a more time-tested way: he married money.

The circumstances under which Coogan met his future bride are lost to history. But on the face of it, the two appeared peculiarly matched. Unlike recent arrival Coogan, Harriet Gardiner Lynch was a member of one of America's oldest and most distinguished families. She was a direct descendent of Lion Gardiner, the English merchant-adventurer granted privileges and property in the colonies by King Charles I in the 1630s. By the time of Harriet's birth more than two centuries later, the Gardiner family had grown large and wealthy, with extensive property holdings in New York, southern New England, and elsewhere.

James J. Coogan c. 1890 (left) and c. 1912.

But interestingly, Harriet's father was a man not unlike James Coogan. Like him, William L. Lynch was an Irish Catholic who had come to America as a youth and prospered in New York City, first as a grocer, thereafter as a tea merchant and importer. How this immigrant of humble origin became acquainted with WASP gentry like the Gardiners is another unknown. By the mid–1840s, however, Lynch had married teenage Sarah Gardiner and started the family that would eventually include eight children, all of whom were raised in their father's Catholic faith.

Harriet was the youngest of the brood, born in Manhattan around 1861. Like her older sisters, she was dispatched to Long Island to be educated, finishing her schooling at the Convent of the Sacred Heart in Manhasset. By the time Harriet returned home, her father had become a wealthy man in his own right,[3] having acquired title to some of the city's choicest real estate (including property in far-north Manhattan that would later become home to the Polo Grounds). As noted, how Harriet became a sweetheart of James Coogan, a man some 16 years her senior in age, is unknown. Whatever the circumstances, their subsequent betrothal was approved by Harriet's parents.[4] The two were married in 1883 at St. Patrick's Cathedral, with no less a Church personage than the Very Rev. Michael Corrigan, the Archbishop of New York, officiating the ceremony.[5] In 1885, son Jay (James Jay, Jr.), the first of the cou-

Harriet Lynch Coogan, around the time of her 1883 marriage (left) and in 1903.

ple's four children, was born.[6] More important for our purposes, the by-now widowed Sarah Gardiner Lynch had entrusted oversight of income-producing family properties to new son-in-law James Coogan. The job was no sinecure, as the holdings were considerable, customarily leased by the family, and rarely sold off. This attachment to property soon brought Coogan into ever-increasing contact with government officials seeking access or title to Gardiner-Lynch real estate (via condemnation or other legal proceedings, if necessary) in order to accommodate ever-growing city expansion/improvement plans.[7]

James J. Coogan and the New York Giants

As Coogan fenced with city bureaucrats, New York Giants founder/owner John B. Day was having his own property problems with officialdom. Since September 1880, Day had leased a meadowland located just north of Central Park in Manhattan from sportsman-socialite James Gordon Bennett, Jr., the owner-editor of the *New York Herald*. Sometime earlier, Bennett had allowed the Westchester Polo Club to enclose a portion of the property so that admission could be charged for its matches. Occasional weekend polo with its small flock of blue-blood patrons was no cause for alarm by the residents of the tony neighborhood. But soon the polo club was gone elsewhere, replaced by summer-long baseball and the noisy, often-uncouth crowds that games brought to the area.[8] This was an entirely different and most unwelcome development. In March 1888, friendly forces on the City Council finally succeeded in pushing through the adoption of a new traffic design plan that remedied the neighborhood's problem with the Polo Grounds by running a city street through the outfield. Rearguard legal action by Day stalled demolition of the ballpark long enough for the Giants to finish the 1888 season with a World Series victory over the American Association St. Louis Browns. Nevertheless, the club boss fully realized that the Polo Grounds was doomed and that he needed to relocate the Giants for the 1889 campaign.

Late that winter, Joseph Gordon, a junior partner in the Giants operation and a Manhattan real estate maven,[9] brought a possible new ballpark site to Day's attention. The property was far-north Manhattan acreage reclaimed via diversion of the Harlem River and owned by the Gardiner-Lynch family.[10] His interest in the property soon brought Day into negotiation with James J. Coogan, the family's estate agent.

By early 1889, it is entirely possible that the two men were already acquainted, as both Day and Coogan were successful downtown Manhattan businessmen, and on the periphery of New York City politics as well. Although not particularly active, Day, a well-heeled cigar manufacturer from Connecticut, was a member of Tammany Hall, the corrupt political machine that controlled Democratic Party affairs in Manhattan. Day had joined Tammany a decade earlier, shortly after he had moved to the city to open a

New York Giants founder/owner John B. Day.

new manufacturing plant on the Lower East Side. While still a principal of Coogan Brothers Furniture, marriage into a wealthy family had afforded Coogan the financial wherewithal to indulge his passion for holding elective office. Because of his frequent business contact with the working classes, Coogan fancied himself a man of the people, and, as such, sought the mayoral nomination of the fringe Socialist Labor Party in 1886. Despite offering to spend $200,000 of his own (meaning his mother-in-law's) money financing his campaign, Coogan's proposed candidacy was roundly rejected by party convention delegates.[11] Two years later, he reentered the political fray with a little more success, garnering the mayoral candidate slot on the United Labor Party ticket. The expenditure of the promised $200,000 in family money did his campaign little good. Coogan was trounced, finishing a distant fourth behind young Tammany Democrat Hugh Grant.[12]

Although far removed from bustling midtown Manhattan, the proposed ballpark site that Day and Coogan dickered over was flat, dry, and already used for pickup baseball games tolerated by the owners. On one side, the site was bounded by a towering escarpment (later dubbed Coogan's Bluff); on the other, the Harlem River.[13] More important, the property was immediately adjacent to a recently constructed north Manhattan railway stop. Given all this, Day thought the spot suitable for a new Giants home and sought a long-term lease to the grounds. But uncharacteristically, the family wanted to unload the property, and it was for sale only. Negotiations soon foundered, prompting Day to place a remarkable notice in the *New York Times*. It read: "I want to find a party to purchase from the present owners, who will not lease, the plot of ground bounded by 8th and 9th Aves., 155th to 157th Sts., which I will lease for five to ten years, at a rental of $6,000 per year. JOHN B. DAY, president New York Base Ball Club, 121 Maiden Lane."[14]

To no great surprise, a property-purchasing angel did not materialize, leaving Day without a ball field as the 1889 season opened. In desperation, the Giants played their first two home games at decrepit Oakdale Park in Jersey City. Day then removed the club to the St. George Grounds on Staten Island, the erstwhile home of the now-defunct New York Mets. But wet weather and the inconvenient locale of the ballpark decimated attendance at Giants games. Quickly, it became clear to Day that playing outside Manhattan was a losing proposition. By now, fortuitously, the Gardiner-Lynch family had relaxed its position on the rental of the north Manhattan site, and negotiations between Day and Coogan resumed. On June 22, 1889, the parties reached agreement on a two-year lease of the grounds.[15] But in an economy that he would soon have cause to regret, Day leased only as much land as he needed for his new ballpark, declining the opportunity to rent the tract in its entirety.

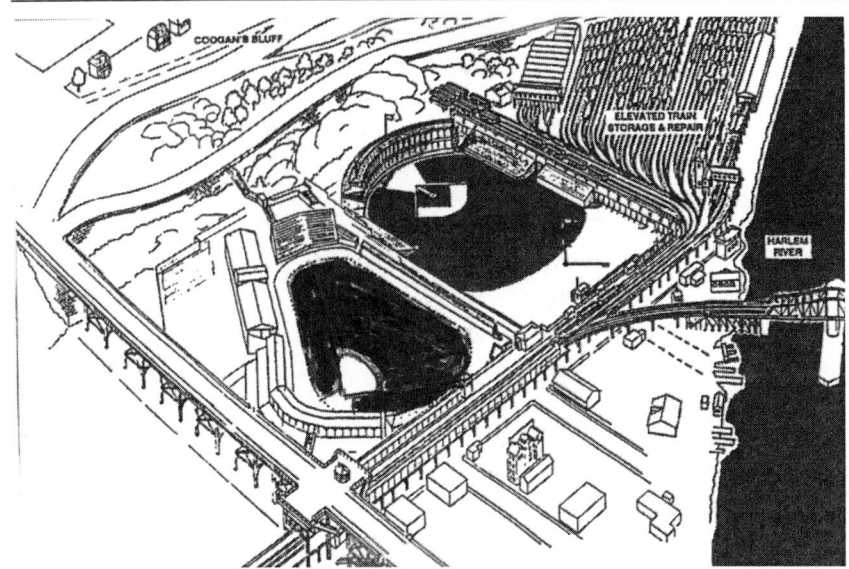

Manhattan Field (below) and the Polo Grounds III.

Working at a furious pace, the small army of workmen that Day loosed on the property erected a usable, if still unfinished, ballpark in a breathless three weeks.[16] The Giants inaugurated their new home field, christened the New Polo Grounds, on July 8, 1889, with a 7–5 win over the Pittsburgh Alleghenies. An estimated crowd of 10,000 paid their way through the turnstiles, while another 5,000 freeloaders watched game action from atop Coogan's Bluff, the Eighth Avenue Viaduct, the Harlem Speedway, and other elevated vantage points. The win augured a New York surge in National League standings that saw the club nip the Boston Beaneaters at the wire for the pennant. The Giants then successfully defended their World Series crown with a post-season triumph over the American Association Brooklyn Bridegrooms. Although he was not known to be a baseball enthusiast, James J. Coogan was impressed by the throngs paying their way into the new ballpark that summer. Consequently, even before the season was done, Coogan made Day a $200,000 offer for the purchase of the Giants.[17] But in another decision that he would soon have reason to second-guess, Day turned Coogan down.

The arrival of the Players League and the havoc which it caused the baseball establishment during the 1890 season is beyond the scope of this article. Suffice it to say that James J. Coogan contributed to the stress endured by the ownership of the NL New York Giants. Although he already had a tenant on site, Coogan felt no compunction about leasing the remainder of

the property to Players League investors headed by young Wall Street financier Edward B. Talcott.[18] Within months, Brotherhood Park, home of the PL
New York Giants, was sitting directly adjacent to the National League Giants
ballpark, their dimensions separated only by a 10-feet-wide passageway and
the stadium walls. While Brotherhood Park was going up, Coogan attempted
to pressure Day into surrendering his lease to the New Polo Grounds, but
was quickly and emphatically rebuffed. Day's ball club was not going anywhere.[19] In fact, only two months after Coogan had tried to force the NL
Giants out of its ballpark, *Sporting Life* reported that "[t]he New York League
club has found a way to vault the obdurate landlord Coogan's stony heart and
has secured a five-year lease of the New Polo Grounds. The terms were not
divulged, but it is safe betting that Coogan didn't get the worst of the bargain
by a very, very long shot."[20]

In the aftermath of the financial bloodbath suffered by both their clubs
and with the Players League headed for oblivion, NL Giants boss Day and
PL Giants leader Talcott agreed to merge their franchises. The consolidated
nine would play the 1891 season as a National League team. Brotherhood
Park, renamed the Polo Grounds, would be used as the club's home base,
while the New Polo Grounds would become Manhattan Field and serve as
a site for non-baseball events. But some weeks after the season's close, Coogan was back on scene to complicate matters. In November 1891, he was approached by representatives of the American Association seeking to place
a club in New York. To that end, they wanted to lease "the land adjoining
the Polo Grounds for a new ballpark." When asked about the AA overture,
Coogan stated, "I told them that I would lease the land and that is all I am
prepared to say."[21] The ensuing demise of the American Association, how-

**Manhattan Field (née New Polo Grounds, foreground) and the Polo Grounds III
(Brotherhood Park, background), c. 1901.**

ever, rendered the matter moot. And within a few seasons, control of the New York Giants passed to a club owner whom Coogan was loath to cross: Andrew Freedman.

Although his election efforts had thus far been fiascos, Coogan's thirst for public office had not been slaked. And it finally occurred to him that the easiest way to achieve his political ambitions was to work his way into the good graces of Richard Croker, the all-powerful and avaricious chief of Tammany Hall—a matter facilitated by Coogan's access to the Gardiner-Lynch family fortune. Given that Freedman was a political protégé, business associate, and close friend of Croker, Coogan took pains not to antagonize the often-prickly club owner. From here on, the Giants' lease to the Polo Grounds/Manhattan Field property was renewed in a timely manner, with minimum fuss.[22]

Before Coogan could much advance his political prospects, the same were threatened by calamity in his business affairs. While more-and-more serving the interests of the Gardiner-Lynch family, Coogan remained a principal in Coogan Brothers Furniture. But a disastrous warehouse fire and a depressed economy (the Panic of 1893) had sent the business into a tailspin. When the brothers could not pay their bills, creditors filed suit.[23] By January 1894, James's finances were in such distress that he was obliged to seek bankruptcy protection. In a humiliating petition filed with the court, Coogan averred that he was penniless; that he was entirely dependent upon his mother-in-law, with whom he, his wife and children lived, for support, and that he could not satisfy the numerous judgments lodged against him.[24]

The failure of Coogan Brothers Furniture subsequently produced an even unhappier event. Edward Coogan initiated a civil suit alleging that his brother James and mother-in-law Sarah Lynch[25] had engaged in conspiracy, fraud, and other improprieties related to the winding-up of the furniture business.[26] In time, the suit was settled out-of-court. During pre-settlement courthouse proceedings, however, it was revealed that Sarah Lynch had been quietly transferring her assets to daughter Harriet Coogan. By now, sadly, seven of Sarah's eight children were deceased, leaving Harriet her sole surviving immediate heir. Dissipation of a person's estate by distribution of assets prior to the testator's death was an effective way to avoid inheritance taxes, and a standard practice of the rich. It was also perfectly legal. By the time the intra-family squabble was resolved, Harriet Coogan had assumed virtually all the wealth of the Gardiner-Lynch family.[27] Given his presumed access to his wife's money, this lent credence to an August 1899 report that Coogan had recently offered "his friend Andrew Freedman" $100,000 for the Giants franchise.[28] If such an offer was, in fact, made, nothing ever came of it.

As Harriet came early into her inheritance, the political fortunes of James J. Coogan were also in ascendance. Having finally ingratiated himself with Boss Croker, Coogan was the Tammany-designated replacement as Manhattan Borough president when incumbent Augustus W. Peters unexpectedly died in office in late–December 1898.[29] The post was largely a ceremonial one, with few official duties to be performed. Coogan got himself into trouble anyway by voting in Southampton, Long Island (not Manhattan), in November 1900 local elections. This put Coogan's place of residence (and thus his continued eligibility for the Manhattan borough president post) in question, and an official inquiry into the issue was briefly conducted.[30] But as long as Tammany held power, Coogan, now a major contributor to Democratic Party campaign coffers, was in little jeopardy.[31] Rather, it took the reform tide of November 1901 NYC municipal elections to sweep him and other Croker vassals from office. That election ended the political career of James J. Coogan, and he more or less retired from working, as well. In the coming years, his much younger wife would handle most of the family's business affairs, including its relationship with the New York Giants.

The Emergence of Harriet Coogan on the Public Stage

As the new century unfolded, Harriet Coogan, rather than her husband, was customarily recorded as the party of interest in family real estate transactions.[32] This included the 1903 foreclosure sale purchase of Whitchall, a Newport, Rhode Island, mansion designed by the famed architect Stanford White.[33] Newport had become the summer playground of the country's Gilded Age millionaires, and ultimately became the site of an epic feud between Harriet Coogan and the resort's society matrons.[34] At first, the newly-arrived Coogans seemed reasonably well-received, with Harriet a frequent presence at art shows, horserace meets, and other social gatherings, while her now-young adult children quickly became popular with Newport's junior set.[35] But Coogan-hosted galas proved second-tier social events, attended by only the lesser local gentry. Their invitations were routinely declined by the Vanderbilts, Belmonts, Whitneys, and other members of Newport's aristocracy. The crème de la crème also avoided socializing with the Coogans at public events.[36]

When the situation was autopsied decades later, the snobbish attitude toward the Coogans was attributed to the elite's disdain of social climbers.[37] But that assessment is farfetched, almost absurd. The Vanderbilt-Belmont

"This is No Coogan's Bluff," Says Mrs. Coogan to Newport

So the Old Mansion in Catherine Street, Where Her Ambitions Were Blasted, Stands Bleak and Dilapidated While Society Protests in Vain

Columbus Dispatch, October 12, 1941.

crowd themselves were parvenus, their fortunes of commercial origin and recently-made.[38] In sharp contrast, Harriet Coogan was a Gardiner, descended from a landed family that traced its wealth back to the reign of seventeenth century Stuart kings.[39] More likely, it was her husband James who was found objectionable: He was Irish, low-born, and a Tammany Hall political hack. And although never mentioned in newsprint, there was also doubtless more than a whiff of society disdain of the Coogans' Catholicism. Whatever its basis, upper-crust Newport's antipathy for the Coogans reached its apogee in 1910.

The event which brought matters to a head was a large dinner party hosted by the Coogans at Whitehall early that summer.[40] Over 400 guests were anticipated, including the Newport aristocracy who, unexpectedly, had accepted invitations to attend. To ensure the evening's success, Harriet pulled out all the stops: musicians, lavish catering, extra wait staff, Whitehall was exquisitely decked-out. Even 40 tuxedo-clad young men were recruited to fill up any empty chairs and to dance with the ladies. Then James and Harriet

Milwaukee Sentinel, October 10, 1941. The caption reads, "'It can rot to its roots,' Mrs. Coogan exclaimed that humiliating night three decades ago as she flounced out of Whitehall, never again to return. And today to the dismay of the proud residents of the resort, it is still rotting."

Coogan waited—until midnight—for the guests who never came. Reportedly acting at the direction of society grand dames bent on humiliation of the Coogans, not one of the 400 invitees showed up.[41] James Coogan, his hide toughened by a life in trade and politics, brushed off the affront. But his wife was not having it.

Whatever satisfaction Newport society derived from the pointed insult, it would soon rue the day that it offended the proud and fierce Mrs. James J. Coogan. Within days, Harriet had collected her family, servants, and staff, and whisked them out of Whitehall, leaving the mansion's furnishings, expensive family wardrobe, art collection, and other valuables behind. She did not even lock the mansion doors, allegedly telling an alarmed personal secretary that the place "can rot to its roots."[42] Predictably, the unprotected Coogan residence was quickly looted. Thereafter, it became a flophouse for vagabonds drawn to the comfort of free shelter among the Newport elite. At the same time, the untended mansion grounds defaced its posh surroundings. A March 1911 Whitehall fire likely started by a drunken squatter then further damaged the premises.[43] All the while, Harriet ignored entreaties to have Whitehall repaired, leaving a decaying, rat-infested eyesore right in the middle of the Newport aristocracy's ritziest neighborhood. And because Harriet ensured that Whitehall property taxes and other municipal assessments were always promptly paid, there was little that her erstwhile neighbors could do about it. For decades thereafter, the abandoned and ever-worsening ruin served as

Whitehall in its glory.

Whitehall abandoned.

Whitehall in ruins.

a vivid reminder of the miscalculation that Newport snobs had made in the summer of 1910.[44]

Perhaps ironically, it was another fire—this time at the Polo Grounds—that returned the Coogan name to the sports pages. In April 1911, an early morning blaze inflicted extensive damage upon the ballpark grandstand and bleacher sections. Current New York Giants owner John T. Brush had assumed the Polo Grounds/Manhattan Field lease when he acquired the club from Andrew Freedman in 1902. But before he invested the $100,000+ likely needed to repair the fire damage, Brush required the long-term security of a lease extension.[45] Fortunately, his real property landlords were happy to oblige, and that May, Brush and Harriet Coogan executed a new 21-year lease on the Polo Grounds.[46] The rent was $50,000 per year.[47] Simultaneously, James Coogan announced that a $6 million amusement venue/amphitheater would be constructed on the now-vacant site of Manhattan Field.[48] Nothing ever came of the project. Nor did New York Highlanders/Yankees owner Frank Farrell take Coogan up on the offer to relocate his club to the former Manhattan Field grounds.[49]

By 1915, James J. Coogan, aging and suffering the effects of heart disease, had largely withdrawn from public life. In March, however, he reportedly tried to interest new Yankees owners Jacob Ruppert and Til Huston, whose American League club had been Polo Grounds sub-tenants of the Giants since 1912, in a proposal to build a new ballpark on the old Manhattan Field site, assuring them that he could get Giants club president Harry Hempstead (son-in-law of the now-deceased John T. Brush and co-trustee of his estate) to go along with the proposition.[50] Like the earlier amusement venue/amphitheater plan, the Coogan scheme came to naught. Seven months later, James Jay Coogan was dead, passing away at the family's residential suite at the Netherland Hotel in Manhattan on October 24, 1915.[51] He was 70. Following a Solemn Requiem Mass concelebrated by Cardinal Terrence Farley at St. Patrick's Cathedral and attended by dignitaries from the New York political and business worlds, the deceased was laid to rest in Calvary Cemetery, Woodside, Queens.

At her husband's death, 54-year-old Harriet Coogan withdrew from society life. With her Ivy League-educated sons out of the house, she and unmarried daughter Jessie moved to smaller quarters in the mid-town Biltmore Hotel. Harriet continued management of Gardiner-Lynch-Coogan real estate interests from offices in a family-owned Manhattan commercial building. On May 1, 1932, she and Charles A. Stoneham, the latest owner of the New York Giants, entered into a new 30-year lease.[52] For the first 15 years, the annual rent would remain $50,000. After March 1947, it rose to $53,000/year. While the Giants continued as owners of the Polo Grounds ballpark, the lease contained a clause forfeiting—without compensation—ballpark ownership to the Coogan family upon a default in rent payment.[53] The lease also prohibited the Giants from demolishing the venerable-but-increasingly-antiquated Polo Grounds without the express consent of the Coogans.[54]

Meanwhile back in Newport, decades of Whitehall neglect finally provoked a public outcry.[55] But even unflattering news articles syndicated nationwide left Harriet Coogan unmoved. She treated attempted press intrusion into her privacy with the same silent contempt visited upon the Newport swells. For its part, the press portrayed Harriet as an eccentric recluse, holed up with a spinster daughter in a tiny hotel suite that she only left late at night to go to her mid-town office. Reportedly, Biltmore Hotel staff had not seen her in years, leaving a once-a-day meal outside her suite door. Still, the elderly Mrs. Coogan was described as invariably cordial when speaking to hotel staffers on the telephone or through a closed door. And she was a very generous tipper.[56] Finally in 1946, eldest son Jay Coogan, his mother's Newport enemies now long dead and with a court order looming, agreed to the razing of Whitehall.[57]

Old and infirm, Harriet Gardiner Lynch Coogan died in her bed at the Biltmore Hotel on December 18, 1947, surrounded by her four children. She was 86. Like her long-deceased husband, she was interred at Calvary Cemetery following a Funeral Mass celebrated at St. Patrick's Cathedral. The Coogan family connection to baseball, however, was not laid to rest with her. For the next two decades, Jay Coogan would oversee family interest in the Polo Grounds. Pursuant to the 30-year lease terms negotiated by his mother in 1932, the Giants continued to pay the $53,000 annual rent on the ballpark—even after the club left for San Francisco at the close of the 1957 season. Thereafter and without a pause in Polo Grounds rent checks, the middle-aged Coogan children began receiving a monthly stipend from the New York Mets, as the expansion club was obliged to use the now-ancient and poorly-maintained ballpark during the 1962–1963 seasons.[58] By then, the City of New York had moved to condemn the Polo Grounds pursuant to the exercise of its eminent domain power. A bitterly fought courtroom battle between the City and the Coogans ensued. In the end, the City prevailed, but was obliged to pay the Coogan family $2,614,175, the court-assessed value of the real property on which the Polo Grounds had been built.[59]

By the time New York's highest court settled the matter, the Polo Grounds was long gone, having been demolished in April 1964. And today, like the vanished North Manhattan ballpark, Polo Grounds real estate landlords James and Harriet Coogan are but a dim memory.

Manhattan Politics, Newport Society, and the Polo Grounds

NOTES

1. James's siblings were Mary Anne (born 1856), Edward (1858), Thomas (1864), Margaret (1866), and Ella (1868).

2. When he stood for election to New York City political office, Coogan maintained that he was a native-born New Yorker. But the sworn passport application that he completed in June 1878 told a different story. Therein, Coogan averred that he had been born in Ireland, had been brought to this country at age seven, and was a naturalized U.S. citizen.

3. Independent of his wife's family wealth, William Lynch had amassed his own fortune, leaving an estate valued in the millions at the time of his death in 1884, as subsequently revealed in "Gives Millions to Daughter: Mrs. Lynch Transfers Her Estate to Mrs. Coogan to Avoid Inheritance Tax," *New York Evening World,* April 30, 1900.

4. According to nationally syndicated gossip columnist *Cholly Knickerbocker* (Maury H.B. Paul) in "Mayfair's Rich Recluse Owns Newport 'Blot'; Scorns Wall Street," *Detroit Times,* October 9, 1941.

5. A year later, the Lynch-Coogan family alliance was further cemented by the marriage of Edward Coogan to Harriet's sister Evelynn, with the nuptial rites again being performed at St. Patrick's Cathedral. See "Married," *New York Times,* June 22, 1884.

6. The other Coogan children were Sarah Jessie (born 1886), W. Gordon (1888), and Gardiner (1892). Another child, born sometime after 1900 and name unknown, did not survive infancy.

7. See, e.g., "Elevated Road Extension," *New York Times,* May 10, 1887, and "Objecting to a Viaduct," *New York Times,* November 19, 1887.

8. The original baseball tenants of the Polo Grounds were Day's first team, the then-independent Metropolitan of New York club. The Mets were admitted to the major league American Association in 1883, while a second Day club, the New York Gothams (later Giants) entered the National League the same season. Both clubs played their home games at the Polo Grounds—occasionally simultaneously, as Day had constructed separate diamonds with grandstands in different corners of the ballpark. At the end of the 1885 season, however, the Mets were sold to amusement entrepreneur Erastus Wiman and relocated to Staten Island. Two seasons later, the Mets were disbanded.

9. Legally speaking, the New York Giants were owned and operated by the Metropolitan Exhibition Company, a closely held corporation controlled by majority stockholder Day. The MEC's three minority stockholders included Gordon, a Tammany Hall friend of Day and formerly the figurehead president of the New York Mets. Although primarily a coal broker, the Manhattan-born Gordon had expansive knowledge of the island's real estate and would later be appointed deputy commissioner of city buildings. Thereafter in 1903, New York Highlanders president Gordon was the one who uncovered the remote rocky mesa in Washington Heights on which Hilltop Park would be built.

10. Sources conflict regarding how the Gardiner-Lynch family obtained the real property that later became the site of the Polo Grounds. The long-prevailing view has been that the property had once been part of a large farm owned for generations by the Gardiner family, and was passed down to Harriet Coogan by her maternal grandmother and mother. See, e.g., "Great Estate Given Away," *Boston Herald,* April 30, 1898. Other sources contend that the Polo Grounds was constructed on 14 acres of Harlem River-reclaimed land purchased for $21,500 by William Lynch at an April 30, 1858 foreclosure sale. See, e.g., Joshua Prager, *The Echoing Green* (New York: Pantheon Books, 2006), 58. The narrative herein favors the latter view.

11. As per "Mr. Coogan's Ambition," *New York Times,* September 3, 1886.

12. See "Another Candidate for New York Mayor," *New York Times,* October 8, 1888; "A Campaign of Bread and Sugar," *New York Times,* October 15, 1888; and "Coogan Has Had Enough," *New York Times,* November 9, 1888.

13. To the chagrin of present and future club owners, the elevation afforded excellent and free viewing of game action below. In time, thousands of freeloaders would take in NY Giants games from atop what was originally called Deadhead Hill. The appellation "Coogan's

Bluff" was coined by an unidentified *New York Times* reporter covering the 1893 Princeton-Yale football game. See "The Orange Above the Blue," *New York Times,* December 1, 1893.

14. *New York Times,* April 8, 1889. An accompanying article explained that "the property referred to is a portion of the Lynch estate controlled by James J. Coogan," and that a long-term lease could not be acquired because "the estate desires to sell this and the adjoining property." Thus, Day was hoping for the intervention of "some capitalist ... [to] purchase the two blocks of land ... and give the [Giants] management a five- or ten-year lease."

15. As reported in the *New York Times, New York Tribune,* and elsewhere, June 22, 1889.

16. Readers should understand that the New Polo Grounds and ballparks subsequently constructed on the adjacent plat were built and paid for by the owners of the New York Giants, and that these ballparks were the exclusive property of the club owners. The real property which lay beneath the ballparks, however, was owned by the Gardiner-Lynch family and had to be leased by Giants owners. When completed over the 1889–1890 winter, the New Polo Grounds was a handsome, if oddly pear-shaped, two-tiered enclosure with a seating capacity of about 14,000 for baseball, and far more for college football, track meets, harness racing, and other attractions that would later use the grounds.

17. See "An Offer for the Giants," *New York Times,* September 6, 1889. At the time, it was estimated that operation of the New York Giants (and Mets) had generated a $750,000 profit for the four-member Metropolitan Exhibition Company during its seven-season existence.

18. See "Leased for the Brotherhood," *Washington Post,* September 9, 1889. The lease was for 10 years, at $24,000 per annum.

19. See "Day in Hard Luck Again," *Chicago Tribune,* February 4, 1890, and "Mr. Day's Voice Still for War," *Chicago Tribune,* February 5, 1890. Both *Tribune* articles stated that Coogan was "financially interested" in the New York Players League franchise, but no evidence of any such Coogan interest has been discovered by the writer. As with other Coogan matters, his motives for pressuring Day are unknown.

20. *Sporting Life,* April 5, 1890.

21. See "To Start a New Park," *Washington Post,* November 8, 1891.

22. After the National League and Players League New York Giants franchises consolidated in September 1890, Manhattan Field was sublet to the Manhattan Athletic Club. Freedman's interest in the Giants stemmed from his subsequent court appointment as receiver for the financially failing MAC. When Freedman gained control of the Giants franchise in January 1895, he assumed the leases for both the Polo Grounds and adjoining Manhattan Field. The dual ballpark leases cost Freedman between $20,000 to $25,000 per year. At the March 1900 National League owners meeting, his fellow magnates agreed to reimburse Freedman the annual cost of the Manhattan Field rental as part of their efforts to appease the Giants boss in the aftermath of the Ducky Holmes affair.

23. See, e.g., "Business Troubles," *New York Times,* January 1894, memorializing a $12,586.36 judgment entered against James J. Coogan and Edward V. Coogan for unpaid business advertising.

24. See "Coogan Is Bankrupt," *New York Times,* January 1, 1894. Coogan's financial distress did not affect the Gardiner-Lynch family fortune, as Sarah Gardiner Lynch had always segregated her family's business interests from those of her son-in-law.

25. As the mother of Edward's late wife Evelynn, Sarah Lynch was also Edward Coogan's mother-in-law.

26. See "J.J. Coogan's Brother Sues Him," *New York Sun,* December 1, 1898; "He Charges Conspiracy," *New York Times,* December 1, 1898.

27. See, e.g., "Great Estate Given Away," *Boston Herald,* April 30, 1900; "Escapes Inheritance Tax," *New Haven* (Connecticut) *Register,* April 30, 1900, and "Millions for Mrs. Coogan," *New York Times,* April 30, 1900. At the time, the value of the property titled over to Harriet was placed in the $15 million-to-$25 million range. In consideration for the transfer of the family wealth, Harriet supposedly gave her mother $2.

28. "Change Not Likely," *Sporting Life,* August 19, 1899.

29. See "New Borough President," *New York Times*, January 6, 1899. The position of borough president was a newly created office, devised after Brooklyn, Queens, the east Bronx, and Staten Island were incorporated into New York City in January 1898.

30. See "President Coogan's Eligibility," *New York Times*, December 18, 1900.

31. The previous May, a $100,000 contribution to the campaign chest of likely Democratic Party presidential candidate William Jennings Bryan had briefly fueled rumor that Coogan was angling for the VP spot on the ticket. See "Coogan's Alleged Gift," *New York Times*, May 27, 1900, and "$100,000 for Bryan," *Washington Post*, May 27, 1900.

32. See, e.g., "The Real Estate Market," *New York Sun*, April 10, 1903; "Million Dollars' Worth of Flats," *New York Evening World*, May 16, 1903, and "Mrs. H.G. Coogan's Venture," *New York Times*, May 17, 1903.

33. As reported in the *Pawtucket* (Rhode Island) *Times*, June 29, 1903, *New York Times* and *New York Tribune*, June 30, 1903, and elsewhere.

34. Previously, the Coogans had summered at Narragansett, another Rhode Island resort. But a new family vacation home was sought after Harriet was accosted by thugs and robbed of jewelry in Narragansett Pier.

35. See, e.g., "The News of Newport," *New York Times*, November 22, 1903; "Mrs. Grosvenor Took Six Firsts," *Pawtucket Times*, September 6, 1905; "Social News from Newport," *New York Tribune*, September 7, 1907; "Snapshots of Social Leaders," *Washington Post*, September 8, 1909.

36. See, e.g., "This Is No Coogan's Bluff, Says Mrs. Coogan to Newport," *San Francisco Chronicle*, November 6, 1932; "Last of Mrs. Coogan's Long Vengeance," *Detroit Times* and *The* (Portland) *Oregonian*, June 9, 1946.

37. Typical was the public complaint of surviving Newport grande dame Maude Wetmore, who declared, Whitehall is a disgrace to our town, It certainly affects property values." See Inez Robb, "Mrs. Coogan's Strange Revenge on Newport," *Milwaukee Sentinel*, October 12, 1941.

38. Even a century later, the Gardiner family patriarch would dismiss the Newport elite and their ilk as "nouveaux riches." See Robert F. Worth, "Robert D.L. Gardiner, 93, Lord of His Own Island, Dies," *New York Times*, August 24, 2004. For more on the pretensions and prejudice of the Newport elite, see Anne DeCourcy, *The Husband-Hunters: American Heiresses Who Married into the British Aristocracy* (New York: St. Martin's Press, 2017), 105–118.

39. Harriet Coogan was also independently wealthy, polished, a stylish dresser, and exceptionally good-looking. But the extent, if any, to which Newport high society matrons were personally jealous can only be speculated upon.

40. Years later, the event was described as a coming-out party for Jessie Coogan. By then, however, Harriet's 24-year-old daughter was well past the debutante stage, and had been out in society since at least 1906. See "Buds to Make Their Bow," *Kansas City Star*, October 3, 1906.

41. As per the articles cited in endnote 37. See also, James Cahill, "Chamber of Horrors," *Columbus Dispatch*, October 12, 1941, and Cholly Knickerbocker, "Mayfair's Rich Recluse Owns Newport 'Blot'; Scorns Wall St." *Detroit Times*, October 19, 1941. Both of the above articles were syndicated and published nationwide.

42. *Ibid.* See also, "Milestones," *Time*, December 29, 1947, and "Necrology," *The Sporting News*, December 31, 1947.

43. See "Newport Home Burns," *New York Times*, March 11, 1911.

44. See again the newspaper articles cited in endnotes 37 and 41.

45. By April 1911, Brush had suffered from the wasting disease locomotor ataxia for years, and was concerned about the financial security of second wife Elsie and teenage daughter Natalie after his passing.

46. As reported in "Two New York Parks," *Sporting Life*, May 13, 1911. See also, "Brush Says Polo Grounds Will Stay," *Springfield* (Massachusetts) *News*, May 5, 1911, and "Long Lease on Polo Grounds Signed," (Boise) *Idaho Statesman*, May 14, 1911.

47. As revealed after the will of the late John T. Brush was admitted to probate. See "Giants Money Making Club," *Springfield News*, January 1, 1915.

48. See "Plan $6,000,000 Park at Coogan's Bluff," *New York Times,* May 6, 1911; "Ninety Acres for Big Park," *Duluth* (Minnesota) *News-Tribune,* May 7, 1911; "Will Seat 50,000 Fans," *Cleveland Plain Dealer,* May 10, 1911.

49. "Two New York Parks," *Sporting Life,* May 13, 1911. See also, "Rival Friends," *Sporting Life,* April 13, 1912. Manhattan Field had been demolished in 1903. Instead of taking up Coogan's offer, Farrell persevered with a boondoggle ballpark construction project in the Knightsbridge section of the Bronx that drained his finances and eventually precipitated the sale of the franchise to Jacob Rupert and T.L. Huston in January 1915.

50. See Joseph Vila, "The Ground Question in New York," *Sporting Life,* March 3, 1915. Brush son-in-law Hempstead had assumed leadership of the Giants franchise shortly after Brush's death in November 1912.

51. "James J. Coogan Dead," *New York Times,* October 15, 1915. The cause of death was given as heart disease.

52. For contract purposes, the lessee was the National Exhibition Company, the NY Giants corporate alter ego.

53. Reputedly, Harriet Coogan did not trust the mails and appeared at the NY Giants mid-town office each month to collect the Polo Grounds rent check in person, per Michael Pollak, "The Man Behind the Bluff," *New York Times,* April 25, 2004.

54. The terms of the Polo Grounds lease became public during litigation instituted by Harriet Coogan's heirs after New York City condemned the ballpark in the early 1960s. A comprehensive overview of the litigation is provided by John Hogrogian in "The Polo Grounds Case: Parts I and II," *The Coffin Corner,* Vol. 11, No. 6, and Vol. 12, No. 1 (1989).

55. According to the 1941 syndicated column of Cholly Knickerbocker cited in endnotes 5 and 41, above.

56. As recounted in extensive and sometimes dubious detail in the circa 1932–1946 newspaper articles and features cited previously. Much of this reportage was dismissed as contrived or hyperbole by her sons when Harriet Coogan died in December 1947. "Mother was not a recluse," maintained son Gardiner. "She withdrew because of her age and infirmity. She was a gracious person who handled everything with perfect amicability," per "Mrs. Coogan Dies; Large Landholder," *New York Times,* December 19, 1947.

57. Per the *Newport* (Rhode Island) *Mercury and Weekly News,* December 26, 1947. The Whitehall grounds, however, remained Coogan family property and stayed unimproved until sold in 1953.

58. See again, Hogrogian, *The Coffin Corner,* above.

59. See *Matter of City of New York v. Coogan,* 20 *N.Y.2d* 618, 233 *N.E.2d* 113 (Court of Appeals, 1967). See also, "Sarah Coogan, Member of Polo Grounds Family," the obituary for S. Jessie Coogan, age 94, published in the *New York Times,* March 7, 1979. The San Francisco Giants were awarded $1,724,714 for improvements made to the Polo Grounds over the years of its tenure there.

John T. Brush and the
Brotherhood War, 1888–1890

David Kathman

John T. Brush is best remembered today for his salary classification plan of 1888, which caused a furor and was a significant factor in the creation of the Players' League a year later. However, Brush was a much more complex figure than his modern reputation as a puritanical skinflint. He was widely admired by players as well as his fellow executives and received virtually no negative publicity at the time for his classification plan. He proposed that plan primarily in response to a major financial crisis facing the Indianapolis Hoosiers, and more broadly as part of his efforts to support small-market teams against the large-market ones. When the National League tried to buy out the Indianapolis franchise as part of its war against the Players' League, Brush initially resisted, causing consternation among his fellow moguls. The deal he eventually struck played a major role in the Players' League war and set the stage for the rest of Brush's long baseball career.

IF JOHN T. BRUSH IS REMEMBERED by baseball historians today, it is usually in connection with the infamous Brush Classification Plan of 1888. This plan, adopted by the National League when Brush was president of the Indianapolis Hoosiers, tied player salaries to a five-level classification system based on performance and character. It caused a furor at the time and was a significant factor in the creation of the Players' League a year later. Brush is often depicted in modern histories as a widely disliked, puritanical skinflint, with the 1888 classification plan being the most prominent example of his tightfisted nature.[1] In fact, Brush was a much more complicated figure

Base Ball 12, pp. 86–109
ISSN 1934-2802 (Print) / ISSN 1934-3167 (Online)
978-1-4766-7473-5 (Print) / 978-1-4766-4112-6 (ebook)

than the caricature would suggest. I have previously documented how he rose from a farm in upstate New York to wealth in Indianapolis as an innovative retailer, to his position as a powerful baseball magnate by 1888.[2]

In the present article, I focus on Brush's role in the baseball labor strife of the late 1880s. Contrary to his modern reputation, Brush was widely respected at the time by his players as well as fellow executives. He proposed his classification plan primarily as a response to a significant financial crisis facing the Indianapolis club, and more broadly as part of his efforts to help smaller-market teams compete against the large-market teams. He received virtually no negative publicity for that plan, but he did cause consternation in the early 1890s by

John T. Brush c. 1890.

initially refusing to let the Indianapolis franchise be bought out by the other National League owners. The deal he eventually struck and its aftermath played a significant role in the Players' League war and laid the foundation for the rest of Brush's long career in baseball.

Brush and the Indianapolis Hoosiers, 1887–1888

Brush had been a prominent member of the group of local businessmen who bought the National League's insolvent St. Louis franchise and brought it to Indianapolis for the 1887 season. He initially kept a low profile as the club's vice president, which allowed him to avoid being tarred by the turmoil that engulfed the team in its first few months. This was made worse by the presence of warring factions on the club's bloated board of directors. Brush finally became president of the Indianapolis baseball club in July 1887, after Louis Newberger resigned in disgust following a scandal in which three of the team's players were arrested in a brothel.[3] Although the team performed poorly for the rest of the season and finished in last place, there were no more significant scandals. The front office, with Brush in charge and a slimmed-down board, was a model of stability compared to the first two months of the season.

On September 26, 1887, two weeks before the end of the National League season, Brush and the Indianapolis directors made a decision that would prove to be fateful. The franchise was now debt-free, but the directors realized that they would need to make substantial investments for the following season if the team hoped to be competitive. A syndicate of nineteen guarantors (including Brush and several other directors) was organized to loan the club $9,250, with most of them contributing $500 each and one contributing $250. The directors pledged the franchise as collateral for the loan, placing it in the hands of three trustees. This money would be invested in the team and paid back to the guarantors in one year. Given that the team had broken even so far even after the early-season chaos, Brush was confident that it could be profitable with a full year of discipline and investments in personnel and infrastructure.[4]

During the 1887–88 offseason, the directors used almost half of the money from the guaranteed loan, $4,546.08, on a new grandstand, which was relocated from the southeast to the southwest corner of the team's grounds.[5] Brush threw himself into promoting the team as he had done with his successful Indianapolis clothing store, touting the grandstand's amenities in the press and often attending home games with local celebrities in his private box.[6] Despite all the hoopla, however, the team remained unsuccessful on the field, and attendance tapered off after July 4. By late September 1888, the club's strained finances were putting its future in danger.[7] The directors had already borrowed $3,000 to pay player salaries, and they would owe another $7,000 in salaries by November 1. In addition, the $9,250 guarantee loan, with the franchise pledged as collateral, was coming due on October 1. If the directors defaulted, as now looked inevitable, the guarantors could legally force them to return the franchise to the National League to repay the loan, and that would be the end of the Indianapolis Hoosiers.

To prevent that from happening, Brush called the guarantors together on October 1 and explained the team's financial situation. He pointed out that if the directors returned the franchise to the league, they would get back $15,000—the $13,000 that the shareholders had paid for the franchise in March 1887, plus two annual $1,000 guarantee payments that the club had made to the league. However, $10,000 of that money would go to repay the debts incurred by the directors for salaries, leaving $5,000 for the guarantors, about 54 percent of what they were owed. Brush promised the guarantors that if they extended the loan for another year, the club would be in much better financial shape by then, and they would get more of their money back. He cryptically promised that at the upcoming National League meeting in November, some action would be taken "that would enable such cities as Indianapolis to live and maintain a ball club without loss."[8] Most of the guarantors did not want to see the club go under, so they agreed to at least wait until after the National League meeting to take any action. They also authorized the directors to borrow $7,000 in three-month bank notes, due just before Christmas, to pay the end-of-season salaries by November 1.

The 1888 Classification Plan and the Rebirth of the Hoosiers

It was in this context that John T. Brush traveled to New York City, along with fellow Indianapolis director John H. Martin, to attend the National League meeting on November 21 and 22, 1888. He was under pressure to demonstrate to the guarantors that he could run the club more economically in 1889, and to that end, he had come up with a classification plan for player salaries. Players would be classified from A (the highest) to E (the lowest) based on "batting, fielding, base-running, battery work, earnest team work, and exemplary conduct, both on and off the field, at all times." Players rated "A" would be paid $2,500, "B" players $2,250, "C" players $2,000, "D" players $1.750, and "E" players the minimum of $1,500.[9] Although Brush's immediate motivations for coming up with the classification plan were specific to Indianapolis, he correctly assumed that the other National League owners, especially those from smaller-market teams, would be receptive to the plan. Player salaries had risen dramatically in the 1880s as the game grew amid a general economic boom, and the rise of the Brotherhood, the first players' union, had made many team owners nervous.

On November 21, the first day of the NL meeting, Brush was appointed to the league's board of directors and the schedule committee. Brush introduced his classification plan the next day, much of which was spent discussing that and other changes to the league constitution. The delegates approved Brush's plan by a vote of 6 to 2, with John B. Day of New York and Arthur Soden of Boston, the two biggest-market teams, the only "no" votes. (As *Sporting Life* noted, "The weaker clubs and Chicago worked together the entire meeting."[10]) The salary plan was to apply only to players who had not already signed contracts for 1889, and with exceptions for players who also served as team captain or manager. When the plan was publicly announced following the conclusion of the closed-door meeting, it "fell like a bombshell among the reporters and players and the celebrities in the corridor."[11] However, Brush managed to keep a low profile publicly. Although today his name is closely identified with the salary classification plan, contemporary reports made virtually no mention of him. Only near the end of its long article about the meeting did *Sporting Life* casually add, "To Mr. Brush, of the Indianapolis Club, belongs the credit of originating the grading of salaries plan adopted by the League."[12]

When he had returned from New York, Brush again summoned the guarantors of the loan, along with the directors (Brush himself was in both groups), and explained the salary classification plan, which he said would save the Hoosiers $6,000 in 1889. The guarantors as a group were still not willing to formally extend the loan for another year, but they agreed not to demand their money until a deal could be figured out. This uneasy status quo persisted until just before Christmas, when one of the directors, H.H. Lee (who was the club's vice president and, like Brush, also a guarantor), decided to force a resolution of the issue. Lee refused to sign a document extending the $10,000 bank debt that the directors had borrowed in late September, thus forcing each of the other six directors to pay one-sixth of the debt individually. At an emergency meeting on December 21, Lee then proceeded to blow up the whole deal.

In the meeting, one of the guarantors, J.H. Holliday, presented a formal proposal whereby the guarantors would extend the loan for one year if the directors would promise to run the club as economically as possible in 1889, with no extraordinary expenses except those approved by the guarantors. This was acceptable to everybody except H.H. Lee, who insisted that he would only agree to this plan if the guarantors assumed unlimited personal liability for the club's expenses in 1889. The other directors told Lee that this demand was absurd, but he would not budge. Nearly all the guarantors had previously seemed amenable to Holliday's proposal, but now several of them were disgusted with the whole process and expressed an unwillingness to wait another year. When Holliday's proposal was formally presented to the group, eleven of the guarantors (including Brush and fellow directors William H. Schmidt and Charles F. Meyer) signed it, but eight of them (including Lee, fellow director Paul H. Krauss, and Holliday himself) refused to sign. The meeting adjourned with nothing resolved.[13]

The stalemate persisted until January 21, 1889, when the press broke the details of the club's financial troubles, which had previously been known only in vague rumors. That same day, Paul H. Krauss notified Brush that he was prepared to sue to collect the $250 he had contributed as part of the guaranteed loan. While the directors were considering this development, they received a telegram from NL president Nick Young, who had seen the press reports and said he needed to know if Indianapolis would be playing in the NL in 1889, since the schedule committee was meeting soon. At this point, the directors realized that there was no way out, so on the afternoon of January 21 they formally notified Young that they were turning the franchise back to the league.[14] On January 31, Brush received a check for $15,000 from Young, of which $10,000 was used to reimburse the six directors who had borrowed that amount for salaries, and the other $5,000 was distributed to the guarantors, $270 for each $500 share of the loan.[15] The original stock in the club became worthless.

The next question was what the National League would do with the franchise. At this late date, awarding it to an entirely new city would present logistical problems, so speculation immediately focused on Indianapolis investors, particularly Brush and his predecessor as team president, Louis Newberger. Brush and club treasurer Charles F. Meyer spent a couple of days putting together a syndicate of ten investors, and on the afternoon of January 24 they formally incorporated with $30,000 in capital stock, after which Brush notified Nick Young of their application for the franchise. The ten investors were Brush, Meyer, William H. Schmidt, R.K. Syfers, George F. Branham, A.B. Meyer, Thomas Taggart, Dr. Henry Jameson, Ford Wood, and Ferd Mayer. The only other application was from the theatrical firm Dickson & Talbott, who proposed to pay all the old club's debts in full, including all the money owed to the guarantors, but who had no experience running a baseball club.[16]

In the end, the National League unanimously approved the Brush-Meyer syndicate's application, and John T. Brush continued as president of the new Indianapolis National League franchise. The club was now much better financed than before, with a smaller ownership group. Brush himself came out of the debacle smelling like a rose, so much so that there were persistent rumors that he had orchestrated the whole thing. The New York *World* reported: "The New York base ball people are unanimous in the belief that President Brush, of the Indianapolis team, is merely trying to squeeze out the large proportion of stockholders who are willing to share a dividend but unwilling to make up a deficit. There is not a more brainy man in the league than President Brush, and it is safe to say that he will come out on top."[17] President Young felt a need to quash the rumors: "The Indianapolis deal was thoroughly honest and fair. Mr. Brush is a thoroughly honorable man, and the way he comes back to the League shows the affair was not prearranged."[18]

Contemporary accounts of the incident and its aftermath are full of similar high praise from Brush's fellow executives. A few days earlier, Young had said: "In having Mr. Brush at the head of affairs the base-ball people of Indianapolis are very fortunate. A clearer-headed man is not connected with base-ball. He has the full confidence of the League, both as to his ability and sterling integrity."[19] Such praise would become commonplace over the next twenty years, contrary to the modern-day image of Brush as a cranky, duplicitous old man. Players and managers tended to have more mixed opinions of him—Brush's reputation as a tough negotiator was not unwarranted—but even they respected him, for the most part. Guy M. Smith wrote:

> Brush tho' often accused of pinching pennies when salaries were involved, was deeply concerned for the comfort of his players. Several Natl. League owners quartered their teams at the cheaper hotels and any jump under 300 miles was made in the ordinary coaches—but Brush moved them in Pullman regardless of distance and registered them at first class hotels. He was once known to affirm, "such practices as certain club owners indulge in tend to keep base-ball in the saloon class."[20]

The 1889 Season: Brotherhood Rumblings

The Indianapolis directors had fired manager Harry Spence after the 1888 season, but Brush had been unable to hire a replacement amid the uncertainty over the club's future. In February, soon after that problem was resolved, Brush offered the manager's job to Jack Glasscock, the team's star player and captain. But a dispute over salary scuttled the deal. Brush offered Glasscock $2,500 as a player, the maximum allowed under the classification plan, plus $1,000 to serve as manager. Glasscock agreed with the $3,500 total, but he wanted to be paid $3,000 as a player and $500 as manager, so that if he were fired as manager, he would still be paid $3,000. Brush refused to violate the classification plan, and so Glasscock declined the promotion and signed a contract just as a player.[21] Brush then brought in his second choice for manager, Frank Bancroft, who was hired on February 16 after being interviewed for several hours by Brush and the other directors.[22] Bancroft had been a well-respected baseball manager for the past decade, including leading the 1884 NL champion Providence Grays.

After starting the 1889 season by splitting their first 12 games at home, the Hoosiers went on a long losing skid, and tensions between Brush and Frank Bancroft gradually increased. Bancroft was not a fan of Brush's salary classification plan and made no secret of the fact. *Sporting Life* reported that Bancroft had said "that salaries are ruinously high, and that the salary limit and classification rules are no good"; the same paper's Albert G. Ovens wrote that "it was a common thing for [Bancroft] to sit around among his players and damn the classification rule and other things of that character."[23] Bancroft clarified that he thought the classification plan made sense in theory, but that it was "a fraud" in practice, with too many loopholes and the major-market teams openly violating it.[24] Personal issues added to Bancroft's stress; on June 29, he accompanied his wife and seriously ill young son to their home in Massachusetts for 10 days, rejoining the team in Philadelphia on July 8 for the start of a road trip.[25] Perhaps the biggest issue was that the Hoosiers were not a good team, and Bancroft could not handle all the losing. The Indianapolis *Journal* reported that "the defeats of the team had a depressing effect on him, and he has frequently said that he wanted to quit."[26]

After a loss in Washington on July 12, Bancroft held a press conference to announce that he was quitting as of the end of the upcoming series in New York. The opinionated A.G. Ovens wrote in *Sporting Life* that Bancroft spoke in the press conference "like a half-witted old woman" and that "the old man had made an ass of himself."[27] Bancroft talked to any reporter who would listen, sounding burned out. He denied rumors that the players had been drinking, or that they had been intentionally playing poorly so that Indianapolis would be thrown out of the National League. He told the Washington *Post* that there was "a fatality with the club," and that "the men in the Indianapolis club will never have a winning team." He told the Indianapolis *News* that "the club is in a rut" and that "the management … may as well dispense with my services. I am sick of the whole business."[28] To replace Bancroft, Brush finally worked out a deal with Jack Glasscock on July 16 to manage the team as well as captain it.[29] The team started playing better under Glasscock, posting a better than .500 record for the rest of the season.

Brush had bigger issues to worry about, for in June the Brotherhood had formally objected to his salary classification plan. In a letter to NL President Nick Young, the Brotherhood, via Giants star shortstop John Montgomery Ward, claimed that the classification rule violated the standard player contract that had been negotiated in 1887 by permitting a player to be reserved at a lower salary than he had been paid the year before. On June 17, the Brotherhood and the NL owners agreed to meet to discuss the issue. An unnamed officer of the Brotherhood (probably Ward) was quoted in *Sporting Life* as saying: "Salary limits and classification systems will be knocked in the head altogether. A ball player is worth all a club can afford to give him, and he will get it. Those schemes are devised by mean managers who want to keep the men down to rock-bottom prices to enable them to pocket big dividends." In the same issue of *Sporting Life*, Brush was quoted as saying that the classification system would "never be repealed," and when asked whether he expected any trouble from the players, he replied, "None at all. If, however, we are to have any, now is just as good a time as any. I am ready for it. I do not think the men are foolish enough to do anything rash."[30]

However, the issue was increasingly out of Brush's control. After much dithering by Albert Spalding of Chicago, who represented the NL owners, the promised summit meeting to discuss the classification rule never happened and the Brotherhood began secretly laying the groundwork for what would become the Players' League.[31] On August 6, while Boston was in Indianapolis playing the Hoosiers, Brush gave a long interview to the Boston *Globe* in which he defended the classification system and denied that his players were underpaid or that Indianapolis might leave the National League.

> Now, let us see. Hines gets more money from us than he ever got from any club before, and but for the classification would be getting less money. Con Daily was asked his terms. They were accepted. Martin Sullivan named his figures, and we gave him what he asked. Henry Boyle is getting $500 more from us than he ever got before in his life. Jack Glasscock is getting a fat salary and is perfectly satisfied. In fact, Jerry Denny is the only man in our team who has any cause for complaint, and he is working with a better spirit this season than ever.[32]

In the same interview, Brush said, "I will tell you what is sure to come, and that is a pooling of all the receipts of the League clubs. That is the only way to keep the League up, as it should be." This idea sounds like an early version of the "baseball trust" idea that Brush would promote more than a decade later, in which all the teams in a league are essentially divisions of one corporate entity.[33] However, Brush said he would be just as happy with a 50–50 division of gate receipts between the home team and the visitors. That would benefit the weaker teams at a time when visiting teams typically got 30 percent of the gate. "The home team should be entitled to all they can make on the extras, such as receipts from the grand stand, score cards, and other privileges.... Either pooling the whole receipts or an equal division of receipts will have to come, and that, too, very soon."[34]

Somewhat surprisingly, John Ward of the Brotherhood had recently expressed almost identical ideas, except that he saw them as alternatives to Brush's classification plan, rather than supplements to it. In the June 8, 1889, New York *Clipper*, Ward acknowledged that teams like Indianapolis and Washington were significantly weaker than the major-market teams, but he noted that the National League clubs as a group still made a healthy aggregate profit, which he estimated at $200,000 to $300,000 annually.

Now, if the National League wishes to carry several weak cities along, why did it not devise some scheme by which the deficiencies in those clubs would be made up out of this enormous profit, instead of taking it out of the pockets of the players in those clubs? If, for instance, the League, instead of attempting the unjust and impossible classification scheme, had simply voted to pay the visiting club 50 per cent, instead of 25 per cent, as at present, the alleged losses of the Indianapolis and Washington clubs would have been made up out of the general profit and there would still be sufficient left to more than compensate the magnates for the capital invested and the risk incurred.[35]

Ward and Brush were both advocating some form of revenue sharing like that found to one degree or another in all the major sports leagues today. Their ideas were similar enough that it is not hard to imagine a compromise being worked out if the parties involved really wanted one. However, there were more significant issues involved, making a settlement between the Brotherhood and the NL owners unlikely. As Ward biographer Bryan Di Salvatore puts it, "by early July, neither Spalding nor Ward were able to rein in their respective runaway wagons."[36]

The Brotherhood War and the End of the Hoosiers

Everyone recognized that Indianapolis was one of the National League's weaker franchises. That meant that Brush had to deal with the real possibility that the Hoosiers might be pushed out of the League. The NL and the American Association both wanted as many strong teams as possible, especially as the threat of a player revolt became more real. On September 19, 1889, the Associated Press reported that the AA's Brooklyn and Cincinnati teams were thinking about jumping to the NL for 1890. The news was even more explosive because Brooklyn was battling for the AA pennant. Two teams had jumped from the AA to the NL before: Pittsburgh in 1887 (replacing Kansas City) and Cleveland in 1889 (replacing Detroit). However, those teams had replaced failing or disbanding franchises, a description that did not fit any of the National League teams in 1889. If Brooklyn and Cincinnati did jump, the NL would either have to play with 10 teams (which nobody seemed to want) or eliminate two teams, with tail-enders Indianapolis and Washington being the obvious candidates. Brush insisted that Indianapolis would be in the NL in 1890, and vehemently denied that the team was for sale. He told the Indianapolis *News*, "I believe I'll get that religious crank who parades the streets bearing a banner inscribed 'Base ball leads to hell' to also post 'This franchise not for sale.'"[37]

On November 4, 1889, after the players' contracts had expired (the standard contract went from April 1 to October 31), the Brotherhood announced at its annual meeting in New York that it was organizing a new league called the Players' National League, or the Players' League for short.[38] Something like this had been widely anticipated, but the formal announcement set off a mad scramble to sign players. The following week, the American Association and the National League considered how to respond to the threat at their annual meetings held concurrently in the same New York hotel where the Brotherhood had met (the Fifth Avenue Hotel). On the morning of Thursday, November 14, Brooklyn and Cincinnati resigned from the AA, as expected, but their representatives had to wait around the hotel while the National League owners discussed the conditions of their admission. Some of the major-market NL teams had been hoping that Indianapolis and Washington would quietly resign to make room for Brooklyn and Cincinnati, but Brush and Washington president Walter Hewitt refused to go. They insisted that they could survive if the rules were changed to give visiting teams 50 percent of the gate receipts, as Brush had suggested in August. The major-market teams (New York, Boston, Philadelphia) were unwilling to give more than 33 percent, but eventually a compromise was reached. Visiting teams would get 40 percent of the gate. The NL would increase to ten teams, including Brooklyn and Cincinnati as well as Indianapolis and Washington and the salary classification rule (favored by the small-market teams) would be eliminated. Thus, Brush's classification plan died a quiet death not quite a year after its creation. The Brooklyn and Cincinnati representatives were tracked down and invited to join the National League, and the other delegates unanimously approved their admission.[39] Brush had once again survived when it had seemed he might be out of baseball for good.

He threw himself with gusto into the war against the Players' League. He got hold of a PL contract and leaked it to *Sporting Life*, accompanied by his detailed criticisms. Among other things, Brush criticized the PL for making all its players sign three-year contracts at the same annual salary and for not guaranteeing player salaries.[40] Brush signed the core of the Hoosier team to 1890 contracts, despite intense pressure on the players to defect to the PL. In the end, only four Indianapolis players jumped to the Players' League: catcher Con Daily; left fielder Emmett Seery; right fielder Jack McGeachy; and center fielder Ed Andrews, who was a leader of the Brotherhood and a close associate of John Ward. (All four of the former Hoosiers would join Ward's Brooklyn PL team.) These defections were by far the fewest of any of the eight National League teams from 1889, some of whom, notably the New York Giants and Pittsburgh Alleghenies, had lost most of their lineups. The Hoosiers who jumped did not hold a grudge against Brush. Seery said, "Mr. Brush is one of the cleverest men in the business, and, go where I may, I will never work for any one I have a higher regard for, or like better, than I do him. I should like to see him at the head of a Brotherhood club. We need just such men as Mr. Brush."[41]

Brush got Jack Glasscock to sign via a cloak and dagger operation worthy of a spy novel. Glasscock had been attending Brotherhood meetings and seemed likely to join the Players' League, but Brush thought he could be kept in the NL fold. Immediately after the November National League meeting in New York, Brush went to Glasscock's hometown of Wheeling, West Virginia, and the two men then got on a train to Indianapolis, arriving at noon on Monday, November 18. They exited the train station through a side entrance and took a carriage to Brush's apartment in downtown Indianapolis. Despite their efforts at secrecy, somebody saw them, and soon there was a crowd of reporters camped outside Brush's apartment.

Meanwhile, John Ward had arrived in Wheeling that same day, but when he realized that Brush had gotten to Glasscock first, he telegraphed his Giants teammate Buck Ewing in Cincinnati and told Ewing to high tail it to Indianapolis. Ewing arrived there Tuesday night, but he was too late. Glasscock, Jerry Denny, Henry Boyle, and Amos Rusie had signed 1890 contracts Monday night in Brush's apartment. Glasscock had already started tracking down other players and trying to convince them to sign.[42] Ewing was furious, as was Brotherhood secretary Tim Keefe, who called Glasscock "a traitor of the worst type" and "a man destitute of honor or decency."[43]

Ward, Ewing, and Keefe had all been members of the New York Giants, who had won the 1889 NL pennant and the World Series against the Brooklyn Bridegrooms. Their departure to form the Players' League, along with most of their teammates, had devastated the Giants, who faced the prospect of fielding a team of scrubs in 1890, and possibly going bankrupt. Everybody recognized that the failure of the National League's New York club, for whom the leaders of the Brotherhood had played, would be a public relations disaster. On the other hand, Brush's success in signing his players had given the Hoosiers a relatively strong roster, even though many people still expected the NL to jettison Indianapolis and Washington to shrink back to eight teams. These developments fueled rumors that Giants president John B. Day was going to buy out the Indianapolis club and transfer its players to New York.[44]

One of the most elaborate versions of this rumor was published in the December 25, 1889, *Sporting Life*, as reported by Chicago correspondent Harry Palmer based on an anonymous source. According to Palmer, Glasscock and Denny had never been happy playing in Indianapolis; "they wanted to get out of a light-weight Western town and play ball with a winning team in a metropolitan city, like Boston, New York, or Chicago."[45] When Brush and Washington president Walter Hewitt arrived at the National League meeting in November, they allegedly had been ready to throw in the towel and sell their teams to the League to make room for Brooklyn and Cincinnati. But

Day and manager Jim Mutrie proposed a secret plan whereby Brush would promise Glasscock and Denny that if they signed contracts with him, they would play in New York in 1890. He would use the same promise to sign the other players. Then, when the NL contracted back to eight teams, which the source considered inevitable, Day would purchase the signed Indianapolis players. The Giants would still have a decent team, the Indianapolis players would get to play in New York, and Brush would get a much bigger payout than if he surrendered his team to the league.[46]

It is appropriate to be skeptical of this story. Until mid–March 1890, Brush continued to vehemently deny the rumors that he was going to sell out to New York, acting for all the world like a man who wanted to keep his franchise at all costs. Even so, the rumors were based on real issues, of which Brush and Day (as well as Glasscock and Denny) were undoubtedly aware. In the end, events in February and March 1890 played out as Palmer's anonymous source had predicted, though (probably) without the conspiracy part.

On February 19, 1890, Day showed up in Indianapolis, along with his associate Joseph Gordon, and announced that he wanted to buy the Indianapolis team and all its players. The pair had just come from Cincinnati, where they had unsuccessfully tried to lure Buck Ewing back to the Giants with the promise of a fat contract, reportedly $33,000 over three years. Speaking to assembled reporters, Day framed his proposed purchase as a matter of Brush helping the National League.

> Mr. Brush is a good base ball man, one of the best in the country, and he must recognize that the good of the League demands that the Indianapolis team be transferred to New York. With that done we will be able to fight the Brotherhood. It will give us the strongest clubs in the best cities, and the organization will be compact and on a sound foundation every way.[47]

Brush forced the pair to cool their heels for several hours. When Day and Gordon finally got in to see him, they never got around to making an offer for the team. The discussion centered on reducing the NL back to eight teams, a necessary preliminary to any dismantling of the Hoosiers, but Brush insisted that Indianapolis was in the League to stay. After three hours with Brush, the New York men left empty-handed.

From March 4 to March 6, 1890, the National League met in Cleveland at a wild affair at which Brush continued his resistance to a sale but also began signaling that he might be willing to sell at the right price. The primary purpose of the meeting was to finalize the NL schedule for the 1890 season, but the schedule committee realized that coming up with a satisfactory 10-team schedule was harder than it looked. The 8-team NL was effectively divided into a 4-team eastern division (New York, Boston, Philadelphia, Washington) and a 4-team western division (Pittsburgh, Cleveland, Chicago, Indianapolis). The schedule alternated between the four eastern clubs going west, the four western clubs going east, and the two divisions playing among themselves. With ten clubs, however, each division would have five teams; that meant that one club in each division would have to be idle each day when the division was playing internally, resulting in more off days and fewer games. The other option would be for the odd teams in each division to play each other during these periods, but this would require a lot more travel and be prohibitively expensive.[48]

After working all day Tuesday, the schedule committee could only come up with a schedule that "suited nobody," according to Francis Richter in *Sporting Life*, so "nearly all the delegates became convinced that an eight-club circuit was an absolute necessity." Wednesday morning was spent in "lobbying, making and breaking deals, all with a view to reducing the membership to eight." Brush was the main object of the other delegates' attention, but he refused to give in despite a full-court press that lasted all day. At one point, there was a rumor that Brush was ready to sell, but when asked about this, Brush told Richter, "There is absolutely no foundation for that report. I have never proposed to sell out, and I don't intend to."[49]

Brush must have realized that he would eventually have to unload the club for the good of the League, but he also had a lot of leverage and wanted to get as much as he could out of the situation. As the meeting extended into Wednesday evening, there were credible reports that Washington had asked for $20,000 to withdraw and that Brush had expressed a theoretical willingness to sell, but only for the absurdly high price of $75,000.[50] As Richter put it, "Even Mr. Hewitt and Mr. Brush admitted that in a financial sense an eight-club league would be the better thing, but they wanted financial salve before they would allow themselves to be offered as burnt sacrifices on the League altar." President Nick Young came out of the meeting room at 9:00 p.m. to tell the assembled reporters that the League had referred the schedule back to the committee and adjourned until 10:00 the following morning, but he then returned to the room, where the discussion continued "fast and furious" until "far into the night." According to Richter, "It was stated that Indianapolis had put a prohibitory price upon her franchise, and the fight was whether to call that bluff on the principle that it will be cheaper in the end than making a fight with ten clubs."[51]

On Thursday morning, the pressure on Brush continued, and he continued to resist. If Brush had really set a $75,000 price on his team, not enough of the other teams were willing to pay it, so the stalemate continued. Finally, in the afternoon, President Young gave up and called the meeting to order.

The delegates adopted a ten-team schedule, even though it was awkward and involved many long and expensive "jumps" between cities. Richter wrote that "[t]he magnates were outspoken in their disgust over the schedule, and even conservative Nick Young said, 'It's a nasty piece of work all round, and very unsatisfactory. It's the best that could be done, however, and that is all there is to it.'"[52] Back in Indianapolis, initial elation at Brush's firmness in saving the team gave way to a realization of how bad the adopted schedule was for the Hoosiers. Brush had asked for his team to be on the road during the June races of the Indianapolis Trotting Association and at home during the Indiana State Fair, but neither request was fulfilled. Brush told the *Indianapolis Journal*, "There's no use denying the fact, this schedule is unjust to us, and the treatment accorded us was neither fair nor what we had reason to expect."[53]

The pressure campaign on Brush was far from over, and he knew it. The bylaws stated that a team could be expelled from the league by a three-quarters vote, but neither Nick Young nor Albert Spalding, the de facto leader of NL team presidents, wanted to do that in the middle of the Brotherhood war. However, their patience would not last forever. After the Cleveland meeting Brush was simply trying to delay the inevitable and get as good a deal as possible. In a telegram to Eli Lilly, president of the Commercial Club of Indianapolis (and founder of the pharmaceutical company that still bears his name), Brush said that "the effort to reduce to eight is so strong that it looks gloomy for us, but you may rest assured that we will surrender only when we are obliged to."[54] In mid–March, Brush met with Jack Glasscock and several other players who had already arrived in Indianapolis for spring training, to discuss their likely transfer to New York. "He foresaw that he was going to be forced to sell out," Glasscock later told *The Sporting News*, "and, of course, he wanted to know whether we would consent to the transfer and what salaries we would demand from New York."[55]

Brush had already gone to Cincinnati and Pittsburgh to make sure all his options were exhausted. There were rumors that Pittsburgh might merge with Cleveland, which would allow Indianapolis to be saved, and Cincinnati president Aaron Stern had seemed shaky about remaining in the League. (It was Stern's franchise that Brush would get a year later.)[56] Neither of those possibilities worked out, so after meeting with the players, Brush and his fellow director and co-owner, William H. Schmidt, traveled to Chicago to meet with Spalding and start negotiating the terms of their surrender. The press had noticed Brush's movements but wasn't sure what he was up to, leading to plenty of rumors. There was even a wild rumor that Brush and Schmidt were in Chicago to meet with Frank Brunell, the secretary of the Players' League, and move the Hoosiers wholesale to the PL.[57]

On Thursday, March 20, Brush and Schmidt took a train to New York. That night at 10 o'clock, they had a secret meeting at the Hoffman House with the committee appointed in Cleveland to solve the ten-club problem: Spalding; Arthur Soden of Boston; and Frank De Hass Robison of Cleveland. John B. Day of New York and Walter Hewitt of Washington were also there. Spalding gave Brush an offer and an ultimatum: if he agreed to sell the Indianapolis players to Day and other NL owners, then he could retain his franchise, meaning he would remain on the NL owners' council and would have the right to buy the first team that became available. If he did not agree within 24 hours, then he would be voted out anyway by the other owners, who were arriving the next day for a formal league meeting. Hewitt was offered the opposite proposition: the League would buy Washington's franchise, but Hewitt could keep his players and join another league if he wanted. (The team had already applied to join the minor-league Atlantic Association.)[58]

At 10:00 a.m. the following morning, March 21, the committee reconvened at the Hoffman House. Brush told Spalding that he agreed to the offer if they could work out a price and other details, so negotiations began, with Robison of Cleveland as the primary negotiator for the League. President Young and the other delegates were at the nearby Fifth Avenue Hotel ready to go into formal session and approve the committee's report, but as the negotiations dragged on through the day and into the evening, the delegates were left "to amuse themselves as best they could," as the Indianapolis *Journal* put it.[59] It was not until midnight, after a marathon 14 hours of negotiations that the committee and Brush finally agreed, after which the National League delegates immediately convened to discuss it. Finally, at almost 5:00 a.m., after forty articles had been drawn up and signed, the delegates unanimously approved the plan, and Indianapolis and Washington were officially dropped from the National League.

Day bought nine of the Indianapolis players for New York: Jack Glasscock; Jerry Denny; Charley Bassett; backup first baseman Mort Scanlan; catchers Dick Buckley and Andy Sommers; and pitchers Henry Boyle, Amos Rusie, and Jesse Burkett. (Burkett, who had just signed with the Hoosiers on January 28, would soon switch to the outfield and go on to a Hall of Fame career.[60]) Paul Hines was initially supposed to go to New York as well, but Day decided not to sign him, so Hines became a free agent on April 1 and signed with Pittsburgh.[61] The other eight players under contract, all rookies ("colts"), went to Chicago, Cleveland, Pittsburgh, and Brooklyn.[62] Although there was no official announcement of the total amount Brush got for these players, it was widely reported at the time to be $67,000, give or take $2,000. Roughly $25,000 of this was in cash, and the other $42,000 was in promissory notes from the eight surviving NL clubs, divided up proportionally according to their projected 1890 home attendance. Thus, each club owed Brush an average of $5,250, with the wealthier clubs owing more and the smaller-market clubs owing less. Day apparently did not have to pay anything up front for the nine players he received, though Col. John Rogers of Philadelphia told reporters that Day was eventually expected to repay half of the money.[63]

Brush told the Indianapolis *Journal:*

> No words can express my regret for the necessity of this move. We have surrendered only when circumstances left no other avenue open.... Our pride in our club and in our city could not be thrown up as a successful barricade against the League's argument backed, as it was, by a belief that in our withdrawal lay their only hope of life.[64]

He told the Indianapolis *News*, "We acted just as any prudent business man would have acted. If a merchant saw water rising in his store, and knew it would keep on rising he would certainly move out."[65] The other NL magnates, on the other hand, were clearly relieved that the ordeal was over. Spalding, talking "like a man relieved of a great weight," told *Sporting Life*, "The Indianapolis Club remains an inactive member of the League, in the councils of which organization Mr. Brush will, however, continue to take an active part. We cannot afford to part with Mr. Brush's advice.... Mr. Brush hopes and expects to enter the League actively again when the war is over, and he undoubtedly will."[66]

When he returned to Indianapolis, Brush had a meeting with the team to explain the deal he had struck, then met individually with each of the players to say goodbye. It was an emotional scene because Brush, contrary to his modern reputation, appears to have been almost universally beloved by the Indianapolis players. As the Indianapolis *Journal* put it, "The players, veterans and youngsters, all declare they never were treated with more consideration and liberality than by President Brush, who, they swear, is the squarest man in the base-ball business." The paper reported melodramatically that Brush's voice got a little shaky as he was saying goodbye to Jack Glasscock, who said, "That's all right, old man. You'll have a team next year that will be hard for any of them to beat out." "That may be, Jack," responded Mr. Brush, "but I won't have you boys with me, and that's what cuts me up."[67]

The 1890 Season: Beginning a New Chapter

By all accounts, Brush's efforts to keep Indianapolis in the National League were sincere, as was his regret when he was ultimately forced to sell out. In retrospect, however, this was the best possible outcome for him. The

The 1890 Players' League Guide.

war between the National League and the Players' League proved to be a bruising affair, with financial losses on all sides as the two leagues competed for a finite universe of baseball fans. In the end, the National League prevailed because its financial backers had deeper pockets than those of the Players' League.

The deal that Brush had negotiated for himself proved to be a godsend: it allowed him to sit out the financially ruinous 1890 season while continuing to participate actively in League meetings and eventually allowed him to take over the Cincinnati franchise after it became available in the 1890–91 offseason, as the Brotherhood war was winding down. The complicated story of that deal belongs to the next chapter of Brush's career and is thus beyond the scope of this paper, but one incident during the 1890 season ended up being enormously important for John T. Brush's future as a baseball executive.

Despite the initial optimism at the merger of Day's New York Giants and the Indianapolis players, the Giants' financial situation deteriorated catastrophically once the season started. Attendance was terrible as New York fans showed little interest in the Hoosier imports, while flocking to see their old favorites in the Players' League.[68] (John Ward led the Brooklyn PL team, and Keefe, Ewing, and the other former Giants played for the New York "Brotherhood Giants.") At the same time, Day was saddled with the generous contracts that Glasscock, Denny, and the other former Hoosiers had negotiated with Brush. By mid–May, it was already apparent that the Giants would go bankrupt before the season was out unless drastic steps were taken.

To prevent that nightmare scenario, Day pleaded for help, aided by Brooklyn president Ferdinand Abell. He telegraphed Brush and several other NL owners, including Albert Spalding of Chicago, Arthur Soden of Boston, and Al Reach of Philadelphia, and summoned them to New York for a secret emergency meeting. At that meeting, which probably took place about May 22, the magnates were briefed on the New York club's finances and were told that Day would need an $80,000 infusion of capital to avoid going bankrupt.[69] All of them agreed to buy stock in the Giants, which provided Day with the cash he so desperately needed but made him a minority owner of his own club. Spalding later recalled that he bought $20,000 worth of stock from Day, and that "Soden and Brush came forward with similar amounts, and the balance was taken by Reach, Abell, and one or two others." Of the $20,000 in stock allotted to Spalding, he sold $5,000 to Cap Anson, $5,000 to his brother Walter Spalding, and $5,000 to "another Chicago gentleman."[70] An 1898 biographical sketch of Brush similarly says that "Mr. Soden, Mr. Brush, and Mr. Spalding subscribed $60,000 and others less sums," but adds that later in

Brotherhood Park and League Grounds, New York City, 1890.

the season "it was found necessary to make further contributions, so that the three who had contributed $60,000 [Soden, Brush, and Spalding] had added $21,000 more, making $81,000 furnished by them."[71] This second round of financing probably took place in July, though like the first round it was kept secret.[72]

Harold and Dorothy Seymour, in their pioneering history *Baseball: The Early Years*, give a similar but slightly different version of the story, based partly on Spalding's account and partly on another source that they, unfortunately, do not cite. The Seymours write:

> The Spalding brothers took $25,000 worth of stock, some of which they parceled out to others, including Anson; Soden of Boston put up the same amount; John T. Brush cancelled $25,000 in notes which he held against the sale of his Indianapolis stars; and F.A. Abel of Brooklyn, a professional gambler, and Al Reach of Philadelphia contributed $6,250 apiece. Day insisted on retaining $20,000 worth of stock for his "sacrifice."[73]

Later writers have misinterpreted the passage to mean that Brush cancelled a single $25,000 promissory note that he held from Day, but that is not what the sentence says; it refers to "notes," plural.[74] As we saw earlier, when the Indianapolis club was bought out in March, Brush got about $42,000 in promissory notes from the eight National League clubs, averaging $5,250

New York Brotherhood League Scorecard, 1890.

each. However, Day was eventually supposed to reimburse the other owners for half of what they had paid Brush, or $21,000, in addition to the $5,250 or so that he owed directly to Brush. This suggests that something like the following took place: Brush agreed to cancel the notes he held from Day, Spalding, Soden, Reach, and Abell, totaling around $25,000; this effectively cancelled Day's debt, and in exchange, Day gave Brush $25,000 in Giants stock. Thus, John T. Brush became part-owner of the New York Giants (up to a 23 percent stake, if the Seymours' figures are correct) without laying out any of his own money directly.

Brush would retain this stake in the Giants throughout the 1890s, even as he bought a controlling interest in the Cincinnati Reds and helped form a new Indianapolis franchise in the Western League. Eventually, in 1902, he used his minority stake in the Giants as a steppingstone to gain a controlling interest in the team, which would be his focus for the remaining decade of his life. The story of Brush's takeover of the Giants is another fascinating tale, full of secret deals and more spy craft, including a clandestine predawn visit to Indianapolis by John McGraw. It was the pinnacle of his career as a baseball magnate, putting him in charge of a winning team in the country's largest market.

Brush reached that pinnacle the same way he had reached other milestones in his life: through a combination of hard work, tenacity, and guile. Those features made him occasional enemies along the way, but they helped him excel in both the business and baseball worlds. Despite his gruff exterior, especially in his later years, Brush's humble origins had made him sympathetic to underdogs and "little guys," and made his relations with his players almost astonishingly harmonious. He was one of the most far-thinking baseball executives of his time, a complicated but ultimately admirable man who deserves to be better known.

Notes

1. This impression has been perpetuated by John Saccoman's influential SABR biography of Brush, which quotes a colorful description by one of Brush's critics: "Chicanery is the ozone which keeps his old frame from snapping, and dark-lantern methods the food which vitalizes his bodily tissues." This description was written by sportswriter Timothy Sharp in 1904 and first quoted by Charles Alexander in his 1988 biography of John McGraw. *Sporting News*, October 29, 1904, 2; Charles Alexander, *John McGraw* (New York: Viking, 1988), 99.

2. David Kathman, "John T. Brush: The Early Years, 1845–1888," *Base Ball 11: New Research on the Early Game* (Jefferson, NC: McFarland, 2019), 118–39.

3. Indianapolis *Sentinel*, July 2, 1887; Kathman, "John T. Brush," 129–31.

4. Indianapolis *Journal*, January 21, 1889, 8; Indianapolis *Journal*, January 22, 1889, 3; Indianapolis *News*, January 22, 1889, 1.

5. Indianapolis *Journal*, January 1, 1888, 2; Indianapolis *News*, April 7, 1888, 1. The cost figure for the grandstand is from the Indianapolis *Journal*, January 27, 1889, 1.

6. Kathman, "John T. Brush," 132–33.

7. The summary in the following two paragraphs is based on the accounts in the *Sporting Life*, January 30, 1889, 3; Indianapolis *Journal*, January 2, 8; January 22, 3; January 23, 8; and January 27, 1888; and the Indianapolis *News*, January 23, 1888, 1.

8. Indianapolis *Journal*, January 22, 1889, 3.

9. *Sporting Life*, November 28, 1888, 1.

10. "A SENSATION! The League Grapples the Salary Evil," *Sporting Life*, November 28, 1888, 1–2.

11. *Ibid.*

12. *Ibid.*

13. *Sporting Life*, January 30, 1889, 3; Indianapolis *Journal*, January 21; January 22, 3; and January 23, 8, 1888; Indianapolis *News*, January 23, 1. The Indianapolis board of directors for 1888 were John T. Brush, H.H. Lee, Charles F. Meyer, Valentine Born, William H. Schmidt, Paul Krauss, and A. Burdsal (Indianapolis *Journal*, March 13, 1888, 5; Indianapolis *News*, March 13, 1888, 4).

14. *Sporting Life*, January 30, 1889, 3; Indianapolis *Journal*, January 22, 1888, 3; Indianapolis *Journal*, January 23, 1888, 8; Indianapolis *News*, January 23, 1888, 1.

15. Indianapolis *Journal*, February 2, 1889, 3.

16. Indianapolis *Journal*, January 25, 1889, 8; Indianapolis *News*, January 24, 1889, 1.

17. Indianapolis *News*, January 24, 1889, 1.

18. Indianapolis *Journal*, February 11, 1889, 8.

19. Indianapolis *Journal*, February 5, 1889, 3.

20. Guy M. Smith, "John T. Brush," photocopy of typescript in the John T. Brush file in the Giamatti Research Center at the National Baseball Hall of Fame and Museum, Cooperstown, New York, 6. See Kathman, "John T. Brush," 136n2.

21. Indianapolis *Journal*, February 13, 1889, 8.

22. Indianapolis *Journal*, February 17, 1889, 9.

23. *Sporting Life*, June 12, 1889, 4; *Sporting Life*, July 24, 1889, 8.

24. *Sporting Life*, June 12, 1889, 8.

25. Indianapolis *Journal*, June 30, 1889, 5.

26. Indianapolis *Journal*, July 17, 1889, 5.

27. *Sporting Life*, July 24, 1889, 8.

28. Indianapolis *News*, July 16, 1889, 4; Indianapolis *News*, July 13, 1889, 8.

29. Indianapolis *Journal*, July 17, 1889, 5.

30. *Sporting Life*, June 26, 1889, 1.

31. Sporting Life, July 10, 1889, 1 ("In No Hurry"); Daniel M. Pearson, *Baseball in 1889: Players vs. Owners* (Bowling Green: Bowling Green State University Popular Press, 1993), 53–54.

32. Indianapolis *Journal*, August 9, 1889, 5.

33. William F. Lamb, "A Fearsome Collaboration: The Alliance of Andrew Freedman and John T. Brush," *Base Ball*, Vol. 3, No. 2 (Fall 2009), 5–20.

34. Indianapolis *Journal*, August 9, 1889, 5.

35. New York *Clipper*, June 8, 1889, 11.

36. Bryan Di Salvatore, *A Clever Base-Ballist: The Life and Times of John Montgomery Ward* (New York: Pantheon, 1999), 265.

37. Indianapolis *News*, September 20, 1889, 2.

38. Di Salvatore, *A Clever Base-Ballist*, 273–75.

39. *Sporting Life*, November 20, 1889, 2.

40. *Sporting Life*, November 27, 1889, 3.

41. Indianapolis *Journal,* February 11, 1890, 5.

42. *Sporting Life*, November 27, 1889, 7.

43. *Sporting Life*, November 27, 1889, 5.

44. The February 2, 1890 Indianapolis *Journal* reported that "The Brotherhood papers still insist that President Brush is remaining in New York to arrange for the transfer of his club to that city" (p. 5).

45. *Sporting Life*, December 25, 1889, 5.

46. *Ibid.* The Washington club was basically an afterthought in the source's story, brought along because teams need to join or leave a league in pairs, in order to maintain an even number of teams.

47. *Sporting Life*, February 26, 1889, 2; Indianapolis *News*, February 19, 1889, 1; Indianapolis *Journal*, February 20, 1889, 5.

48. I am indebted to Richard Hershberger for this explanation of the unfeasibility of scheduling a 10-team league. By the time the NL and AL each expanded to 10 teams in the early 1960s, air travel had made the logistical problems less severe.

49. *Sporting Life*, March 12, 1890, 1.

50. The $75,000 figure comes from Francis Richter in *Sporting Life* (March 12, 1890, 1); the Indianapolis *Journal* reported "between $50,000 and $75,000" (March 6, 1890, 5).

51. *Sporting Life*, March 12, 1890, 1.

52. *Sporting Life*, March 12, 1890, 1.

53. Indianapolis *Journal*, March 9, 1890, 7.

54. Indianapolis *Journal*, March 7, 1890, 5.

55. *Sporting News*, March 29, 1890, 1.

56. Indianapolis *News*, March 7, 1890, 1; Indianapolis *Journal*, March 13, 1890, 5; Indianapolis *Journal*, March 16, 1890, 3.

57. Indianapolis *Journal*, March 21, 1890, 8.

58. Indianapolis *Journal*, March 23, 1890, 1; *Sporting Life*, March 26, 1890, 1.

59. Indianapolis *Journal*, March 22, 1890, 7.

60. Indianapolis *Journal*, January 28, 1890, 2.

61. *Sporting Life*, April 5, 1890, 2 ("Washington Whispers"); Indianapolis *Journal*, April 5, 1890, 5.

62. Indianapolis *Journal*, March 27, 1890, 3; *Sporting Life*, April 2, 1890, 1.

63. Indianapolis *Journal*, March 23, 1890, 1; *Sporting Life*, April 2, 1890, 2; *Sporting Life*, April 5, 1890, 8 ("The Indianapolis Deal"); *Sporting Life*, November 15, 1890, 4. Cincinnati's share of the money owed to Brush was $5,500, a fact that became publicly known when owners Aaron Stern and Harry Sterne sold the club to Al Johnson of the Players' League in October 1890 (New York *Clipper*, October 11, 1890, 88).

64. Indianapolis *Journal*, March 23, 1890, 1.

65. Indianapolis *News*, March 26, 1890, 1.

66. *Sporting Life*, April 2, 1890, 1.

67. Indianapolis *Journal*, March 27, 1890, 3.

68. James D. Hardy, Jr., *The New York Giants Base Ball Club: The Growth of a Team and a Sport, 1870–1900* (Jefferson, NC: McFarland, 1996), 22.

69. The 1898 New York *Clipper* bio of Brush (cited below) says that the meeting happened "after the season had advanced nearly two months in 1890," when the season traditionally started on April 1. Brush was certainly in New York on May 22, when a *Sporting Life* correspondent talked to him in the stands at the Polo Grounds (*Sporting Life*, May 24, 1890, 1).

70. *Spalding's Official Base Ball Guide* (1895), 123.

71. *The Complete New York Clipper Baseball Biographies*, ed. by Jean-Pierre Caillault (McFarland, 2009), Vol. 1, 77 (profile of Brush from the March 26, 1898 *Clipper*).

72. Spalding only mentioned one meeting and recalled that it happened "along in July, I think," and on this basis most historians have dated the rescue mission to that month. But if the rescue mission had two parts, as the Brush bio says, then the first part was probably in late May, for the reasons cited above, and the second part was in July.

73. Harold Seymour and Dorothy Seymour, *Baseball: The Early Years* (Oxford: Oxford University Press, 1960), 238.

74. Hardy, *The New York Giants Base Ball Club*, 110, writes that "Day, however, did not have the money to pay for his nine new men, and the Indianapolis owner, John Bush [*sic*], took a note for $25,000." Charles C. Alexander, *Turbulent Seasons: Baseball in 1890–1891* (Dallas: Southern Methodist University Press, 2011), 63, writes that "John T. Brush's contribution was to cancel the $25,000 that Day owed him."

"He will do just what is best, no doubt"

William Hulbert's Calculated Dismantling of the Chicago Base Ball Association

JACK BALES

In the summer of 1876, fans of the Chicago White Stockings professional baseball team (now the Chicago Cubs) wondered why Chicago Base Ball Association President William A. Hulbert and other officers were making no efforts to acquire ballplayers for the team's next season. As it turned out, the club could not offer a contract to any player, as the Association's three-year charter, approved by the state in 1873, had expired earlier that spring. Hulbert and two of his friends quietly formed the Chicago Ball Club and filed a new corporate charter. Had Hulbert deliberately let the Association's previous charter expire just so he could start a new club, structured the way he wanted it? What happened to the shareholders in the old company? Using primary sources such as newspapers, the corporation's 1876 charter, and Hulbert's letters, business records, and other documents, the author details how the baseball executive dismantled the Chicago Base Ball Association and, in so doing, disenfranchised many of its investors. By late 1876, William Hulbert was president and one of the principal stockholders of the Chicago Ball Club. As for the Association, it had ceased operations, its assets transferred to the flourishing new organization.

Base Ball 12, pp. 110–125
ISSN 1934-2802 (Print) / ISSN 1934-3167 (Online)
978-1-4766-7473-5 (Print) / 978-1-4766-4112-6 (ebook)

WHEN WILLIAM A. HULBERT, president of baseball's National League, died on April 10, 1882, newspapers praised his devotion to the sport and his leadership as the founder of the league six years earlier. Stockholders, officials, and ballplayers of the Chicago Ball Club—of which Hulbert was also president—emotionally presented their own eulogies. One of several resolutions they unanimously adopted affirmed that the club stockholders had lost "a zealous and trustworthy custodian of their interests, who was ever true to the trusts submitted to his care."

These heartfelt sentiments notwithstanding, some of the shareholders of the old Chicago Base Ball Association (the predecessor of the Chicago Ball Club) might well have objected if they had heard Hulbert referred to as a "trustworthy custodian of their interests." As president of both the local organization and the National League, he had been a dedicated—but also demanding—business executive. Obituaries and eulogies had singled out his "strong will," "commanding presence," "impressive directness of speech," and "strong personality." They had also mentioned his "unerring instinct of right," but Hulbert's sense of what was "right" sometimes meant only what was right for him. In running his baseball club, for example, he had brooked no interference, and in 1876 had run roughshod over many of the stockholders as he sought to restructure the Chicago ball club to his liking.[1]

William Hulbert and the Formation of the Chicago Base Ball Association

Born in 1832 in Burlington Flats, New York (some fifteen miles west of Cooperstown), William Ambrose Hulbert was two years old when his parents moved to Chicago. After attending a college preparatory school in Beloit, Wisconsin, for one year, he returned to Chicago, where he became successful in the coal industry, wholesale groceries, and as a grain dealer, obtaining a position on the Chicago Board of Trade. Energetic, self-confident, and proud of his hometown, he often remarked that "I would rather be a lamp-post in Chicago than a millionaire in any other city."

Although he was not an athlete himself, Hulbert was also proud of Chicago baseball, and in 1870 he had purchased a share of stock in the city's fledgling professional baseball franchise. That year the Chicago White Stockings defeated the New York Mutuals, 7–5, in a controversial match and claimed the championship of the National Association of Base Ball Players. The Chicago Fire of October 1871 incinerated several square miles of the city, as well as the White Stockings' stadium and grounds and the homes and possessions of most of the players. The team's chances of finishing the season also went up in smoke, but a year later, Hulbert and others interested in bringing professional baseball back to the city formed the Chicago Base Ball Association, with Hulbert elected as a director.[2]

Hulbert soon began to take an active role in the affairs of the new organization. In the wake of a media outcry about the New York Mutuals allegedly throwing the August 5, 1874, game to the Chicago White Stockings, the Association's officers all resigned, and Hulbert was elected chairman of a temporary board of directors. "It now becomes the duty of the stockholders to elect permanent officers," Hulbert told them, adding that it was therefore "very desirable that all the stockholders" attend a special meeting on August 18. With members casting 52 votes in his favor, Hulbert was elected a club director. Edwin F. Dexter, who received 44 votes, joined him on the five-man board of directors, along with Philip Wadsworth (42), George W. Gage (39), and Charles S. Bartlett (34). Hulbert also became secretary, soon handling with efficiency the team correspondence and other details associated with player contracts. Businessman and city park commissioner Gage was elected president, replacing Norman T. Gassette, a well-known local government official and Mason. When Gage unexpectedly died a year later, Hulbert was elected as his successor.[3]

A New Season for the White Stockings

White Stocking fans were certainly looking forward to the start of the 1876 season. In July 1875, Hulbert had quietly signed Boston's ace pitcher, Albert G. Spalding, who would not only join the White Stockings in 1876 as field manager (captain) but would also assume the club's secretarial responsibilities. Hulbert also had received commitments from Spalding's teammates Ross Barnes, James "Deacon" White, and Cal McVey, as well as a star of the Philadelphia Athletics, Adrian Anson.

The White Stockings' first six games were all on the road, and the ballplayers returned to Chicago boasting a record of 5–1. They next took five out of six home games. On July 8 the White Stockings defeated the Hartford Dark Blues by the score of 9–3, thus beginning an 11-game winning streak that on August 1 put them solidly in first place, 7½ games in front of the St. Louis Brown Stockings.

Unlike several of their rival clubs, however, the White Stockings directors were making no efforts to acquire ballplayers for the next season. On July 30, the *Chicago Daily Tribune* had printed a list of men signed to various clubs and added that "this may be a good place to drop a paragraph in answer to several letters addressed to THE TRIBUNE asking why the Chicago Club management don't engage their team for next year. The answer is that Mr. Hulbert is doing just what is wisest under the circumstances; and, as he should be given the credit for assembling the only first-class team Chicago ever had, so he should be let alone in his movements for 1877. He will do just what is best, no doubt."[4]

Plans for a New Baseball Club

There is little doubt that what occurred was just what was best for William Hulbert. An article in the Chicago *Inter Ocean* relates that the

THE COMMISSIONERS duly authorized to open Books of Subscription to the Capital Stock of The Chicago Ball Club.
pursuant to license heretofore issued bearing date the Twenty first *day of* July
*A. D. 187*6, *do hereby report that they opened books of subscription to the Capital Stock of said Company, and that the said stock was fully subscribed; that the following is a true copy of such subscription, viz: We, the undersigned, hereby severally subscribe for the number of shares set opposite our respective names to the Capital Stock of* The Chicago Ball Club
and we severally agree to pay the said Company, on each share, the sum of One Hundred *Dollars.*
at such time or times and in such installments as shall be required by the Board of Directors

NAMES.	SHARES.	AMOUNT.
Albert G. Spalding	30	$3000
Roscoe C. Barnes	30	3.000
Wm H. Murray	50	5000
Calvin A. McVey	5	500

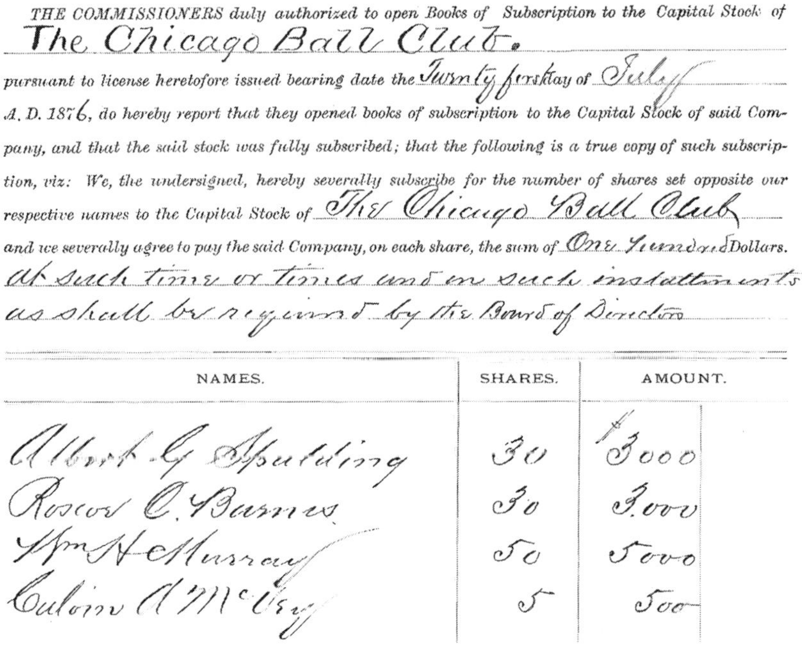

The Chicago Ball Club's 1876 corporate charter states that the capital stock was $20,000 and the amount of each share was $100. The principal shareholders among the 32 investors included Albert G. Spalding (30 shares), second baseman Roscoe "Ross" Barnes (30), William H. Murray (50), and William A. Hulbert (22; not shown here). First baseman Cal McVey bought five shares (Secretary of State, "Dissolved Domestic Corporation Charters," Record Series 103.112, Illinois State Archives).

Chicago Base Ball Association's three-year charter, approved by the state in 1873, had expired in the spring of 1876. The newspaper explained that the club could not operate as a legal enterprise and "it therefore follows that [Association officers] were not in a position to make any contracts for 1877, and the cause for the supposed dilatoriness is thus at once shown." The officers were "fully empowered to wind up the affairs of the old company," so Hulbert and director Edwin F. Dexter, a bookseller and stationer, got to work. William H. Murray, a grain dealer like Hulbert, assisted them.

The men filed a corporate charter with the state of Illinois, which outlined their plans for a new baseball club. Its purpose, they wrote, was "to foster and elevate our National sport—the game of base-ball." The charter was approved and it was filed with the Secretary of State on July 21. Hulbert, not surprisingly, was elected president of the organization. Other board members of the fledgling Chicago Ball Club included Spalding (Secretary), Dexter, Murray, and grain dealer John B. Lyon. The club's capital stock was fixed at $20,000, divided into 200 shares of $100 each.

The *Inter Ocean* went on to state that "the success of this year's work so far has been unexampled in the history of the game, and there was naturally little difficulty in placing the shares." Murray headed the list of 32 subscribers with 50 shares, followed by Spalding (30), second baseman Ross Barnes (30), Hulbert (22), and Lyon (20). Newspaper articles named other prominent subscribers, including Dexter, Norman Gassette, Chicago banker John DeKoven, and Charles S. Bartlett, a railroad executive and a director of the Chicago Base Ball Association. First baseman Cal McVey purchased five shares. It was not unusual that he, Spalding, and Barnes were included as stockholders, for the plan was that other ballplayers, based on their success on the field, would also be invited to join the new organization. "Whenever a member of the nine proves himself a steady, reliable, and valuable man," a Chicago sportswriter noted, "he can have the privilege of taking stock in it, thus giving him in addition to his salary an interest in the profits of the club, which profits depend to a degree upon his individual play."[5]

Interestingly enough, Hulbert was not the majority stockholder, but with his friends on board, perhaps he did not feel it necessary to have a controlling interest. By this time, he was signing players for the 1877 season, though he was keeping most of the details under wraps. In mid–September 1876 a reporter complained that "any attempt to get an answer to a question from him about the future policy of the organization, of which he is the only visible head, is as fruitless as it would be to attempt to perceive a prominent bone in his well-fed body."

The directors of the Chicago Base Ball Association held a special meeting on November 2, 1876. As recorded in Secretary Albert Spalding's minutes, they decided that since the Chicago Base Ball Association "has ceased by limitation" and because "a new corporation has been duly organized under the laws of Illinois styled 'The Chicago Ball Club,'" the Association's assets would "be transferred to and held by the said 'The Chicago Ball Club'" (Chicago History Museum, ICHi-176530-001.)

Taking Control of the Chicago Base Ball Association

It all seemed to be a nice and cozy setup for Hulbert, the officers, and the new stockholders—but certainly not for the investors in the old Chicago Base Ball Association who were not shareholders in the new Chicago Ball Club. One journalist declared that a few of the original officers had known early on that the organization would be losing its status as a legal corporation, so they "quietly set to work, obtained a charter for a new association, elected officers, issued new stock, which was all disposed of before some twenty or thirty old stockholders were aware of the movement."

Naturally, these disenfranchised individuals objected to being shut out of the new group. They placed newspaper ads in Chicago papers urging all stockholders of the Association to attend a special meeting on the evening of August 1 to discuss "important business." About a dozen of the stockholders met, but according to the *Chicago Evening Journal*, much animated discussion produced only "meager results." The *Chicago Times* reported that some of the disgruntled investors wanted a legally appointed receiver to take charge of the club, and they all agreed to hire an attorney "to ascertain what their rights are and fight for them."[6]

The stockholders, however, probably did not have much time for legal skirmishes. On the day of the meeting, Hulbert and the officers wrote National League Secretary Nicholas Young that "we wish to place on file in your office—not to be by you promulgated until further notice—an application on behalf of the 'Chicago Ball Club[,]' successors of the Chicago Base Ball Association, to become a member of the National League of Professional Base Ball Clubs." Hulbert was moving quickly, and although he was not exactly aboveboard ethically, up to a point he had done nothing wrong legally. In addition, newspapers reported no sense of moral outrage among their readers, as Chicagoans were pleased that a team would take the field in 1877. Hulbert may have, however, been walking on thin legal ice when he acquired the new ballplayers. They belonged to the old Association, and he could have been charged with deliberately letting the organization lose its right to operate so he could sign the men for his new venture.

A Baseball Executive's Stock Transactions

To perhaps protect himself from any lawsuits, Hulbert systematically bought the stock from many of the investors of the old Association. Some of the men, such as William H. Murray, were his friends and would be share-

581

[handwritten memorandum]

Chicago Sept 15th 1876

Memorandum shares stock in Chicago Base Ball Association in the hands of W A Hulbert

Original Certificate #6 to W.A.H		1 share
do #66	do	15	
do 67	do	2	
do 68	do	5	
Orign' Cert #20 assign'd by J R Smith	1	
" 12 " " H J Culver	1	
" 21 " " A M Boynton	1	
" 3 " " W B Walker	1	
" 65 " " A C Campbell	1	
" 9 " " N M Wadsworth	1	
" 41 " " C H Houg k	1	
" 5 " " W H Murray	1	
Assignment by J M Thacher	1	
do " W H Wadsworth	1	
Total	33 Shares

I certify the foregoing to be correct list of shares as set forth all of them standing in the name of W A Hulbert

Wm L Finley

This memorandum shows that on September 15, 1876, William A. Hulbert owned 33 shares of stock in the Chicago Base Ball Association. The "original certificate #6" refers to the first share that he had purchased in 1870; by the end of July 1876 he had acquired 22 more. The memorandum lists the names of investors from whom he purchased additional shares. Hulbert's personal secretary, William L. Finley, signed the document and declared that "I certify the foregoing to be correct list of shares as set forth all of them standing in the name of W A Hulbert." The "do" under a few words is an abbreviation of "ditto" (Chicago History Museum, ICHi-176531-002).

Above and opposite: By November 1, 1876, Hulbert held the controlling interest in the Chicago Base Ball Association with 36 shares of stock; the other 30 stockholders owned just 33 shares. Association Secretary Albert Spalding included in his list of stock owners of the Chicago Base Ball Association the stock certificate numbers, shareholders' names and addresses, and the number of shares each person owned. At the end of the document Spalding wrote: "I certify the foregoing to be a correct list of Stock owners as shown by the books of the Association" (Chicago History Museum, ICHi-176531-003 and ICHi-176531-004).

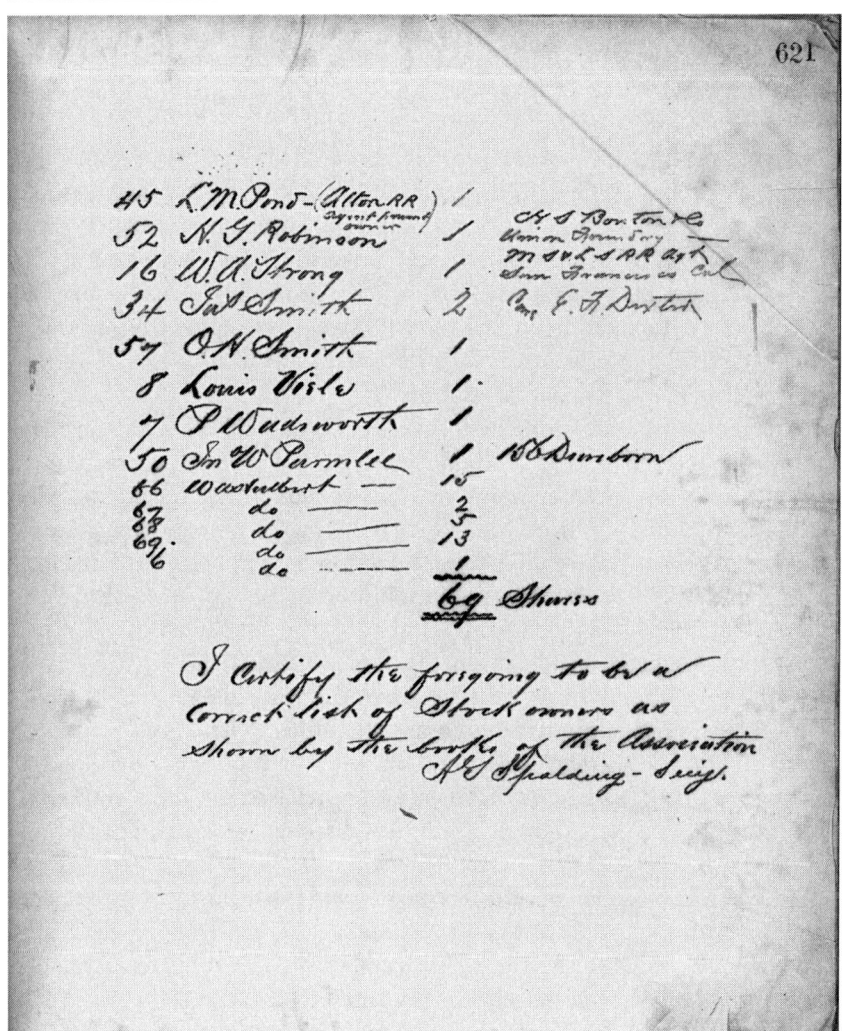

holders or officers in the new club anyway. Chicago Cubs historian Ed Hartig believes that Hulbert's strategy was to "buy out the big guys—the ones who had clout—and the lesser would soon follow. The more stock in the old company held by Hulbert, the less likely things would end poorly for him."

Stockholders familiar with the strong-willed Hulbert (and perhaps recalling his bold signing of the five ballplayers the previous year) probably acquiesced when they realized what Hulbert's plans were and that the "big guys"—to quote Hartig—were selling their stock. What also might have worked in Hulbert's favor were the financial difficulties of the New York

Mutuals and the Philadelphia Athletics. The fact that both teams lacked the funds to play their road games and finish out the season was hardly a secret at that time, and worried Chicago investors may have been eager to sell while they had someone at hand who was willing to buy.

Perhaps, too, some of the shareholders sold their shares because they did not see eye to eye with Hulbert and simply wanted out. For instance, after investing in the new club, former Association President Norman Gassette told him he wished to sell all his stock. One cannot help but wonder what sort of falling-out led to Hulbert's somewhat cryptic reply: "I assure you I am heartily sorry you have determined to withdraw your capital from base ball, … but I am willing to believe it is not because of dislike for myself—con[s]ciously I have always tried to please you."[7]

Hulbert's papers and other Chicago club documents at the Chicago History Museum (formerly the Chicago Historical Society) reveal numerous details about his stock transactions. The Chicago Base Ball Association's ledger pages indicate that 59 investors had owned 70 shares of stock in the early summer of 1876. By the end of July, Hulbert had purchased 22 shares from among the other backers. A memorandum dated September 15 shows that his stock holdings had increased to 33 shares, which included the one share (certificate number 6) he had originally purchased in 1870.

The baseball club records disclose that Albert Spalding had once owned one share of stock, although the phrase "Cancelled, Oct. 30–1876," is written alongside the stock holdings notation, with both the word "one" and his name crossed out. Apparently Hulbert had purchased the share and retired (canceled) it. This share did not appear in subsequent stock listings and represented no ownership in the club.

By November 1, Hulbert held 36 shares and the majority of stock, as the other investors—now down to 30—retained just 33 shares. Secretary Spalding compiled a list of the 31 stockholders and their 69 shares, noting the stock certificate numbers, the owners' names and addresses, and the number of shares each person owned. At the bottom of the document Spalding wrote: "I certify the foregoing to be a correct list of Stock owners as shown by the books of the Association."

The Demise of One Baseball Club and the Introduction of Another

With Hulbert controlling the stock, he could now officially sever all ties to the defunct Chicago Base Ball Association. The directors held a "special

State of Illinois, } ss.
Cook County.

To George H. Harlow, Secretary of State:

We, the undersigned *William A. Hulbert*, *William H. Murray, and Edwin F. Dexter*

propose to form a Corporation under an act of the General Assembly of the State of Illinois, entitled "An Act Concerning Corporations," approved April 18, 1872; and that for the purposes of such organization we hereby state as follows, to-wit:

1. The name of such Corporation is The *Chicago Ball Club*

2. The object for which it is formed is *to foster and elevate our National sport – the game of base-ball*

3. The Capital Stock shall be *Twenty thousand dollars*
4. The amount of each share is *One hundred dollars*
5. The number of shares *Two hundred*
6. The location of the principal is in *the City of Chicago* in the County of *Cook* State of Illinois.
7. The duration of the Corporation shall be *Twenty five* years.

William A. Hulbert
William H. Murray
Edwin F. Dexter

After the Chicago Base Ball Association's three-year charter expired in the spring of 1876, Association President William A. Hulbert and two of his friends, William H. Murray and Edwin F. Dexter, filed a corporate charter with the state of Illinois that outlined their plans for a new baseball club. The object for which it was formed, they wrote, was "to foster and elevate our National sport—the game of base-ball" (Secretary of State, "Dissolved Domestic Corporation Charters," Record Series 103.112, Illinois State Archives).

meeting" on November 2, five weeks after the Chicago Ball Club's White Stockings clinched the National League's inaugural pennant. Attending the meeting were President Hulbert and Directors Albert G. Spalding, Edwin F. Dexter, and Charles S. Bartlett. With the following resolution, recorded by Secretary Spalding in his minutes, Hulbert and his friends formally transferred the assets of the old Association to the new Ball Club:

> And whereas the duration of the powers and corporate existence of said Chicago Base Ball Association, under the charter heretofore obtained pursuant to law, has ceased by limitation (except for the purpose of closing the affairs of said corporation as provided by law). And whereas a new corporation has been duly organized under the laws of Illinois styled "The Chicago Ball Club," which association is hereby the successor of "[T]he Chicago Base Ball Association," a majority of the stockholders and officers being the same persons who owned the stock and were officers of the late C[hicago] B[ase] B[all] Association and have employed for the year 1877 most of the players in the Chicago Base Ball Club of 1876. Therefore it is Resolved that the membership of the said Chicago B[ase] B[all] Club in the said National League of Professional Base Ball Clubs and the said championship Pennant of 1876 be transferred to and held by the said "The Chicago Ball Club" in the same manner as though said "Club" had been in existence during the season of 1876 and had employed and controlled the said Chicago Nine of this year.[8]

Hulbert did not waste any time contacting stockholders and settling accounts. "The affairs of the Chicago Base Ball Association have been finally closed up," he wrote to Association and Chicago Ball Club investor Thomas E. Courtney the following day. Hulbert had purchased three shares of stock from Courtney for $75 each, and the baseball executive said he was enclosing with his letter a final dividend check. (He valued the stock at $91.60 per share "after discharging all obligations.") Hulbert and the new club were also "closing up" accounts—and probably warding off potential lawsuits—by agreeing to pay dividends on remaining shares of the Association's stockholders. Researcher Preston D. Orem, who pored over many newspapers while compiling a detailed history of nineteenth-century baseball, concluded that "matters were apparently fixed up" between Hulbert and the shareowners, and that the baseball official "was obviously just scuttling some individuals he considered undesirables."[9]

"Hulbert made all the decisions"

Naturally, Hulbert had no intention of admitting any "undesirables" to the Chicago Ball Club. "I think all of this can be boiled down to Hulbert wishing to gain control," Ed Hartig observed, "to limit the stock to those he thought he could control and to eliminate those whom he couldn't. In short, control what you can, minimize what you can't." His plan also made sense strategically: dissolve an association with too many shareowners, start a new club with a smaller group of handpicked investors, and buy out the members of the old organization.

And when the dust settled, William Hulbert was the one in charge, just as he was during the National League's inaugural season of 1876. Morgan G. Bulkeley of the Hartford club may have been the league's head, but as John Thorn, official historian of Major League Baseball, points out in his article on the founding of the National League, Bulkeley was merely the "titular president," for "Hulbert made all the decisions." Moreover, Hulbert continued to assert his authority, as he was elected league president for the following year and presided over both it and the White Stockings until his death. It is clear that whatever else had guided his vision in the Chicago club's reorganization, one principal aim was to consolidate his already considerable control and influence over all aspects of the game and business of baseball.[10]

NOTES

1. Obituaries, eulogies, and resolution are in *Spalding's Base Ball Guide and Official League Book for 1883* (1883; repr., St. Louis: Horton Pub. Co., 1988), 5–11; "Obituary," *Chicago Daily Tribune*, April 13, 1882, 8.

2. Information on William Hulbert is in Robert Knight Barney and Frank Dallier, "'I'd rather be a lamp post in Chicago, than a millionaire in any other city': William A. Hulbert, Civic Pride, and the Birth of the National League," *NINE: A Journal of Baseball History and Social Policy Perspectives* 2 (Fall 1993): 40–58; Tom Melville, "A League of His Own: William Hulbert and the Founding of the National League," *Chicago History* 29 (Fall 2000): 44–57; David Ball and David Nemec, "Hulbert, William Ambrose/'Will' 'William,'" in *Major League Baseball Profiles, 1871–1900*, vol. 2, 35–36; Michael Haupert, "William Hulbert," SABR Baseball Biography Project, Society for American Baseball Research, accessed October 28, 2019, http://sabr.org/bioproj/person/d1d420b3; Jack Bales, *Before They Were the Cubs: The Early Years of Chicago's First Professional Baseball Team* (Jefferson, NC: McFarland, 2019), 76–77, 82. Hulbert's "lamp-post" quotation is from Albert G. Spalding, *America's National Game: Historic Facts Concerning the Beginning, Evolution, Development and Popularity of Base Ball* (1911; repr., Lincoln: University of Nebraska Press, 1992), 207–208. Hulbert as a stockholder in 1870 is in "William A. Hulbert [...]," *Chicago Daily Tribune*, April 11, 1882, 6. Hulbert as owner of one share of stock is in Minutes of August 18, 1874, meeting of the stockholders, Record book of stockholders' meetings, Chicago Base Ball Association, Chicago Cubs Records, box 5, folder 4, 1, Chicago History Museum. Controversial game is in "Sporting," *Chicago Times*, November 3, 1870, 4; "Who Are the Champions for 1870?," *New York Clipper*, November 12, 1870, 250. The end of the White Stockings season is in "Games and Pastimes," *Chicago Tribune*, November 13, 1871, 6; "Games and Pastimes," *Chicago Tribune*, November 26, 1871, 2. Hulbert as director of Association is in "Base Ball," *Chicago Tribune*, July 23, 1872, 2.

3. August 5 game is in an unsigned editorial, *Chicago Daily Tribune*, August 6, 1874, 4; "Base Ball," *Chicago Daily Tribune*, August 6, 1874, 8. Hulbert's positions in the Chicago Base

"He will do just what is best, no doubt"

Ball Association are in "Sporting News," *(Chicago) Inter Ocean*, August 20, 1874, 5 (mentions Gassette's resignation and Gage's election); "The Chicago Club," *New York Clipper*, December 12, 1874, 290 (mentions correspondence, contracts, and Hulbert as "efficient secretary"); "William A. Hulbert [...]," *Chicago Daily Tribune*, April 11, 1882, 6. Stockholders meeting details and Hulbert quotations are in Minutes of August 18, 1874, meeting, 1–5 (see note 2). Gassette's occupation is in "Death of N.T. Gassette," *Chicago Daily Tribune*, March 27, 1891, 9. George Gage is also in "George W. Gage," *Chicago Daily Tribune*, September 26, 1875, 12 (occupation and death). Manager James Wood alluded to the game cheating in a letter: "It is our intention of engaging a nine for next year that will be a credit to play with. Chicago is <u>disgusted</u> with <u>bummers</u>, will have nothing hereafter <u>but Gentlemen</u>." James Wood to Scott Hastings, 2 September [187]4, Letterbook of the Board of Directors, Chicago Base Ball Association, Chicago Cubs Records, box 1, folder 7, Chicago History Museum. See also Larry Names, *Bury My Heart at Wrigley Field: The History of the Chicago Cubs* (Neshkoro, WI: Angel Press of Wisconsin, 1996), 120–21.

4. Hulbert signing ballplayers is in Minutes of July 3, 1875, and July 16, 1875, meetings of the Directors of the Chicago Base Ball Association, Record book of the Board of Directors, Chicago Base Ball Association, Chicago Cubs Records, box 4, folder 4, Chicago History Museum; "Base-Ball," *Chicago Daily Tribune*, July 20, 1875, 5; "Base Ball," *Chicago Daily Tribune*, July 24, 1875, 2. Games won and lost and standings of teams are in http://www.retrosheet.org/. "This may be" quotation is from "Next Year's Engagements," *Chicago Daily Tribune*, July 30, 1876, 3.

5. *Inter Ocean* quotations and details of new club, including names of stockholders, are in "Bats Are Trumps," *(Chicago) Inter Ocean*, July 31, 1876, 8 (article reprinted in Bales, *Before They Were the Cubs*, 104–106). Names of board members are in "Field and Turf," *Chicago Daily Tribune*, March 18, 1877, 7. Occupations of men are in *The Lakeside Annual Directory of the City of Chicago, 1875–6* (Chicago: Donnelley, Loyd and Co., 1875), 153 (Bartlett); 309 (DeKoven); 315, 1147 (Dexter); 736 (Murray); 1199 (both Murray and Hulbert in "Grain Dealers" section). Interestingly enough, Hulbert had married one Jennie Murray in 1860. See also "John B. Lyon," *Chicago Daily Tribune*, May 12, 1874, 8; "W.H. Murray Dies in Mississippi," *Chicago Daily Tribune*, December 27, 1893, 11. "To foster and elevate" quotation is from "Report of Commissioners of the Chicago Ball Club," filed August 14, 1876, in Secretary of State, "Dissolved Domestic Corporation Charters," Record Series 103.112, Illinois State Archives (report includes "Statement of Incorporation of the Chicago Ball Club," filed July 21, 1876, as well as the names of the stockholders, the number of shares they purchased, and the names of the club's board members, who were elected on August 12 in a meeting in Hulbert's office). Date of July 21 is also in "Official Crop Reports from Ninety-Five Counties of Illinois," *Macomb (IL) Journal*, July 27, 1876, 1. See also Philip Wadsworth to [Illinois Secretary of State] George H. Harlow, 12 August 1876, Letterbook of the Board of Directors, Chicago Base Ball Association, Chicago Cub Records, box 2, folder 1, 543, Chicago History Museum: "Enclosed find certificate of the organization of the Chicago Ball Club duly signed and executed by the Commissioners. I have to request that there will be no delay in sending to the address of Mr. Hulbert (as shown in the report) the Certificate of Organization to file for record in this county." "Whenever a member" quotation, which originally appeared in "a Chicago paper," is quoted in "Sports and Pastimes," *Brooklyn (NY) Daily Eagle*, August 15, 1876, 3.

6. Signing players and "any attempt to get" quotation are from "Pastimes," *Chicago Daily Tribune*, September 17, 1876, 7. "Quietly set to work" and "meager results" quotations are from "Base Ball," *Chicago Evening Journal*, August 2, 1876, 4. "Important business" quotation is from "Miscellaneous," *Chicago Daily Tribune*, July 30, 1876, 15. A dozen stockholders and "to ascertain what" quotation are in "Base Ball," *Chicago Times*, August 2, 1876, 2.

7. "We wish to place" quotation is from W.A. Hulbert, W.H. Murray, and E.F. Dexter to N.E. Young, 1 August [187]6, Letterbook of the Board of Directors, Chicago Base Ball Association, Chicago Cub Records, box 2, folder 1, 533, Chicago History Museum. Team taking the field in 1877 is in "Bats Are Trumps." Hulbert possibly being charged is in Names, *Bury My Heart at Wrigley Field*, 141. Ed Hartig quotation is from Ed Hartig, email message to author,

September 25, 2019. New York Mutuals and Philadelphia Athletics are in "Philadelphia Gossip," *Chicago Daily Tribune*, August 6, 1876, 7 (Athletics); "Pastimes," *Chicago Daily Tribune*, September 24, 1876, 3 (Mutuals). For information on Gassette, see "Death of N.T. Gassette," *Chicago Daily Tribune*, March 27, 1891, 9. "I assure you" quotation is from W.A. Hulbert to N.T. Gassette, 9 October [187]6, Letterbook of the Board of Directors, Chicago Base Ball Association, Chicago Cubs Records, box 2, folder 1, 607, Chicago History Museum.

8. The Hulbert documents cited in this note are from the Chicago Base Ball Association's record and letterbooks in the Chicago Cubs Records at the Chicago History Museum. Ledger pages are in "Stockholders Chicago Base Ball Association," Record book of stockholders' meetings, box 5, folder 4, 50–53 (Spalding's "cancelled" share is on pp. 52 and 53). William L. Finley [Hulbert's personal secretary], Memorandum, September 15, 1876, Letterbook of the Board of Directors, box 2, folder 1, 581. November 1 list of stockholders is in A.G. Spalding, "List of Stock Owners C[hicago] B[ase] B[all] Assn," Letterbook of the Board of Directors, box 2, folder 1, 620–21. Meeting and resolution are in Minutes of November 2, 1876, special meeting of the Directors of the Chicago Base Ball Association, Record book of stockholders meetings, box 5, folder 4, 9–12. Clinching the pennant is in "The Deciding Game," *Chicago Evening Journal*, September 27, 1876, 4.

9. The Hulbert documents cited in this note are from the Chicago Base Ball Association's record and letterbooks in the Chicago Cubs Records at the Chicago History Museum. "The affairs of" quotation is from W.A. Hulbert to Thos E. Courtney, 3 November [187]6, Letterbook of the Board of Directors, box 2, folder 2, 1. Stock purchase price of $75 is in "Acct Purchases Chicago Base Ball Assn Stock," Letterbook of the Board of Directors, box 2, folder 1, 558. "After discharging" quotation is from W.A. Hulbert to H.E. Swartwout, 3 November [187]6, Letterbook of the Board of Directors, box 2, folder 2, 4. Payment of dividends is in Minutes of November 2 meeting, 11–12. "Matters were apparently" quotation is from Preston D. Orem, *Baseball (1845–1881): From the Newspaper Accounts* (Altadena, CA: Preston D. Orem, 1961), 259. See also Names, *Bury My Heart at Wrigley Field*, 139–42.

10. Ed Hartig quotation is from Ed Hartig, email message to author, September 30, 2019. "Titular president" quotation is from John Thorn, "History Awakens: February 2, 1876, and the Founding of the National League," in *Base Ball 11: New Research on the Early Game*, ed. Don Jensen (Jefferson, NC: McFarland, 2019), 108. See also "Field and Turf," *Chicago Daily Tribune*, March 18, 1877, 7: The new club's advantages "are its compactness of interest, and the fact that it contains within its small number of stockholders all the best elements of the support of the game in this city."

Brooklyn Baseball

The Missing Years

Brock E. Helander

Writers of nineteenth century baseball often overlook or discount base-ball activity in Brooklyn, third most populous city, after the Mutuals of New York were expelled from the National League for failing to complete its 1876 schedule. The Mutuals had actually played on the Union Grounds in Brooklyn. (New York proper did not host a major league team until 1883.) Yet in the wake of the Mutuals' expulsion, various promoters did endeavor to assemble teams to play in Brooklyn. This article examines the sundry efforts made to maintain high-level baseball play in that city outside the confines of the National League. Hundreds of box scores and game accounts were examined to determine the constituencies of the teams, and various biographical resources and listings at Baseball-Reference.com were utilized to confirm team membership.

BROOKLYN, UNTIL 1898 AN INDEPENDENT CITY, was one of the early hubs of organized baseball. Nine of the sixteen clubs represented at a May 1857 meeting assembled to discuss the formation of a national baseball organization hailed from the city: the Atlantic; Harmony; Eckford; Excelsior; Putnam; Continental; Bedford; Nassau; and Olympic. Nine Brooklyn clubs attended the March 1858 meeting that produced a written set of by-laws, rules, and a constitution, christening the organization of the National Association of Base Ball Players (NABBP).[1]

The Atlantics, Eckfords, and Excelsiors were mainstays of the organiza-

Base Ball 12, pp. 126–142
ISSN 1934-2802 (Print) / ISSN 1934-3167 (Online)
978-1-4766-7473-5 (Print) / 978-1-4766-4112-6 (ebook)

tion, competing every year from 1858 to 1870. The Atlantics were especially successful, posting winning records every year except 1862. Initially strin gently amateur, the NABBP, at their 1868 convention, allowed clubs to pay their players, opening the professional era of baseball. The Atlantics and Eckfords played professionally in 1869 and 1870.

The NABBP was superseded by the National Association of Professional Base Ball Players (NAPBBP) in 1871, but the two Brooklyn entries fared poorly. The Eckfords were members in 1872 and the Atlantics from 1872 to 1875. Neither posted a winning record and the Atlantics' record for 1875 was an abysmal 2–42.

After Brooklyn was excluded from the formation of the National League (NL) in 1876, various efforts were made by baseball promoters to re-establish baseball in Brooklyn. Two men, William Cammeyer and Billy Barnie, repeatedly attempted to form Brooklyn baseball clubs. Finally in 1883, enthusiasts George Taylor and Charles Byrne were able to establish a minor league Brooklyn team.

William Cammeyer was born in New York on March 20, 1821. His father John was engaged in the leather business for many years and invested heavily in Brooklyn real estate, amassing a vast fortune. William worked in his father's leather business and moved to the Williamsburg section of the city in 1849. In 1861 he leased the ground bound by Harrison and Marcy Avenues and Rutledge and Lynch Streets and transformed it into a winter skating pond. In the spring of 1862, Cammeyer laid out a baseball ground on the property and enclosed it with a six-and-a-half-foot fence, thus enabling him to charge admission. The Union Grounds, as it was called, hosted its first baseball game on May 15. The early occupants of the Grounds were the amateur Eckford, Constellation, and Putnam clubs. According to the *New York Clipper*, the Atlantics and the notoriously corrupt Mutuals began to play on the Union Grounds in 1867. Cammeyer was president of the Mutuals in 1875 and 1876 and managed the team in 1876.[2]

Billy Barnie was a baseball "lifer" and one of the prominent baseball "hustlers" of the nineteenth century. Born in New York on January 26, 1853, he moved with his parents to Brooklyn around the age of two. Barnie began playing with amateur clubs in Brooklyn at the age of twelve. He joined the amateur Nassau club of Brooklyn in 1870, stayed through 1873, then briefly joined the Atlantics. He accepted his first professional engagement with Hartford in 1874. A true baseball vagabond, Barnie subsequently played for teams in Keokuk, Iowa; New York (the Mutuals); Columbus, Ohio; Louisville; Cincinnati; and Buffalo. Barnie also managed baseball teams for 18 consecutive seasons, 14 of them in the major leagues.[3]

Union Grounds, Brooklyn, 1865. The Union Grounds hosted baseball games from 1862 to 1882.

Early Efforts

Before the scheduled annual March 1 meeting of the NAPBBP, the National League of Professional Base Ball Clubs (NL) formed in New York on February 2, 1876. The National League members included six NAPBBP clubs and two strong independent clubs from the West, Cincinnati and Louisville. Several NAPBBP clubs were excluded, including New Haven, the Atlantics of Brooklyn, the Red Stockings of St. Louis, and two Philadelphia clubs, one known as the Centennials, the other as the Pearls or Philadelphias. The National League constitution provided that no co-operative clubs (that is, teams dependent on gate-money as opposed to those comprised of salaried players) be admitted. This ruled eliminated eliminating the Atlantics of Brooklyn.[4] The New Haven club requested admission to the National League and the club's secretary met with the president of the Chicago club, William Hulbert, but to no avail. The *Brooklyn Eagle* reported on February 15 that the Philadelphia club invited the "cooperation of all the organized base ball clubs of the country ... to be held in New Haven on March 1...." However, on February 26, the New Haven Base Ball Club withdrew from the National Association.[5]

The March 1 meeting took place as scheduled. Participants included the Centennial and Philadelphia clubs and the Atlantics of Brooklyn, represented by James McColgan, one of the directors of the Philadelphia club. Officers were elected and a rules committee was appointed. The convention adjourned to meet again on April 3 in Philadelphia.[6] At that meeting of the organization, referred to as the National Professional Association, the Atlantics were again represented by McColgan and the Brooklyns of Brooklyn by Peter H. Garland. Officers were elected, rules adopted, and committees formed.[7] However, no evidence exists that the teams of the association ever played an official game. In November, the *Chicago Tribune* noted derisively that "the Professional Association ... opened the season of 1876 so vigorously—on paper— but never played a game."[8]

Peter Garland persisted. He formed a cooperative club known as the Brooklyns, served as manager and selected players from Brooklyn amateur clubs of 1875. Among the last-name-only players on the team were eight members of the amateur Tuttle and Bailey club of 1875, including Dooley, Sullivan, and Valentine.[9] The team began play in April, with Brooklyn-born Terry Larkin as pitcher into May.[10] The club withdrew from the Professional Association in June, reverting to amateur status.[11] Due to "general bad conduct, viz.: Dooley, Sullivan and Valentine," the team abandoned its New York state tour and returned home July 11.[12]

Hartford of Brooklyn, Then Cammeyer and Barnie

The year 1877 was a difficult one for the National League. The prior year, the Mutuals of New York and the Athletics of Philadelphia had ceased play on September 16, before season's end, leading to their expulsion at the League convention at Cleveland in early December. Neither League and Hartford president Morgan Bulkeley nor William Cammeyer attended the meeting. Hartford Manager Robert Ferguson acted as the Hartford representative. Chicago club president William Hulbert was elected president of the league.[13]

The Hartford club was formally transferred to Brooklyn on March 4, 1877.[14] The club, known as the Hartfords of Brooklyn, included seven regular players from the Hartfords of 1876: manager-third baseman Ferguson, catchers Bill Harbridge and Doug Allison, second baseman Jack Burdock, shortstop Tom Carey, and outfielders John Cassidy and Tom York. Ferguson, Burdock, Cassidy, and York had been born in Brooklyn. Burdock and Cassidy had played for NAPBBP Atlantic teams, as had Ferguson, who also played for the Atlantics from 1866 to 1870 and managed and played third base for the Atlantics from 1872 to 1874. York had played for the Eckfords of Brooklyn and Ferguson, Allison, Burdock, and Carey had played for the Mutuals of New York.[15]

The new members of the team were pitcher Terry Larkin and first baseman Joe Start, both born in Brooklyn, and outfielder Jim Holdsworth. Veteran Start had played for the Atlantics from 1862 to 1870 and the Mutuals from 1871 to 1876.[16] Holdsworth had played for the Eckfords in 1872 and the Mutuals in 1873, 1875, and 1876. The Hartfords of Brooklyn concluded their sole stint in the National League on September 29, finishing in third place, with a record of 31–27. Following the season, Larkin, Harbridge, Start and Cassidy went with Ferguson to the Chicago NL club.

One other team played in Brooklyn in 1877, probably as a cooperative. This Brooklyn club was formed in April, with John Garvey as president and William Dennen as secretary.[17] The team played from at least May 3 until September 28.

In April 1878, the *Brooklyn Eagle* announced: "What with the Atlantic nine of the Western District and Cammeyer's Brooklyn nine for the Eastern, we ought to have some old time rivalry on the field."[18] Both cooperatives, William Cammeyer's Brooklyns played on the Union Grounds, while Billy Barnie's Atlantics played on the Capitoline Grounds, which had opened for baseball two years after the Union Grounds.[19] The Atlantics played field games in March and April.[20] The players included catcher Barnie and pitcher William "Candy" Cummings, the reputed inventor of the curve.

However, the Atlantic team was hijacked by Ben Douglas, who had "resigned" from his position as manager of NL Providence "on account of difficulties growing out of the former's alleged indiscretion in communicating and making dates with International (Association) clubs unauthorized by the directors."[21] Within days, "Benjamin went to Hartford, leased the ball-grounds there, then went to New Haven and engaged the ball-grounds there, and finally went to Brooklyn and gobbled up the new Atlantic nine."[22] Douglas entered New Haven in the International Association and moved it to Hartford in May, only to have it expelled from the Association in July.[23]

Cammeyer fared little better. His team included veteran pitcher and captain Bobby Mathews (who had played for the Mutuals from 1873 to 1876), outfielder Eddie Booth, catcher Edward McGlynn, and third baseman James Farrell.[24] Five of the players had manned the amateur Chelseas of Brooklyn in 1877, including catcher John Curran, second baseman Ben Laughlin, and outfielder Pete Treacey.[25]

Brooklyn played its first game on April 20 and played through May 11, as the property of the Union Grounds had been sold for building purposes, the first of a number of threats to the existence of the ballpark. Mathews and McGlynn subsequently went to IA Worcester, while Curran went to IA Springfield, Massachusetts, and Laughlin and Treacey to the Flyaways of Brooklyn.[26]

In December 1878, the *New York Clipper* announced that "(b)oth the Union and Capitoline grounds, Brooklyn, will be cut up into building lots next spring."[27] Nonetheless, Billy Barnie organized a cooperative Atlantic team to play on the Union Grounds, although several sources state that veteran John Chapman managed the club.[28] The team included three Brooklyn-born players: Jake Knowdell, Henry Kessler, and Bill Schenck.

The inclusion of two other players poses one of the problems of identification in nineteenth century baseball: infielders Farrell and Lavin. According to the *New York Clipper*, Joseph Farrell played for the Hudsons of Brooklyn in 1877 and 1878, "playing under the name 'Lavin,' to distinguish himself from his cousin, Joseph Farrell, both of whom played with the Hudsons at the time."[29] Joseph Farrell's obituary in the *Clipper* years later observed that the other Joe Farrell was "the then noted catcher of that name."[30]

The Atlantics began play in April 1879, with Schenck leaving in May.[31] Later that month, Chapman was appointed manager of the Holyoke, Massachusetts, club of the National Association, which had superseded the International Association when the two Canadian clubs dropped out.[32] The *Clipper* announced: "The Flyaways will take the place of the disbanded Atlantics in the local cooperative nine."[33] Lavin and Farrell then played for the Flyaways. Barnie went west, debuting with the Knickerbockers of San Francisco on June 1.[34]

The year 1880 was a wild one for fans of Brooklyn baseball. In March, at William Cammeyer's request, the *Clipper* stated the Union Grounds would be open and that a cooperative nine would immediately be organized. The Grounds became available because of a delay in legislative action regarding its use for the 47th Regiment Armory.[35] Thus, the facility was available for baseball until August. The team played several practice games in April. Five players were members of the 1879 Atlantics, including Henry Kessler, Bill Schenck, and Jake Knowdell, each Brooklyn-born. The new players were Brooklyn-born Jake Schappert and New York-born outfielder Jim Clinton, who had played for the Eckfords in 1872 and the Atlantics in 1874 and 1875.

Extant box scores show only road games for Brooklyn, most often against the college teams of Yale and Princeton. In May, arrangements for laying the foundation for the armory were in progress and the Brooklyns were to be transferred to the enclosed grounds of the Elysian Fields of Hoboken, New Jersey. The team played one game there, on May 31, losing to the Jersey Citys by 7 to 3.[36]

In August it became clear that the completion of the reconstruction of the Union Grounds would be delayed until October.[37] Cammeyer quickly arranged for a series of games there between the Rochesters and Nationals of Washington of the withering National Association. The first series took place on consecutive days, August 11 through 14, with the final game being contested at Brighton Beach race course.[38]

Cammeyer then organized and managed his own team, the Unions. The players included two members of earlier Brooklyn teams, Bill Schenck and Jim Clinton. Others included two New York-born veterans, outfielder Lipman Pike, who had played for the Mutuals and the Atlantics, and shortstop John "Candy" Nelson, who had played for the Eckfords and the Mutuals.[39] The new players were two New York-born men, catcher Charlie Reipschlager and second baseman John "Dasher" Troy. Joe Farrell played first base.[40]

A new series of games at the Union Grounds among the Rochesters, the Nationals, and the Unions commenced August 18 and concluded August 24. Rochester won all four of its games, the Nationals won two and lost two, and the Unions lost all four of its games. Yet another series at the Union Grounds among the three teams took place August 26 through 28, with the Unions defeating the Rochesters on August 26 and losing to the Nationals on August 27.[41] The Unions soon began playing against Jim Mutrie's newly formed club, initially known as the New Yorks, later as the Metropolitans, on the Union Grounds September 5 through 16. Their game on September 6 was held in Hoboken.[42]

The Metropolitan-Union game of September 16 proved a competitive and financial disaster. For the previous day's game, Farrell, Nelson, Pike, and Troy did not play for the Unions, Farrell and Nelson having joined the Metropolitans.[43] According to one account, all of the Union players were present but refused to play.[44] According to another, the cause was "some difficulty about money matters drawing from the seven absentees the declaration that they would not play until it was settled."[45] The *Clipper* reported that Clinton, Hayes, Schenck, Reipschlager, and McManus "declined to play because they were not placed upon equal terms in sharing the gate-receipts with the salaried and uniformed regular team of the Metropolitans. Cramer and Farrell then assembled an ad hoc team to play the game, committing numerous errors and losing 15–0."[46]

The fate of the Union club is uncertain. In a review of the game of September 18 in the *Clipper*, the article was headlined "METROPOLITAN vs. UNION," while the box score showed the teams as Metropolitan and Brooklyn.[47] Who was the manager? Was it merely an ad hoc team? Was this a players-only team? Regardless, the team played only one more game, on September 21, losing to the Metropolitans 14–4.[48]

Billy Barnie was back on the scene in 1881. In March, the *Brooklyn Eagle* reported that Barnie, assisted by Lipman Pike, was reorganizing the Atlantics a cooperative.[49] On April 11, the Eastern Championship Association was formed at Earle's Hotel in New York. Delegates included Barnie of the Atlantics, William Warren White of the Nationals of Washington, John Kelly of the New York club, and James Mutrie of the Metropolitans.[50] The clubs benefited from the proximity of other clubs, but players jumped from team to team.

Among the early-season players for the Atlantics in 1881 were five veterans of prior Brooklyn teams: Lip Pike, "Candy" Nelson, Terry Larkin, Bill Schenck, and "Dasher" Troy. Troy, Larkin, and Schenck remained the entire season, while Pike and Nelson moved to NL Worcester in August.[51] New members included John Driscoll and two Brooklyn-born players, pitcher John Valentine and outfielder James "Chief" Roseman. Others to subsequently join were slugger Dan Brouthers (briefly) in May, catcher Charlie Reipschlager in June, and outfielder Bill Harbridge and second baseman Bill Smiley in July. Brooklyn-born first baseman Oscar Walker came in August.

The Metropolitans' Polo Grounds, opened the previous September, was the premier facility for baseball in the area, yet the Union Grounds, continuing to survive the threat of the armory's construction, was used occasionally. However in August, the *Clipper* observed: "So great (was) a demand for grounds early in the season that the overflow from the thirteen ball fields at the Parade Grounds, Prospect Park, Brooklyn, found its way to the Union Ground, and crowded out the Atlantic professionals from the field."[52] This development may have prompted Barnie to consider other arrangements.

Barnie found a welcome solution thanks to rising interest in baseball in the West, due to the efforts of O.P. Caylor, sporting editor of the *Cincinnati Enquirer*, and Alfred Spink, sporting editor of the (St. Louis) *Missouri Repub-*

lican.[53] In his history of early baseball published in 1911, Spink stated: "Later I wrote to Horace B. Phillips, then managing the Athletics of Philadelphia, and to William Barnie, then operating the Atlantics of Brooklyn. Both the Athletics and the Atlantics ... were willing to come all the way to St. Louis to meet the St. Louis Browns for a division of gate receipts."[54]

Barnie later reminisced:

> Horace Phillips and myself then formed the idea of organizing a big league. We learned through the papers that large audiences were being attracted by base ball teams in Cincinnati, Louisville and St. Louis and began negotiating for a trip to those cities. The Western clubs guaranteed us more than enough to pay our expenses on the road trip. We accepted and both the Atlantics and Athletics took the journey.[55]

On their way west, the Atlantics played the Athletics in Philadelphia on September 14 and 15, losing both games.[56] By then, the Atlantics consisted of Larkin, Reipschlager, Schenck, Smiley, and Walker, plus Jim Clinton, Joe Farrell, and John Schappert. Between September 17 and October 9, they played the Eclipse and Eagles (one game only) of Louisville and the Browns and Reds (one game only) of St. Louis. The *Clipper* later reported that the Atlantics had played fourteen games on their Western tour, winning nine and losing three of their five games against the Eclipse.[57] The Atlantics closed out the season against the Metropolitans on the Polo Grounds. In November, the *Eagle* posted a list of their victories only (some unconfirmed) numbering 30.[58] An examination of box scores (likely incomplete) shows losses at 36.

In September 1881 the *Philadelphia Times* reported: "Mr. Phillips, manager of the Athletic Club, said last evening, upon his return from the West, that the movement was meeting with great favor in St Louis, Pittsburg, Louisville and Cincinnati, and that a meeting was to be held in Pittsburg on October 10 to consider the formation of the new league."[59] Who attended the meeting is a matter of conjecture. The day following the meeting, numerous newspapers published virtually identical accounts, possibly authored by Frank Wright of the *Cincinnati Enquirer*, who reportedly did attend.[60] The report was replete with misspellings and name-dropping, perhaps to impress prospective members.[61] The *New York Clipper* was more circumspect: "An informal meeting was held Oct. 10 in Pittsburg in the place of the proposed convention of clubs to organize a new Association, at which there were but two or three of the representatives of the clubs present who were to have sent delegates. After some talk together, it was resolved to hold a meeting for a permanent organization at the Gibson House, Cincinnati, on Nov. 2."[62]

Indeed, the American Association of Base Ball Clubs (AA) formed in Cincinnati on November 2, 1881. The Association would allow the sale of alcohol in the ballparks and play baseball on Sundays (circumstances not allowed by the National League), and charge only twenty-five cents admission (compared to the League's fifty cents). The clubs admitted to membership were Cincinnati, St. Louis, the Alleghenys of Pittsburgh, the Eclipse of Louisville, and the Atlantics of Brooklyn (represented by Barnie). Philadelphia was represented by two different delegates: Charles Fulmer of the Athletics and Horace Phillips of the Philadelphia club. (Phillips had been released by the Athletics in October.[63]) Fulmer was admitted and Phillips excluded.[64]

At the December meeting of the National League in Chicago, the dormant League Alliance was resurrected. (The League Alliance formed in 1877 under the auspices of the National League to extend its power over independent clubs across the country while protecting the sanctity of player contracts.[65]) Clubs could join the Alliance by paying $25. Only one club could join from any city. League Alliance clubs were prevented from playing any non–League club in a League Alliance city. The Metropolitan club was declared to be the League Alliance club of New York and the Philadelphia club, managed by Phillips, was recognized as the other member of the League Alliance.[66]

In December, the *Clipper* announced that the Atlantics would be reorganized as a stock company.[67] The *Clipper* interviewed Barnie in January and noted that he "… was in a somewhat doubtful position as to where he would be found in April next, whether as a member of the American Association … or as a member of the League Alliance. One of his objections to entering the American Alliance is that rule which gives to each club the whole of receipts from matches played on their own grounds … in lieu of the customary division of receipts. On the other hand, Manager Barnie is debarred from any benefit accruing from his becoming a League Alliance club member by the fact that the Metropolitan League Alliance club has entire control of the district of country which extends four miles from the corporate limits of the City of New York, which law deprives him League Alliance membership in the City of Brooklyn."[68]

In February, Barnie announced the withdrawal of the Atlantics from the American Association.[69] He finally secured the Union Grounds later in the month, making arrangements with Mr. Cammeyer.[70] The prior December the *Brooklyn Eagle* had stated that "(t)he Union Grounds if used will require a new fence and new stands. The fence … is now rotting away."[71] Later the *Clipper* noted the Union Grounds "is in a very dilapidated condition at present, but is to be fitted up in March."[72]

At the March meeting of the American Association in Philadelphia, the resignation of the Atlantic club was announced. The stated reason was that the club was "improperly admitted … by reason of the club not having its full complement of members at the time of the election of their representatives."

A Baltimore club, represented by Henry Myers and Charlie Wiatt, was admitted in its stead.[73]

The Atlantics persevered as an independent club and began practice play in March. Early season team members included six men who had played for prior Brooklyn teams: John Cassidy, Jim Clinton, Jim Holdsworth, Bill Schenck, and John Valentine, with Barnie as change-catcher. New players included Brooklyn-born utility player Bill Morgan,[74] outfielder Dan O'Leary, shortstop Charles "Pop" Smith, and infielder Harry Spence. By June Schenck had gone to AA Louisville, Smith to the AA Athletics, Cassidy to NL Troy, and Clinton and O'Leary to NL Worcester. Added were veteran third baseman Joe Battin and first baseman Jimmy Knowles.

In late July, Horace Phillips resigned as manager of the Philadelphia club, now referred to as the "Phillies."[75] Barnie was engaged as the team's manager.[76] Jack Silsby took over the Atlantics as manager and the team played into August.[77]

Another Brooklyn team played in 1882. Organized by Charles Endler and run as a cooperative, the Brooklyns played at the Union Grounds, competing into late August. For the season, they won 28, lost 15, with two draws.[78]

A New Beginning

In late 1882, two minor leagues were organized, the Interstate Association (ISA) and the Northwestern League.[79] With William Cammeyer out of baseball and Billy Barnie elsewhere, George Taylor, night editor of the *New York Herald*, emerged as the newest proponent of Brooklyn baseball.[80] After an early investor backed out, Taylor contacted lawyer John Brice, who mentioned the scheme to Charles H. Byrne, a former sportswriter then involved in the real estate business. Byrne met with his brother-in-law, Joseph J. Doyle, who owned a casino on Ann Street in Manhattan. Doyle furnished the early funding and brought in Ferdinand Abell, who owned a casino in Rhode Island.[81]

By January 1883, the new Brooklyn club had begun draining and grading the site of the old Washington skating pond in south Brooklyn for a new ballpark.[82] In early March, the Brooklyn club was incorporated with directors Byrne, Taylor, Doyle, Abell, and John M. Kelly, with capital of $20,000, $14,000 of which had already been spent. Byrne became the president and Taylor the secretary and manager.[83] The Brooklyn club finally applied for membership in the Interstate Association on March 24 and was admitted on March 31.[84]

The early season team members included two familiar names, Bill Schenck and Oscar Walker. New players included pitcher John Doyle, catcher John Farrow, English-born second baseman Tim Manning, shortstop Bill Geer, and outfielder Tom Dolan. Joining later were outfielder Edgar Smith and handsome pitcher William "Adonis" Terry.

On July 23, Brooklyn was in fourth place, well behind the league-leading Merritts of Camden, New Jersey. However on July 20, the Merritts disbanded. At a meeting at the Bingham House in Philadelphia on the evening of July 22, "(George) Taylor was on hand ... while Manager (Billy) Barnie of Baltimore, (Alfred) Reach of Philadelphia, (Lew) Simmons of the Athletics and (Jim) Mutrie of the Metropolitans were there...."[85] According to one source, Byrne had already met with State Senator Albert Merritt, the majority owner of the club, regarding the players and dispatched Taylor to complete negotiations.[86] The club picked up five players: catcher Jack Corcoran, infielder Frank Fennelly, outfielder-second baseman Bill Greenwood, pitcher Sam Kimber, and first baseman Charles Householder.[87]

The name Householder presents another one of the conundrums of nineteenth century baseball, though not as confusing as that of Lavin and Farrell: there were two Charlie Householders. Charles F. Householder was born in Harrisburg, Pennsylvania, and played principally with Harrisburg teams. Charles W. Householder was born in Philadelphia and manned northeastern teams before playing with Philadelphia and Baltimore teams from 1879 to 1882.[88]

The five new players helped propel Brooklyn to the Interstate championship. For the season, Brooklyn played 107 games. Overall, they won 66 and lost 40 games, with one draw. In Interstate games, they won 46 and lost 30, with one draw.[89]

Charles Endler was at it again after the 1883 season. In October, the *Clipper* stated that the new Brooklyn club of the Union League (formed in Pittsburg on September 12) would field a team the next year, managed by Endler.[90] At the October meeting of the league, two more clubs were wanted in addition to the six already admitted. Preference was given to the clubs of Brooklyn and Indianapolis, both of which had promised to join the American Association.[91] In November, President Von Der Ahe of the St. Louis AA club announced that the Association would add four new teams, Brooklyn, Indianapolis, Toledo, and Washington, which occurred at the December AA meeting in Cincinnati.[92]

In January, the Union League changed its name to the Eastern League to avoid confusion with the outlaw major league Union Association.[93] Endler's Atlantic club did not receive coverage until July, when it was admitted into the Eastern League, taking over the schedule of the resigned Harrisburg club.[94] Playing at Queens County Park in Long Island City, the Atlantics hosted the Virginia of Richmond team on July 14 and 15, losing both games. On July 16, the Atlantic club, a mere cooperative club, was expelled by the

Washington Park board game.

Eastern League "for nonpayment of the guarantee money due the Richmond Club...."[95]

Over the winter, the National League had adopted the National Agreement to govern baseball in order to achieve harmony with the American Association. Player contracts of member associations would be guaranteed, while the number of players reserved by each club would rise to eleven, virtually an entire team.[96] The American Association adopted the National Agreement on December 12 and seven other leagues subsequently signed the agreement. Thus, seventy-one clubs, major and minor, opened the professional season of 1884.[97]

Back in the Major Leagues

For the 1884 season Brooklyn retained eight players from the 1883 Interstate team: catchers Jack Corcoran and John Farrow, pitchers "Adonis" Terry and Sam Kimber, first baseman Charlie Householder, second base-

Washington Park hosted Brooklyn professional baseball from 1883 to 1889.

man Bill Greenwood, shortstop Billy Geer, and outfielder Oscar Walker. Two Brooklyn-born players manned the outfield, veterans John Cassidy and Jack Remsen.

The Brooklyn team finished ninth in the twelve-team American Association. Three of the clubs added for the season, Washington/Richmond, Indianapolis, and Toledo, were eliminated when the Association contracted to eight teams. The Columbus club was also dropped, with virtually the entire team moving to Pittsburg for 1885. Although the Brooklyn club fared poorly, it marked the ascension of Brooklyn to permanent major league status.

Afterword

Several men who played for Brooklyn teams during the missing years extended their careers into the late-1880s, including Jim Clinton, Bobby Mathews, "Candy" Nelson, and Charlie Reipschlager. "Adonis" Terry played for Brooklyn major league teams from 1884 to 1891, winning more than twenty games in 1889 and 1890.

Brooklyn's rich baseball history includes numerous league championships and World Series appearances. The team won the American Association pennant in 1889 and promptly switched to the National League for 1890, winning another championship. Brooklyn would win National League pennants in 1899, 1900, 1916, 1920, 1941, 1947, 1949, 1952, 1953, 1955, and 1956, losing the World Series to Boston in 1916, Cleveland in 1920, and the New York Yankees in 1941, 1947, 1949, 1952, 1953, and 1956. Brooklyn won its sole World Series in 1955.

Sources and Acknowledgments

One of the essential elements of research for this article are box scores from a variety of publications, including the *New York Clipper, New York Herald, New York Tribune, New York Times, New York Sunday Mercury, Brooklyn Eagle, Philadelphia Inquirer, Washington Post, St. Louis Globe-Democrat, Cleveland Herald, Harrisburg* (Pennsylvania) *Patriot,* and *Trenton* (New Jersey) *Gazette.* Birthplace information comes from baseball-reference.com.

Special thanks to John Thorn and Mark Fimoff of the Society for American Baseball Research's Pictorial History Committee for providing the graphics for this article. Also, thanks to Reed Howard, the dean of nineteenth century baseball player team affiliations, for his research on Joe Farrell, Joe Lavin, and the two Charlie Householders.

NOTES

1. Marshall D. Wright, *The National Association of Base Ball Players, 1857–1870* (Jefferson, NC: McFarland, 2000), 5–7, 15–16.
2. *New York Times,* January 19, 1881, 5; *New York Times,* September 7, 1898, 7; Philip J. Lowry, *Green Cathedrals* (New York: Walker & Company, 2006), 34; Ed Maher and Frederick Ivor-Campbell, "William Cammeyer," *Baseball's First Stars* (Cleveland: Society for American Baseball Research, 1996), 21; *New York Clipper,* September 17, 1898.
3. *New York Clipper,* June 11, 1892; *Brooklyn Daily Eagle,* April 26, 1896, 16; *New York Clipper,* July 28, 1900; Jack Kavanagh, "William Harrison Barnie," *Baseball's First Stars,* 6.
4. *Chicago Daily Tribune,* February 7, 1876, 7.
5. *New York Times,* February 13, 1876, 2; *Chicago Daily Tribune,* February 20, 1876, 10; *Brooklyn Daily Eagle,* February 15, 1876, 1; *New York Clipper,* February 19, 1876; *Chicago Daily Tribune,* February 27, 1876, 9.
6. *Brooklyn Daily Eagle,* March 4, 1876, 2; *New York Clipper,* April 11, 1885; *Chicago Daily Tribune,* March 5, 1876, 12.
7. *Brooklyn Daily Eagle,* April 6, 1876, 1.
8. *Chicago Daily Tribune,* November 12, 1876, 7.
9. *New York Clipper,* April 1, 1876; *St. Louis Globe-Democrat,* April 9, 1876, 2.
10. *Brooklyn Daily Eagle,* April 14, 1876, 4.
11. *New York Sunday Mercury,* June 25, 1876, 5.

12. *New York Sunday Mercury*, July 16, 1876, 5; *New York Clipper*, July 22, 1876.

13. *New York Clipper*, December 16, 1876; *New York Clipper*, December 23, 1876.

14. *New York Clipper*, March 10, 1877.

15. Frank V. Phelps, "Robert V. Ferguson," *Nineteenth Century Stars* (Kansas City, MO: Society for American Baseball Research, 1989), 43; Richard A. Puff, "Thomas J. York," *Nineteenth Century Stars*, 142; baseball-reference.com.

16. Frederick Ivor-Campbell, "Joseph Start," *Nineteenth Century Stars*, 117.

17. *New York Sunday Mercury*, April 29, 1877, 5; *New York Sunday Mercury*, May 13, 1877, 5.

18. *Brooklyn Daily Eagle*, April 8, 1878, 4.

19. *New York Clipper*, April 13, 1878.

20. *New York Clipper*, March 3, 1878; *New York Clipper*, April 20, 1878.

21. *Chicago Daily Tribune*, April 14, 1878, 7.

22. *New York Clipper*, April 27, 1878.

23. *New York Clipper*, April 27, 1878; *Chicago Daily Tribune*, May 26, 1878, 7; *Buffalo Commercial*, July 19, 1878.

24. *New York Clipper*, April 6, 1878; *New York Tribune*, May 24, 1878, 8.

25. *Brooklyn Daily Eagle*, March 21, 1878, 3; *New York Clipper*, April 20, 1878; baseball-reference.com.

26. *New York Tribune*, May 24, 1878, 8.

27. *New York Clipper*, December 7, 1878.

28. *New York Clipper*, April 12, 1879; *Brooklyn Daily Eagle*, April 13, 1879, 4; *New York Clipper*, April 19, 1879.

29. *New York Clipper*, July 14, 1883.

30. *New York Clipper*, April 29, 1893.

31. *New York Clipper*, May 3, 1879; *New York Clipper*, May 17, 1879.

32. *New York Clipper*, May 31, 1879.

33. *New York Clipper*, May 24, 1879.

34. *New York Clipper*, June 14, 1879.

35. *New York Clipper*, March 20, 1880.

36. *Brooklyn Daily Eagle*, May 14, 1880, 1; *New York Clipper*, June 5, 1880; *New York Clipper*, June 5, 1880.

37. *Brooklyn Daily Eagle*, August 12, 1880, 3; *New York Clipper*, August 14, 1880.

38. *New York Clipper*, September 4, 1880; *New York Times,* August 15, 1880, 2.

39. Joseph M. Overfield, "Lipman Emanuel Pike," *Nineteenth Century Stars,* 103; Richard Puff, "John W. Nelson," *Baseballs First Stars*, 117.

40. *New York Clipper*, August 17, 1880.

41. *New York Clipper*, September 4, 1880.

42. *New York Clipper*, September 11, September 18, and September 25, 1880.

43. *New York Herald*, September 16, 1880, 5.

44. *New York Herald*, September 17, 1880, 8.

45. *New York Times*, September 17, 1880, 2.

46. *New York Clipper*, September 25, 1880.

47. *New York Clipper*, September 25, 1880.

48. *New York Times*, September 22, 1880, 8.

49. *Brooklyn Daily Eagle*, March 25, 1881, 1.

50. *New York Herald*, April 12, 1881, 11.

51. *New York Clipper*, August 27, 1881.

52. *New York Clipper*, August 13, 1881.

53. Alfred H. Spink, *The National Game* (Carbondale, IL: Southern Illinois University Press, 2d ed., 2000), 46.

54. Spink, 48, 50.

55. *Brooklyn Daily Eagle*, January 30, 1898, 9.

56. *New York Clipper*, September 24, 1881.

57. *New York Clipper*, October 22, 1881.

58. *Brooklyn Daily Eagle*, November 8, 1881, 3.

59. *Buffalo Express*, September 14, 1881, citing the *Philadelphia Times*.

60. *Pittsburg Dispatch*, November 9, 1889, 6.

61. *Cincinnati Enquirer*, October 11, 1881; *Cincinnati Daily Gazette*, October 11, 1881, 9; *Chicago Daily Tribune*. October 11, 1881, 7; *Cleveland Herald*, October 11, 1881, 3; *St., Louis Globe-Democrat*. October 11, 1881, 6.

62. *New York Clipper*, October 22, 1881. See also Brock Helander, "Prelude to the Formation of the American Association," *The National Pastime* (Phoenix, AZ: Society for American Baseball Research, 2013), 7–12.

63. *New York Clipper*, October 8, 1881.

64. *St. Louis Globe-Democrat*, November 4, 1881, 2; *New York Clipper*, November 12, 1881.

65. Brock Helander, "The League Alliance," sabr.org/bioproject.

66. (Cleveland) *Plain Dealer*, December 9, 1881; *New York Clipper*, December 17, 1881.

67. *New York Clipper*, December 17, 1881.

68. *New York Clipper*, January 28, 1882.

69. *New York Clipper*, February 18, 1882.

70. *Brooklyn Daily Eagle*, March 1, 1882, 3.

71. *Brooklyn Daily Eagle*, December 9, 1881, 3.

72. *New York Clipper*, March 4, 1882.

73. *New York Clipper*, March 18, 1882.

74. *Brooklyn Daily Eagle*, April 21,1883, 2.

75. *Philadelphia Inquirer*, April 14, 1882, 2; *New York Clipper*, July 29, 1882.

76. *New York Clipper*, August 5, 1882.

77. *New York Clipper*, June 3, 1882; *New York Clipper*, February 24, 1883.

78. *New York Clipper*, March 31, 1883; *Brooklyn Daily Eagle*, April 7, 1883, 2.

79. *Philadelphia Inquirer*, November 10, 1882, 8; *New Haven Register,* November 1, 1882, 2.

80. *New York Clipper*, December 1, 1883.

81. "THE BROOKLYN CLUB, Its Origin and the Many Deals Which Have Made It Famous," *New York Clipper*, March 4, 1889; Andy McCue, "A History of Dodger Ownership," *The National Pastime*, Number 13 (Cleveland: Society for American Baseball Research, 1993), 34–35; Andy McCue, "Charles H. Byrne," *Baseball's First Stars*, 19; Ronald G. Shafer, "Charles Byrne," sabr.org. bioproject.

82. *New York Clipper*, January 20, 1883.

83. *New York Clipper*, March 10, 1883; *New York Clipper*, March 17, 1883.

84. *New York Clipper*, March 31, 1883; *New York Clipper*, April 7, 1883.

85. (Wilmington, Delaware) *Daily Gazette*, July 23, 1883, 1; *New York Clipper*, July 28, 1883.

86. *Brooklyn Daily Eagle*, July 24, 1883, 3.

87. *New York Clipper*, November 10, 1883.

88. Personal communication with Reed Howard, November 10, 2014; *Boston Herald*, March 5, 1888, 8.

89. *New York Clipper*, November 10, 1883.

90. *New York Clipper*, September 22, 1883; *New York Clipper*, October 13, 1883.

91. *New York Times*, October 21, 1883, 2; *Washington Post*, October 21, 1883, 1.

92. *New York Times*, November 14, 1883, 5; *St. Louis Post-Dispatch*, December 13, 1883, 2.

93. *New York Times*, January 5, 1884, 1.

94. *New York Times*, July 9, 1884, 2.

95. *Brooklyn Daily Eagle*, July 17, 1884, 3.

96. *New York Clipper*, November 10, 1883; *New York Clipper*, December 1, 1883.

97. *New York Clipper*, December 22, 1883; *New York Clipper*, April 26, 1884.

Flyin' High

A Comparison of the Brooklyn Superbas
and the Pittsburgh Pirates, 1900–1909

Bill Scheeren

In 1899, the Brooklyn Superbas were the best team in baseball and the Pittsburgh Pirates were just an also-ran in the 12-team National League. By the end of the 1909 season, the Pirates were the World Champions and the Superbas were among the dregs of the Senior Circuit. What happened? This article traces the decline of the Superbas and the rise of the Pirates as the first baseball dynasty of the 1900s. It finds that this reversal can be attributed to several factors: the purchase of the Pirates by Barney Dreyfuss and the movement of Louisville's best players to the Pirates; poor personnel decisions by Brooklyn; the rise of the American League, which cost the Superbas many of their best players; and the aging of the Brooklyn team (although by 1909 the Pirates were aging also). This research also shows that the most significant factors driving these changes were the poor personnel decisions made by Brooklyn and the excellent ones made by Pittsburgh.

WHEN CONSIDERING THE THREE major sports in the United States (baseball, football, and basketball—hockey can be considered a Canadian sport for this article) we would only recognize baseball if we were to attend a game from each in the period 1890–1910. At that time football was still in its infancy and the rules in effect in the 1890s would make it unrecognizable to us. Basketball was "invented" by James Naismith at Springfield College in 1891 and was a totally different game than what exists today. Baseball, on the other hand, would be familiar, albeit with some modifications: parks were

Base Ball 12, pp. 143–164
ISSN 1934-2802 (Print) / ISSN 1934-3167 (Online)
978-1-4766-7473-5 (Print) / 978-1-4766-4112-6 (ebook)

constructed of wood and had an annoying habit of burning down (These included the South End Grounds and many surrounding homes in Boston in 1894, Robison Field in St. Louis in both 1892 and 1898, Philadelphia Base Ball Park in 1894, Eclipse Park in Louisville in both 1892 and 1898, and League Park in Cincinnati in 1900); players had no numbers to identify them; the pitching distance was increased to 60'6" in 1893; the foul strike rule, under which some foul balls are counted as strikes against the batter, was not in effect; and after 1891 there was only one twelve-team league, the National. But these changes aside, baseball was still a game that involved pitching and hitting the ball, three outs for each team per inning, and usually nine-innings for each contest. These things we would recognize.

Before 1900

The purpose of this article is not to go into the historical detail of major league baseball in the 1890s. But to set the stage for understanding the rise and fall of the Pittsburgh Pirates and Brooklyn Superbas (later Dodgers)—the goal of this article—some examination of the teams' performances in the '90s is needed. Beginning in 1892, the first year of the twelve-team National League, the standings show that both Brooklyn and Pittsburgh were decidedly mediocre. Brooklyn had one first division finish (third in 1892) as did Pittsburgh (second in 1893). Other than in those two seasons, neither club finished above fifth place in any year through 1898. Overall, the average final standing for both Brooklyn and Pittsburgh from 1892 until 1898 was sixth place.

The year 1899 was a watershed year for the Superbas. They set a major league record for improvement by going from tenth place, 46 games behind the pennant winner in 1898, to first place in 1899, winning 101 games. What happened? Briefly put, syndicate baseball: the practice in the National League in the 1890s, which permitted ownership of several teams in the league. Such a practice made possible a rapid transformation in a team's fortunes if an owner wanted to concentrate talent in one club.

Certainly, Brooklyn was not the only team affected by this practice. (The Robison brothers, owners of the Cleveland Spiders and St. Louis Perfectos, decided that a good team in St. Louis would draw more fans, so they transferred most of the Cleveland stars, including future Hall of Famers Cy Young, Jesse Burkett, and Bobby Wallace, as well as manager Patsy Tebeau, to St. Louis. The Spiders went 20–134.) Moreover, other factors were at play. In the National League's twelve-team alignment in the 1890s, not all teams made money due to the general economic downturn, and the fact that they were just bad teams. It thus was difficult for fans to generate enthusiasm for the hometown club, as the 1899 Cleveland Spiders demonstrated, when a team is far behind the league leader by the Fourth of July.

In addition to the Cleveland Spiders, the teams most affected by syndicate baseball were the Baltimore Orioles, the St. Louis Perfectos, and Brooklyn Superbas. To make the most money, many of the stars of the Orioles moved to the Superbas for the 1899 season. These included: Ned Hanlon, Dan McGann, Hughie Jennings, Joe Kelley, and Willie Keeler, and pitchers Jay Hughes, Doc McJames, and Al Maul. Also added was shortstop Bill Dahlen from Chicago and, in 1900, Joe McGinnity and Jimmy Sheckard from Baltimore.

The 1899 Pirates were an also ran despite finishing two games over .500. But some of the pieces were already in place for the Pirates dynasty of the 1900s: Bones Ely, Jimmy Williams, Ginger Beaumont, Sam Leever, Jesse Tannehill, and Jack Chesbro. The Pirates' subsequent move to the top of the National League was a result of two things. First, the Pirates were bought by the owner of the Louisville Colonels, Barney Dreyfuss, in December 1899. Second, a monumental trade the same month that brought 12 players to the Pirates, including Chief Zimmer, Claude Ritchey, Deacon Phillippe, Tommy Leach, and future Hall of Famers Rube Waddell, Fred Clarke, and Honus Wagner. (Pitcher Jack Chesbro was sent to Louisville, along with George Fox, Art Madison, and John O'Brien plus cash in the deal but he came back to Pittsburgh when the Louisville team folded before the 1900 season.) Although Dreyfuss's club is not generally thought of as part of syndicate baseball, he probably sensed that Louisville would be one of the teams leaving the National League as the circuit consolidated at the end of the decade.

The Brooklyn Superbas, on the other hand, had a great 1899 season, winning 101 games and beating out the Boston team by eight games. As a team, the Superbas hit .291 that year, which ranked third in the National League. Three regulars (Tom Daly, Willie Keeler, and Joe Kelley) hit over .300. The real strength of the team, however, was the pitching. The Superbas had three pitchers (Jack Dunn, Jay Hughes, and Brickyard Kennedy) who won more than twenty games, with Doc McJames winning 19.

The Rise of the Pirates Ten-Year Dynasty...

While historians have paid much attention to the fortunes of the Giants and the Cubs during this period, the data show that the Pirates were one of the first modern baseball dynasties. During the period 1900–1909, the Pirates won 930 games, as opposed to 809 for the Giants, 763 for the Cubs, and

649 for the Superbas. In that same ten-year period, the Pirates won four pennants, the Cubs three, the Giants two, and one for the Superbas. During this decade attendance in Pittsburgh consistently ranked third in the National League, generally exceeded only by the much larger New York and Chicago.

Below is a statistical comparison of the Superbas and Pirates which shows Pittsburgh's excellence and the decline of Brooklyn's record. Also of note are the attendance figures, which show that the Pirates drew well despite their home city's small size. The Pirates attendance after 1900 eclipsed that of the much larger Brooklyn every year.

Pittsburgh

Year	Won	Lost	Percentage	Place	Attendance/ Rank	City Population Rank
1899	76	73	0.510	7	251,834/6 of 12	13
1900	79	60	0.568	2	264,000/3 of 8	11
1901	90	49	0.647	1	251,955/3 of 8	11
1902	103	36	0.741	1	243.826/3 of 8	11
1903	91	49	0.650	1	326,855/4 of 8	11
1904	87	66	0.569	4	340,615/5 of 8	11
1905	96	57	0.627	2	369,124/3 of 8	11
1906	93	60	0.608	3	394,877/3 of 8	11
1907	91	63	0.591	2	319,506/3 of 8	11
1908	98	56	0.636	2	382,444/4 of 8	11
1909	110	42	0.724	1	534,950/3 of 8	11
1910	86	67	0.562	3	436,586/3 of 8	8
Composite	1100	678	0.619	2.4		

Brooklyn

Year	Won	Lost	Percentage	Place	Attendance/ Rank	City Population Rank
1899	101	47	0.682	1	269,641/4 of 12	4

Year	Won	Lost	Percentage	Place	Attendance/ Rank	City Population Rank
1900	82	54	0.603	1	183,000/7 of 8	4
1901	79	57	0.581	3	198,200/7 of 8	4
1902	75	63	0.543	2	199.868/6 of 8	4
1903	70	66	0.515	5	224,670/6 of 8	4
1904	56	97	0.366	6	214,600/6 of 8	4
1905	48	104	0.316	8	227,925/7 of 8	4
1906	66	86	0.434	5	277,400/7 of 8	4
1907	65	83	0.439	5	312,500/4 of 8	4
1908	53	101	0.344	7	275,600/6 of 8	4
1909	55	98	0.359	6	321,300/5 of 8	4
1910	64	90	0.416	6	279.321/7 of 8	4
Composite	814	946	0.463	4.6		

...And the Decline of the Superbas

In one of his most famous songs, *That's Life,* Frank Sinatra lamented that "[y]ou're riding high in April" and "Shot down in May."[1] If we apply those lyrics to the fortunes of the Superbas, it will begin to show the reasons for the fall of the Brooklyn team.

The 1900 season marked the beginning of their decline. Although the Pirates only increased their win total by three that season, from 76 to 79, Brooklyn's win total declined from 101 to 82, even though they won the pennant. (The National League schedule had been reduced from a scheduled 154 games to a scheduled 140 games.)

The decline for Brooklyn and the rise of Pittsburgh is better illustrated by comparing their winning percentages in 1899 and 1900: Brooklyn declined from .682 to .603 while Pittsburgh increased from .510 to .568. Two other facts are of note. First, Brooklyn's attendance declined about 86,00 from 1899 to 1900, dropping from a ranking of fourth of the 12 teams in 1899 to seventh of eight the next year. Pittsburgh, on the other hand, increased its attendance by about 12,000 and rose from sixth to third in rank of National League attendance despite being the smallest of the National League cities.

Why Did This Occur?

Differences in team performance may have been due to differences in the teams' average age. At the beginning of the decade, the Superbas were substantially older than the Pirates. The Superbas average team age in 1900 was 29.8 years, with ten players over 30. The Pirates, in contrast, had an average age of 27.7, with only four players 30 or older.

Below are presented two charts representing the two teams' average age from 1900 to 1909. As one examines the ages of the Pirates and Superbas, it is notable that Brooklyn had a higher average age through 1903, but then Pittsburgh overtook them. This could reflect the decline and loss of veteran players for Brooklyn and the Superbas experimenting with younger players, while the Pirates had settled on players who were their base for the rest of the decade. In this writer's opinion, a stable lineup exhibited by the Pirates was a key to their success in the decade; an unstable lineup had much to do with Brooklyn's lack of success. As will be noted later, Brooklyn was adding and deleting players at a much higher rate than the Pirates.

Brooklyn–Pittsburgh Age Comparison

Years	Brooklyn	Pittsburgh
1900	29.8	27.7
1901	29.6	27.9
1902	28.6	27.5
1903	27.7	26.9
1904	26.4	27.4
1905	26.1	28.9
1906	28.1	29
1907	28.2	28.7
1908	27.1	29.7
1909	26.6	28.6
	27.82	28.23

Another factor that might have led to the decline of the Superbas and the rise of the Pirates could have been that the Dodgers underachieved, or the Pirates overachieved based on the performance of their managers or other

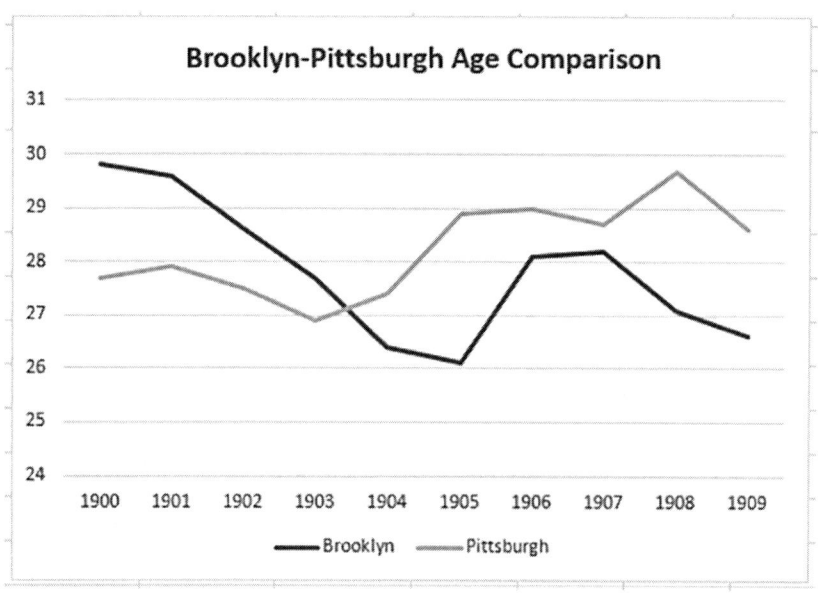

factors. Shown above is a Pythagorean comparison of Brooklyn and Pittsburgh wins between 1899 and 1909. While the differences are statistically significant, Brooklyn's actual wins during this period exceeded their projected Pythagorean wins eight times and Pittsburgh's actual wins exceeded their Pythagorean projection five times. This would indicate that Brooklyn overachieved late in the decade.[2]

Year	Brooklyn Actual Wins	Brooklyn Pythagorean Wins	Pittsburgh Actual Wins	Pittsburgh Pythagorean Wins
1899	101	94	76	80
1900	82	76	79	81
1901	79	81	90	92
1902	75	74	103	103
1903	70	67	91	86
1904	56	62	87	86
1905	48	45	96	90
1906	66	60	93	96

Year	Brooklyn Actual Wins	Brooklyn Pythagorean Wins	Pittsburgh Actual Wins	Pittsburgh Pythagorean Wins
1907	65	63	91	92
1908	53	55	98	93
1909	55	53	110	105

Home and Away Performance

The difference in home and away performance in the first decade of the twentieth century by the Pirates or the Superbas also could explain the difference in the fortunes of the two clubs.[3] The following table shows that winning and losing teams win at a higher percentage at home than on the road. The number that stands out is the high winning percentage on the road for Pittsburgh teams for the period 1900–1909.

Year		Home Win	Home Lost	Home Winning %	Away Win	Away Lost	Away Winning %	Scheduled Games
1900	Pittsburgh	42	28	0.600	37	32	0.536	140
	Brooklyn	43	26	0.623	39	28	0.582	
1901	Pittsburgh	45	24	0.652	45	25	0.643	140
	Brooklyn	43	25	0.632	36	32	0.529	
1902	Pittsburgh	56	15	0.789	47	21	0.691	140
	Brooklyn	45	23	0.662	30	40	0.429	
1903	Pittsburgh	46	24	0.657	45	25	0.643	140
	Brooklyn	40	33	0.548	30	33	0.476	
1904	Pittsburgh	48	30	0.615	39	36	0.520	154
	Brooklyn	31	44	0.413	25	53	0.321	
1905	Pittsburgh	49	28	0.636	47	29	0.618	154
	Brooklyn	29	47	0.382	19	57	0.250	
1906	Pittsburgh	49	27	0.645	44	33	0.571	154

Year		Home Win	Home Lost	Home Winning %	Away Win	Away Lost	Away Winning %	Scheduled Games
	Brooklyn	31	44	0.413	35	42	0.455	
1907	Pittsburgh	47	29	0.618	44	34	0.564	154
	Brooklyn	37	38	0.493	28	45	0.384	
1908	Pittsburgh	42	35	0.545	56	21	0.727	154
	Brooklyn	27	50	0.351	26	51	0.338	
1909	Pittsburgh	56	21	0.727	54	21	0.720	154
	Brooklyn	34	45	0.430	21	53	0.284	

The final statistical comparison in this article between Brooklyn and Pittsburgh for the period 1900–1909 is team performance, first in offensive categories and, second, in pitching categories.

The chart below shows that after the 1900 and 1901 seasons, the Superbas rarely exceeded the Pirates in any batting category except for home runs, which played a small part in the game during the first decade of the twentieth century. These rankings reflect the fall of the Superbas and the rise of the Pirates. While not a cause, but rather a result, it is evident that the Pirates outstripped the Superbas in nearly all other batting performances.

Pittsburgh-Brooklyn Batting Rank Comparison

Year		AB	R	H	2B	3B	HR	SB	BB	SO	BA	OBP	SLG	OPS	TB	HBP
1900	Pittsburgh	7	5	7	4	1	6	8	8	4	6	6	5	5	6	5
	Brooklyn	6	1	2	2	4	6	1	2	1	1	1	1	1	2	1
1901	Pittsburgh	3	2	2	4	3	4	2	2	2	2	1	3	1	3	3
	Brooklyn	4	3	3	1	2	3	5	6	1	1	3	1	2	2	7
1902	Pittsburgh	1	1	1	1	1	2	2	2	2	1	1	1	1	1	1
	Brooklyn	4	4	3	3	3	1	6	5	6	4	4	3	3	3	2
1903	Pittsburgh	1	1	1	2	1	1	4	6	1	2	3	1	2	1	4
	Brooklyn	8	5	6	6	6	5	1	1	7	6	1	6	3	6	3

Year		AB	R	H	2B	3B	HR	SB	BB	SO	BA	OBP	SLG	OPS	TB	HBP
1904	Pittsburgh	3	3	2	5	1	7	6	4	4	2	2	2	2	3	4
	Brooklyn	8	7	8	6	7	7	3	2	8	8	6	8	7	8	6
1905	Pittsburgh	2	4	3	2	2	4	3	6	4	3	3	3	3	3	8
	Brooklyn	6	7	5	6	7	2	4	7	6	6	7	6	7	6	7
1906	Pittsburgh	2	3	2	3	5	6	6	4	1	2	3	2	3	2	5
	Brooklyn	7	6	7	5	4	1	4	6	6	6	6	4	5	6	7
1907	Pittsburgh	4	1	1	6	2	3	1	2	2	1	2	1	1	1	4
	Brooklyn	5	7	7	4	4	4	7	7	8	7	7	7	7	6	7
1908	Pittsburgh	2	3	3	4	1	2	4	2	2	3	3	2	2	1	6
	Brooklyn	7	7	8	8	4	1	8	7	7	8	8	8	8	8	8
1909	Pittsburgh	2	1	1	1	1	2	4	3	3	1	2	1	1	1	5
	Brooklyn	5	7	7	4	5	5	7	8	7	7	8	7	7	7	8

Legend

Pittsburgh with better ranking

Brooklyn with better ranking

The pitching comparison for Pittsburgh and Brooklyn during the era is even more telling. Even in their last pennant winning season of the period, 1900, Brooklyn rarely ranked better than the Pirates in measures of pitching performance. The Suberbas often led the Pirates in complete games, but one could make the case that Brooklyn's secondary pitchers were less competent than Pittsburgh's. Brooklyn's pitchers ranked more highly than Pirates pitchers several times in saves (only an official category much later) and strikeouts.

Pittsburgh-Brooklyn Pitching Rank Comparison

Year		ERA	CG	SHO	SV	IP	H	R	ER	HR	BB	SO
1900	Pittsburgh	1	6	2	4	5	1	1	1	2	1	1
	Brooklyn	6	8	5	1	6	3	2	5	6	6	6
1901	Pittsburgh	1	5	1	3	5	2	1	1	3	1	6
	Brooklyn	4	8	5	1	8	4	4	4	1	8	2

Year		ERA	CG	SHO	SV	IP	H	R	ER	HR	BB	SO
1902	Pittsburgh	2	2	1	3	2	2	1	2	1	1	1
	Brooklyn	5	2	3	3	4	1	4	5	3	7	2
1903	Pittsburgh	2	5	1_4	3	2	2	3	2	1	5	4
	Brooklyn	6	4	2	4	6	4	5	6	4	3	6
1904	Pittsburgh	6	6	3	7	5	4	4	6	1	4	7
	Brooklyn	5	5	5	3	8	5	6	4	7	6	8
1905	Pittsburgh	4	8	4	2	4	3	3	4	1	4	7
	Brooklyn	8	4	8	4	8	7	8	8	5	8	3
1906	Pittsburgh	2	6	2	6	3	4	2	2	3	1	6
	Brooklyn	7	4	3	2	6	7	7	8	5	6	8
1907	Pittsburgh	2	6	2	3	4	3	3	2	2	1	5
	Brooklyn	3	2	5	8	5	5	6	4	4	7	7
1908	Pittsburgh	2	5	3	3	4	2	4	2	2	3	6
	Brooklyn	6	1	5	6	7	3	5	6	4	8	3
1909	Pittsburgh	2	5	2	2	3	2	2	2	3	1	5
	Brooklyn	6	1	3	8	6	6	6	6	8	7	4

Legend

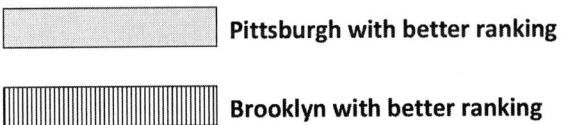

Pittsburgh with better ranking

Brooklyn with better ranking

Player Movement

The final possible explanation of the rise of the Pirates and the decline of the Superbas was player movement. As one reviews the movement, as shown below, this is the primary reason for the clubs' reversal in fortunes. In short, the Superbas lost most of their best players and added less able players, while the Pirates added by far better players as their roster changed, including two Hall of Fame players (Clarke and Wagner) who were the cornerstones of the team throughout the decade. Two factors affected these trends. First, losses of players to the American League decimated Brooklyn and the players added did not measure up. The Pirates, however, made a great trade with Louisville that replaced mediocre players with much better talent.

Brooklyn Player Additions and Losses, 1900

There was little change in Brooklyn position players between 1899 and 1900. However, the addition of Hugh Jennings at first base in mid-season 1899 and Lave Cross at third base provided more offense than did Dan Mc-Gann and Doc Casey in 1899. The major difference was in the pitching. The Superbas had great success with Joe McGinnity, who won 28 games in his rookie year, and the continued success of Brickyard Kennedy. Further, the retirement of Doc McJames who won 19 games in 1899, the contract problems and injuries to Jack Dunn, who fell from 23 wins to three wins, and the absence of Jay Hughes, who went from 28 wins to none—he stayed on the West Coast after getting married and pitched in the California League—were large negatives for the Superbas. (Hughes returned in 1901 but was never the same pitcher as he was in his prime.)

Pittsburgh Player Additions and Losses, 1900

After Barney Dreyfuss purchased the team on December 6, 1899, he immediately made a trade that led to the creation of the Pirates dynasty of the first decade of the twentieth century. Pittsburgh sent Jack Chesbro, catcher Paddy Fox, and outfielders John O'Brien and Art Madison, along with $25,000, to Louisville in exchange for pitcher Rube Waddell, pitcher Deacon Phillippe, outfielder Tommy Leach, outfielder/infielder Honus Wagner, outfielder Fred Clarke, second baseman Claude Ritchey, first baseman Mike Kelly, catcher Tacks Latimer, catcher Chief Zimmer, pitcher Walt Woods, and two other players. What a trade! In exchange for three players, the Pirates little needed and a pitcher who eventually returned to Pittsburgh, the Pirates received three future Hall of Famers: Clarke, Wagner, and Waddell. They also obtained two quality pitchers, a second baseman, a future shortstop, and two starting outfielders. Of the 11 players the Pirates lost before the 1900 season only two, Patsy Donovan, who was near the end of his career, and Frank Bowerman continued as successful major leaguers. Five players moved to the American League from Pittsburgh, but in 1900 the American League was still considered a minor league.

Brooklyn Player Additions and Losses, 1901

The year of 1901 was a year of disastrous player losses for Brooklyn. They lost their best pitcher (Joe McGinnity), two second-line pitchers (Jerry Nops and Harry Howell), Lave Cross, their starting third baseman, and Fielder Jones to the new American League. This would not be the last Superba losses to the American League. Hugh Jennings, Gene DeMontreville, and Jack Dunn were moved to National League teams for failure to report or to decrease salary but were not significant losses. Other than Tom McCreery, who was obtained from the Pirates, none of their newly acquired position players were major additions. Jay Hughes was an important contributor, winning 17 games after coming back from California, but Doc McJames and the arrival of Doc Newton from Cincinnati only produced a total of 11 wins.

Pittsburgh Player Additions and Losses, 1901

For the Pirates, 1901 was a memorable season. They won their first National League championship, with a winning percentage of .643, the first of three-consecutive pennants for the Pirates and the first of four during the first decade of the twentieth century. The only significant player loss was 38-year-old shortstop Bones Ely, who was released by the Pirates and then signed with the Philadelphia Athletics. This was addition by subtraction as it opened the shortstop position for Honus Wagner. There were five player additions for 1901, but only three were to see extensive action. Kitty Bransfield solved the Pirates first base problem for several years, arriving from Worcester of the Eastern League. Lefty Davis was claimed on waivers from Brooklyn and occupied one of the outfield slots for half the season. Ed Doheny was a solid addition, signed as a free agent after being released by the New York Giants.

Brooklyn Player Additions and Losses, 1902

In 1902 the Superbas continued their fall from the top of the National League. While they finished second to the Pirates, they were 27½ games behind the Pittsburgh juggernaut. Player additions for the Superbas had little effect, with only Tim Flood taking a regular position, second base, while hitting .218, low even for the Deadball Era. The player losses were again substantial in 1902, as the American League raided the Superbas again. After the 1902 season, Willie Keeler, Cozy Dolan, Duke Farrell, Bill Donovan, and Frank Kitson all decamped to the new league. These were devastating losses for Brooklyn, but for club performance, the worst was still to come.

Pittsburgh Player Additions and Losses, 1902

Of the four players added by the Pirates for the 1902 season, two—Smith and Phelps—became part of the merry-go-round of catchers manager Fred Clarke employed, joining Jack O'Connor and Chief Zimmer. They hit .189 and .213, respectively. Jimmy Sebring joined Pittsburgh late in the season and assumed a regular outfield job in 1903. Wid Conroy came from the American League Milwaukee Brewers for the 1902 campaign and then just as quickly moved back to the New York Highlanders. After the 1902 season, the American League made inroads into Pirates personnel. Pittsburgh losses to the New York Highlanders included shortstop Wid Conroy, pitchers Jesse Tannehill and Jack Chesbro (a total of 48 wins), and O'Connor. For most teams, this would have spelled complete disaster, but for the Pirates, it was just a bump in an overall pattern of success.

Brooklyn Player Additions and Losses, 1903

In 1903, Brooklyn won 70 games while losing 66, falling to fifth place in the National League. This was the last time the Superbas finished above .500 through the end of the decade. When one looks at the players for Brooklyn, one must wonder if they won even these 70 games with smoke and mirrors, as their roster was filled with over-the-hill or never-were players. Of their eight position players, Jack Doyle and Jimmy Sheckard were the leaders. Doyle was 33, and a refugee from the American League. Sammy Strang was an adequate third baseman who arrived on the scene for the 1903 season.

The Superbas did add two quality pitchers from the California League for the 1903 season, Oscar Jones and Henry Schmidt. Schmidt checked in with 22 wins while Jones clocked 19. This would be the high point of Jones's career, but Schmidt, who came east when he was 30, did not sign a Brooklyn contract for 1904 and never pitched another game in the major leagues. These were the high points of players added by Brooklyn for the 1903 season. After the season, Doyle moved to the Phillies in 1904, and Bill Dahlen, 33 years old, transferred to the Giants. Four of the players who left after 1903 left Organized Baseball for good, a sign of their minimal worth.

Pittsburgh Player Additions and Losses, 1903

The 1903 Pirates won their third straight National League championship and participated in the first modern World Series, losing to the Boston Pilgrims, five games to three, with all three wins credited to Deacon Phillippe.

The 1903 Pittsburgh Pirates in the dugout at Huntington Avenue Grounds during the 1903 World Series (Digitalcommonwealth.org, Massachusetts Collections Online).

The player gains for the Pirates for the 1903 season were not particularly noteworthy. Otto Krueger, who came from St. Louis, was a useful utility infielder and remained with Pittsburgh through the 1905 season. Brickyard Kennedy was an interesting acquisition, signing as a free agent after much time with Brooklyn. Kennedy's last year in the majors was 1903, winning nine games for the Pirates and starting a World Series game. The primary loss was Ed Doheny. (Apparently a drinker, his sanity was questioned during the 1903 season and he was placed under a doctor's care.) Although Jimmy Sebring hit the first World Series home run, he was not the easiest teammate to get along with and had several tiffs with teammates in 1904. Barney Dreyfuss ran out of patience and traded Sebring to the Reds in August 1904. Sebring died an early death, passing from Bright's disease in 1909.

Brooklyn Player Additions and Losses, 1904

The 1904 Superbas were beginning to scrape the bottom of the National League. They lost 97 games, 50 games behind the pennant-winning New York Giants, and only finished that high because the hapless Boston Beaneaters (98 losses) and Phillies (100 losses) were even worse. There were, however, a couple of noteworthy additions to the club. Bill Bergen came to Brooklyn, where he spent eight years as the lead catcher. He must have been a whiz on defense because he never hit above .200 in those eight years. Harry Lumley was a solid contributor to the Superbas, but his performance tailed off during the 1908 season, despite his being only 28 years old. The Dodgers added three pitchers, Jack Cronin, Ed Poole, and Doc Scanlan. Their combined record was 26 wins and 43 losses. It is some reflection on the Superbas' poor selection of players in that seven of the nine players on the roster in 1904 were in the minor leagues in 1905. The only player who left Brooklyn after 1904 who made any further impact was Sammy Strang, who became a good pinch-hitter and semi-regular for John McGraw's Giants.

Pittsburgh Player Additions and Losses, 1904

The 1904 Pirates posted their worst record of the decade and slipped to an 87–66 record, a fourth-place finish. The main cause of their decline was pitching, as both Deacon Phillippe and Sam Leever (both 32 years old) fell off from their previous performances. Patsy Flaherty and Mike Lynch, with 19 and 15 wins, respectively, attempted to take up the slack but were not wholly successful. Moose McCormick was a useful extra player and the Pirates career of Howard Camnitz began in late 1904. Other than the trade of Jimmy Sebring to the Reds, there were two other significant player losses for 1905: Catcher Ed Phelps was traded to the Reds for Heinie Peitz; and Kitty Bransfield was traded to the Phillies, opening up a revolving door at first base that continued through the decade. No fewer than 25 different players, including the immortal Wagner, tried their hand at the first for the Pirates from 1905 to 1920.

Brooklyn Player Additions and Losses, 1905

The year 1905 was a disaster for the Brooklyn Superbas. The team won 48 games while losing 104, and finished eighth, 56½ games behind the pennant winning New York Giants. The keystone combination of Phil Lewis and Charley Malay was added but was not satisfactory. Lewis stayed with Brooklyn for two more years but could hardly be classified as an all-star. John Hummel made his debut and was a productive member of Brooklyn through the 1915 season. Three pitchers were added for 1905: Harry McIntire, Elmer Stricklett, and Mal Eason. Harry McIntire was 8–25, the first of three 20-loss seasons. Stricklett was 9–18, with a three-year Brooklyn record of 35–50. Mal Eason's record in 1905 was 5–21, in his second-to-last season in Brooklyn. Doc Gessler, purportedly an outfielder, played mainly a first base for the Superbas and was traded to the Cubs during the 1906 season. After the 1905 season,

Jimmy Sheckard was traded to the Cubs, where he was a mainstay through the 1912 season.

Pittsburgh Player Additions and Losses, 1905

The 1905 edition of the Pirates produced a sterling 96-win, 57 loss record, one of the best Pittsburgh records of the decade. Unfortunately, they were nine games behind the New York Giants who won 105 games and overpowered the Philadelphia Athletics four games to one in the World Series.

The Pirates acquired several players who were regulars or at least semi-regulars in 1905. Heine Peitz came in a trade from the Reds and caught more than half their games. The big acquisition was catcher George Gibson, only a part-timer in 1905, but was the long-term answer at that position. David Brain was acquired from the Cardinals in July but just as quickly rotated out of Pittsburgh after that season. Otis Clymer was a semi-regular in the outfield, but his career is more remembered as a member of the Washington Senators. Three pitchers, Charlie Case, Patsy Flaherty, and Chuck Robitaille, who had some degree of success in 1905, winning a total of 29 games, were dispatched. Del Howard, one of the revolving players at first base, was traded to Boston after the 1905 season.

Brooklyn Player Additions and Losses, 1906

Brooklyn had one of their best records of the decade in 1906, winning 66 games. Unfortunately, this put them 50 games behind the Chicago Cubs juggernaut that won 116 games before being upset by the "Hitless Wonders" Chicago White Sox in the World Series. The Superbas added three players from the Cubs in the trade in December 1905 for Jimmy Sheckard. All became regulars. Unfortunately, except for Jack McCarthy, none were wonderful hitters. Tim Jordan arrived on the scene for the 1906 season, and was the regular first baseman through 1909, hitting several home runs, unusual for the Deadball Era, but also striking out more than 70 times in three separate seasons, also unusual. Whitey Alpermann was the regular second baseman through 1909, never hitting above .252. Jim Pastorius was an effective pitcher in both 1906 and 1907 but then fell completely apart. Mal Eason lost 17 games in his swan song in MLB.

Pittsburgh Player Additions and Losses, 1906

The Pirates were only 23½ games behind the Cubs in 1906—they were in third place, but some player acquisitions were building blocks for a resurgence in 1907–1909. Ed Phelps was reacquired from the Reds, where he had been traded in 1904 and was the backup catcher to George Gibson. Tommy Sheehan played more than 90 games at third base and Joe Nealon joined the merry-go-round at first base.

The two most significant acquisitions by the Pirates in 1906 were two pitchers, future Hall of Famer Vic Willis, acquired in a trade from Boston, who thought his career was done, and Lefty Leifield, a mainstay on the Pirates pitching staff through 1911. Bob Ganley was sold to Washington after the season. Dutch Meier, Heinie Peitz, and Otis Clymer also departed, but the big move was trading two long-time Pirates mainstays to Boston, Claude Ritchey and Ginger Beaumont, in exchange for Ed Abbaticchio. In the final analysis, this was probably a pretty even trade as all three players were on the downside of their careers, although Abbaticchio provided solid work at second base for several years.

Brooklyn Player Additions and Losses, 1907

The year of 1907 was another mediocre year for the Superbas. They finished in fifth place, 40 games behind the Chicago Cubs, winning 65 games. Al Burch played 40 games in the outfield and then was dispatched to Rochester after the season. Two newly acquired pitchers, George Bell and Nap Rucker, were more important to the team. Although having a career record of 43 wins and 79 losses, Bell was an inning-eater for several years. Nap Rucker was a different story. He became the Superbas ace through 1915 after being acquired from Augusta, where he was a teammate of Ty Cobb. Doc Casey was the day-to-day third baseman but was off to Montreal at the age of 37. The year of 1907 was the swan song in the major leagues for Emil Batch and Elmer Stricklett. Doc Scanlan was out of Organized Baseball in 1908, completing his medical studies, but came back to Brooklyn in 1909.

Pittsburgh Player Additions and Losses, 1907

The Pirates finished second in 1907, winning 91 games, 17 games behind the Chicago Cubs. Abbaticchio became a part of the Pirates in 1907 and played 147 games at second base. Goat Anderson was a regular outfielder but departed Pittsburgh for Rochester after the 1907 season. Alan Storke played games at third base but became a part-timer in 1908. Neither Henry Swacina nor Danny Moeller were integral parts of the 1907 team. Joe Nealon was returned to the Pacific Coast League whence he came, not having solved the club's eternal first base problem. This problem had begun in 1904 with the trade of Kitty Bransfield and continued for another decade until Charlie Grimm came to the Pirates as a regular in 1920. Hallman and Sheehan were not particularly effective nor ineffective and left Pittsburgh after the 1907 season. Otis Clymer was sold to Washington in June.

Brooklyn Player Additions and Losses, 1908

The 1908 Superbas were again a complete disaster. They won only 53 games and finished a stunning 46 games behind the Cubs. If it was any consolation, they did not finish last as the St. Louis Cardinals managed to win only 46 games. Most players acquired by Brooklyn were hardly of major league caliber. Perhaps sweeping all out and finding all new players would have been an improvement. Harry Pattee played 80 games, hit .216, and returned to the minors. Tommy Sheehan finished his career hitting .214. Tommy Mc-Millan, Tom Catterson, Joe Dunn, Alex Farmer, and Jim Holmes were not major league players in quality. Pattee, Sheehan, and Farmer were dispatched to the minor leagues after the 1908 season. Billy Maloney played 135 games in the outfield, hitting .195—goodbye Brooklyn, hello Rochester. Phil Lewis and Lew Ritter's careers in the major leagues were over.

Pittsburgh Player Additions and Losses, 1908

What could have been! In one of the most exciting pennant races in National League history, the Pirates and the Giants tied, one game behind the Chicago Cubs, each winning 98 games. Actually, the Pirates substantially overachieved as their Pythagorean wins only called for 93 wins. Much has been written about the Giants-Cubs pennant race, but an equally exciting story would be the Pirates, who had a far greater winning percentage on the road than at home. The Pirates kept rotating players in (and out after the season) in their pursuit of the Giants and Cubs. The veteran Roy Thomas was a regular in the outfield for one year. Chief Wilson came to the Pirates and was a regular through 1913, setting the major league record for triples along the way. Alan Storke, Warren Gill, and Jim Kane split time at first base, while Spike Shannon came from the Giants in July. Charlie Starr, Beals Becker, Paddy O'Connor, and Irv Young were tried and discarded. Nick Maddox, along with Vic Willis, were the aces of the Pirates pitching staff, each winning 23 games. Unfortunately, after 1908 Maddox only won 15 more games in the Major Leagues.

The Pirates moved several players after the season who had contributed in 1908. The core of the team was aging, and the widespread opinion—correct as it turned out—was that a few new players could put them over the top.

Brooklyn Player Additions, 1909

Brooklyn's 1909 season was their usual less than wonderful season. They finished in sixth place but only won 55 games, finishing 55½ games behind the Pirates. The Superbas brought in nine new players before the 1909 season, but other than Zack Wheat, who began his illustrious career with the Dodgers in 1909, there was little quality as shown by their 55 wins. Ed Lennox was adequate at third base, hitting .262. Wally Clement was a part-time outfielder in his last major league year. Pryor McElveen, Jul Kustus, Doc Marshall, George Hunter, and Red Downey were all tried and found wanting, with batting averages ranging from .256 (Downey) to .145 (Kustus). Jimmy Sebring, the former Pirates player, was back from the outlaw Tri-State League and hit .099.

Pittsburgh Player Additions, 1909

In 1909 the Pirates won the National League pennant, with 110 victories, before beating the Detroit Tigers in the World Series four games to three. Little did Pirates fans and administration realize that this was the last year of their dynasty, since five of their most reliable players, including Fred Clarke and Honus Wagner, were over 30 years old. During the next ten years, the Pirates would not win another pennant and would finish in the second division four times. In 1909 they added three regulars. Bill Abstein was acquired and appeared to solve the problem at first base, but his abysmal performance in the World Series spelled his end in Pittsburgh. Dots Miller came from the minors and became the regular second baseman, a position he held for four seasons. Jap Barbeau began the season at third base but was traded to St. Louis for Bobby Byrne, who solidified the infield. Ham Hyatt was a useful utility player who hit .299 and was a good pinch-hitter. Ward Miller, Mike Simon, and Chuck Brandom played minor roles on this great Pirates team. The sleeper in the new players was Babe Adams, who won 12 regular season games and because of the ineffectiveness of Camnitz and Willis was forced into World Series action and won three games.

Outlook

For the Superbas, there was some improvement in the years 1910–1920. They won pennants in both 1916 and 1920, but also finished in the second division eight times. They continued to be mediocre throughout the rest of the 1920s and 1930s, finishing second, third, fourth, and fifth twice each, sixth nine times, and seventh three times. During the 1930s a shortage of funds hurt the club. The dynastic years of the Superbas (then called the Dodgers) did not begin until the 1940s.

For Pittsburgh the decade of the 1910s was far less successful than the 1900s. Barney Dreyfuss placed great importance in the team finishing in the first division, but for four consecutive years (1914–1917) the Pirates slid to the second division of the National League. For the Pirates, great improvement came in the 1920s, when they won two pennants, one World Series, and were never out of the first division. First division finishes continued through the 1930s and into the '40s, but Pirates fans would have to wait until 1960 for another pennant.

NOTES

1. "That's Life." https://www.musixmatch.com/lyrics/Frank-Sinatra/That's-Life. Accessed July 25, 2019.

2. Bob Bailey, "Barney Dreyfuss Buys Pittsburgh," *Baseball Research Journal*, Vol. 48, No. 1 (2019), 86–91.

3. Stanley Rothman. "A New Formula to Predict a Team's Winning Percentage." *The Baseball Research Journal*. Vol. 43, no 2 (2014): 97–105. It was Bill James who in the mid–1990s first noticed the non-linear relationship between runs scored, runs allowed, and wins. It turned out to be relatively easy to predict a team's win-loss record using a simple formula, which very closely resembles trigonometry's Pythagorean Theorem:

$$\text{win}\% = \frac{\text{runs scored}^2}{\text{runs scored}^2 + \text{runs allowed}^2}$$

The formula has been updated frequently (generally by changing the exponent) to match empirical results, but there is a statistical reason for the relationship as well. Regardless, what we need to know for now is that there is both an empirical and logical relationship between runs scored, runs allowed, and wins, and they agree down to some very small details.

BIBLIOGRAPHY

Ahrens, Arthur H. "Crowds of Days Gone By." *The Baseball Research Journal*, Vol. 1 (1972).

Alexander, Charles C. *Our Game: An American Baseball History*. New York: Holt, 1991.

Anderson, David W. *More than Merkle: A History of the Best and Most Exciting Baseball Season in Human History*. Lincoln: University of Nebraska. 2000.

Antonucci, Thomas J. "Them Wonderful Bums." *Brooklyn Dodgers Baseball*. St. Louis: Historical Briefs, 1992.

Baseball-Reference.com. Last accessed July 24, 2019.

Bailey, Bob. "Barney Dreyfus Buys Pittsburgh." *The Baseball Research Journal*, Vol. 48, no.1 (2019).

Bailey, Bob. "Four Teams Out: The NL Reduction of 1900." *The Baseball Research Journal*, Vol. 19 (1990): 45–48.

Bevis, Charles W. "1901 Boston Americans." *The National Pastime*, Vol. 10 (1990): 27–32.

Bjarkman, Peter C. *Baseball's Great Dynasties: The Dodgers*. New York: Smithmark, 1990.

Cohen, Stanley. *Dodgers!: The First 100 Years*. New York: Birch Lane, 1990.

Cunerd, Stephen "Viv Willis: Turn-of-the-Century Great." *The Baseball Research Journal*, Vol. 18 (1989).

Dabilis, Andy, and Nick Tsiotos. *1903 World Series: The Boston Americans, the Pittsburg Pirates, and the "First Championship of the United States."* Jefferson: McFarland, 2004.

Devaleria, Dennis, and Jeanne Burke Devaleria. *Honus Wagner: A Biography.* New York: Holt, 1996.

Dubbs, Gregg. "Jim Sheckard: A Live Wire in the Dead-Ball Era." *The Baseball Research Journal,* Vol. 9 (1980).

Eckhouse, Morris. *This Date in Pittsburgh Pirates History.* New York: Stein & Day, 1980.

Elinich, Joe. "Pittsburgh: June 1903." *The Baseball Research Journal,* Vol. 25 (1996). 103–105.

Finoli, David, and Bill Ranier. *Pittsburgh Pirates Encyclopedia.* Chicago: Sports Publishing, 2015.

Golenbock, Peter. *Bums: An Oral History of the Brooklyn Dodgers.* New York: Putnam, 1984.

Graham, Frank. *Brooklyn Dodgers: An Informal History* (Writing Baseball). Carbondale: Southern Illinois University Press, 2002.

Graham, Frank. *New York Giants: An Informal History of a Great Baseball Club* (Writing Baseball). Carbondale: Southern Illinois University Press, 2002.

Honig, Donald. *Brooklyn Dodgers: An Illustrated Tribute.* New York: St. Martin's, 1981.

Katz, Lawrence S. "Pittsburgh's Pitching Twins." *The Baseball Research Journal,* Vol. 26 (1997). 133–135.

Krell, David. *"Our Bums": The Brooklyn Dodgers in History, Memory and Popular Culture.* Jefferson, NC: McFarland, 2015.

Lancaster, Donald G. "Forbes Field Praised as a Gem When it Opened." *The Baseball Research Journal* Vol. 15 (1986).

Lieb, Frederick G. *Pittsburgh Pirates* (Writing Baseball). Carbondale: Southern Illinois University Press, 2003

McCollister, John. *Bucs!: The Story of the Pittsburgh Pirates.* Lanham: Taylor Trade, 1998.

McCue, Andy. "History of Dodger Ownership." *The National Pastime,* Vol. 13 (1993): 34–42.

McGee, Bob. *Greatest Ballpark Ever: Ebbets Field and the Story of the Brooklyn Dodgers.* New Brunswick: Rutgers University Press, 2005.

Murphy, Cait. *Crazy '08: How a Cast of Cranks, Rogues, Boneheads, and Magnates Created the Greatest Year in Baseball History.* New York: Harper, 2007.

Neil, William F. *Dodgers Encyclopedia.* Chicago: Sports Publishing, 2012.

Niese, Joe. The Long Way to Philadelphia: The Strange Route Leading Rube Waddell to Join the Philadelphia Athletics. *The National Pastime,* Vol. 43 (2013).

Rothman, Stanley. "A New Formula to Predict a Team's Winning Percentage." *The Baseball Research Journal.* Vol. 43, no 2 (2014), 97–105.

Smizak, Robert. *Pittsburgh Pirates: An Illustrated History.* New York: Walker & Company. 1990.

Snyder, John. *Dodgers Journal: Year by Year and Day by Day with the Brooklyn and Los Angeles Dodgers Since 1884.* Clerisy Press: Covington, 2009.

Soderholm-Difatte, Bryan. "1906–1910 Chicago Cubs: The Best Team in National League History." *The Baseball Research Journal,* Vol. 40, no.1 (2011).

Spalding and Reach Guides, 1899–1910.

Steinberg, Steve. "1908's Forgotten Team: the Pittsburgh Pirates." *The Baseball Research Journal,* Vol. 47, no.2 (2018).

Story of the Brooklyn Dodgers. Bantam Books, 1949.

Stout, Glenn, and Richard A. Johnson. *Dodgers: 120 Years of Dodgers Baseball.* New York: Houghton Mifflin Harcourt, 2004.

"That's Life." https://www.musixmatch.com/lyrics/Frank-Sinatra/That's-Life. Accessed July 25, 2019.

Wagner, Bill. "The League that Never Was." *The Baseball Research Journal,* Vol. 16 (1987): 18–21.

Ward, Geoffrey C. *Baseball: An Illustrated History, including The Tenth Inning.* New York: Knopf, 2010.

Zinn, John G. *Charles Ebbets: The Man Behind the Dodgers and Brooklyn's Beloved Ballpark.* Jefferson, NC: McFarland, 2018.

Baseball, Boating, and Gymnastics
Who Was William Wood?
JOHN THORN

Artifacts tell tales for those with ears to hear. In this instance, a tattered pillbox cap of the 1890s contains, in its lining, a clue to a time when baseball was so new that no formal clubs had yet arisen. In the 1820s and 1830s, New York sportsmen were inflamed by boxing and fencing but especially by boating and gymnastics. In telling the story of pioneer oarsman and gymnast William Wood, famous long ago but unknown today, the author sets the scene (as Wood had created the seedbed) for the rise of our national game. This is a story of early New York: its cyclical epidemics of yellow fever and cholera, and the physical exercise movement—pugilistic, gymnastic, aquatic, and field sport—that spurred young clerks to leave their desks.

A Mears online auction of December 1, 2018, included an offering that struck my interest. I recall opening the bidding at $100, knowing I had little hope of winning with that amount. The item shown above bore this listing notice:

Offered is a game worn pillbox style baseball cap likely dating to circa the 1890s-1900s. Hat is constructed of grey wool with a pair of burgundy stripes circling the exterior with some fabric loss revealing the woven backing. Interior features a leather sweatband and a screened logo for "Wm. Wood Mfr. & Importer High Grade Sporting Goods 25 W. 125th St. NY."

The pillbox cap was intriguing because so few from this period survive, even in museums. What made it stand out for me beyond its rarity was its

Base Ball 12, pp. 165–175
ISSN 1934-2802 (Print) / ISSN 1934-3167 (Online)
978-1-4766-7473-5 (Print) / 978-1-4766-4112-6 (ebook)

merchant, about whom I knew a thing or two for his role in popularizing gymnastics and for his 1867 book, *Manual of Physical Exercises.* That book bore a key citation of baseball in New York as played in *1832*—long before the Knickerbockers—that astounded me when I discovered it 35 years ago:

Pillbox cap, Mears Auction, December 1, 2018.

> The history of the present style of playing Base Ball (which of late years has been much improved) was commenced by the Knickerbocker Club in 1845. There were two other clubs in the city that had an organization that date back as far as 1832, the members of one of which mostly resided in the first ward, the lower part of the city, the other in the upper part of the city (9th and 15th wards). Both of these clubs played in the old-fashioned way of throwing the ball and striking the runner, in order to put him out.

The first ward in New York City consisted of the lowermost part of the island, from the Battery to Maiden Lane, while the ninth and fifteenth wards were both located between Houston and 14th Streets, the whole of which was then called Greenwich Village. It is perhaps noteworthy that the influx of wealthy New Yorkers into then rural Greenwich Village was so great after the yellow fever epidemic of 1822 that an additional

Wood's *Manual of Physical Exercises.*

ward, the fifteenth, was created from the ninth in 1832, a year ahead of the great cholera epidemic.

That outbreak of yellow fever in 1822 may well have been what prompted the first recorded game of baseball played by that name in New York in the very next year.

First, let me say that I did not win the auction. After 22 bids, the pillbox cap closed at $1,826—but it pleased me to think that none of the bidders was moved as I had been by its purveyor. So … was the "Wm. Wood" of the pillbox cap the same William Wood who wrote that 1867 book and, if so, how did gymnastics and baseball relate? Indulge me in some admittedly roundabout

Dedicated to the New York Boat Clubs, Nathaniel Currier, 1838.

rumination, which is the way I sometimes arrive at a new understanding of how baseball came to be our game.

Despite his obscurity today William Wood, it turns out, was a very big deal in the rise of interest in sport in New York and the nation. He was in some measure responsible for what was, briefly, a boating mania in New York in the 1830s, then moved on with the times to bursts of enthusiasm for boxing and gymnastics and, finally, baseball. Col. Tom Picton wrote entertainingly of those boating days in the *Clipper* in 1868 (as "Paul Preston, Esq." in "Reminiscences of a Man About Town"):

> I remember when the boat club fever raged, when every grown up man and half grown hobbledehoy aspired to the dignity of an aquatic championship. Merchants' clerks, bank actuaries, dry goods assistants, printers and every tradesman's apprentice went into the boat club mania, and not a day passed without some lively contest between a dozen or so of ambitious boats' crew. All the town identified themselves with the merits of rival oarsmen; the press teemed with praises of the athletic amateurs; the populace turned out in huge masses along the Hudson to witness oft repeated displays of aquatic skill, while the names of the contending barges became as household words in the mouth of universal fame. We talked nothing but boating and rigged ourselves out in striped shirts and fancy jackets in the faint hope of becoming jolly young watermen through inspiration. We had each our favorite barge upon which we pinned our faith as to invincibility and not a ferry house or private bulkhead along either river but was adorned with half a dozen or so of boat houses from the center of whose carpeted floor dangled the favorite of their club.

William Wood in 1881.

The *Clipper* ran a substantial profile of William Wood in its issue of July 30, 1881:

This week we present the portrait and the biography of one who has been spoken of as the father of physical training in this country, having been among the first to persistently advocate its great importance, not only by his practical teachings, but also by his publications upon the subjects of rowing, running, walking and other athletic branches. William Wood was born on Christmas-day, 1818 [possibly as early as 1813—jt], in the First Ward of this city, and near the Battery—in fact, within two hundred yards of Whitehall Slip, famous for watermen whose skill and powers of endurance were then known almost the world over. Although now in his sixty-third year, yet he is as hale and hearty as most men are at half that age; and thus in his person, no less than in his books, he demonstrates the paramount importance of proper physical training.... As early as June 9, 1836, when he was but eighteen years old, he was matched to row four miles in seventeen-foot working-boats against James Varick, over whom he gained an easy victory.... [A long discussion of Wood's professional rowing exploits follows, until we get to the year 1856.]

It was also in 1856 that Mr. Wood first turned his attention practically to the subject of gymnastics and physical training. At the outset he joined hands with the late Charles F. Ottignon in the old Crosby-street gymnasium, but in the Winter of 1858 a partnership was entered into between himself and dead-and-gone Mat Gooderson, a great favorite with the New York public, and they fitted up a gymnasium and training and sparring rooms at 8 Sixth avenue, opposite Eighth street....

Another early gymnastics instructor who was a documented baseball player—with the pioneering Knickerbockers—was James L. Montgomery, who had begun teaching in 1856, at the rooms of Wood's partner Ottignon. Like Wood, Montgomery became Ottignon's partner and brought to

Baseball, gymnastics, aquatics: William Wood did it all.

CHARLES F. OTTIGNON'S
SPARRING ACADEMY
58 West 30th Street,   -   -   New York.

OTTIGNON'S GYMNASIUM & SPARRING ROOMS.

Ottignon's Gymnasium at Canal and Elm Streets, 1845, when Wood was a member and not yet a partner.

the gymnasium a new emphasis on weight-lifting. According to one account, he "introduced the fashion of using dumb bells, and when he curled and put up the 100 pound bell all New York wondered." A cast of one of Montgomery's biceps was even reproduced in *The American Phrenological Journal and Repository of Science* in 1858, along with an explanation of how "judicious practice" in the gymnasium had turned a slender teenager into a man capable of extraordinary feats of strength.

William Wood, called "The Grandfather of Athletics in the United States" in his *New York Times* obituary, died on September 20, 1900, at the age of 86. The *Times* averred that he had had instructed more than 75,000 aspiring gymnasts. In 1886, having grown too old for hands-on athletic instruction, he set up his sporting-goods store in Harlem, where he sold the pillbox cap that has given rise to this story.

In his obituary notice Wood was credited with founding the first gymnasium ever built in New York. As we have seen above, that was not quite so. Besides Ottignon's, preceding gymnasia in New York included those of

John B. Rich, M.D., who established his Institute for Physical Education at 159 Crosby Street "for the promotion of health by means of systematic physical training." William Fuller's gymnasium was even earlier, having formed at least by 1831. The gymnasium of Professor George M. Coulon, who also taught fencing and dancing, was earlier yet, in 1826.

Scant months before the yellow fever epidemic of 1822 there opened perhaps the very first gymnasium in the city—*previously unnoted in the literature*—the New York Gymnastic Institution, at whose opening Dr. Samuel Latham Mitchill's lofty remarks held an audience spellbound before the evening devolved into "feats of skill and dexterity in fencing and boxing." It was noted that the ubiquitous Mitchill—author of the first travel guide to New York in 1807—"appears to be *apropos* to every thing in New York, from science down to sour krout."

The latter was a reference to his role as President or Grand Krout of

James L. Montgomery and Dumb Bell, *Clipper,* **May 17, 1856.**

a social gathering of descendants from the original settlers of New York City. The insignia of his office, typically worn during an address, were said to be a crown of cabbage and a mantle of its leaves, as depicted below, perhaps fancifully.

Another description of the Grand Krout's insignia, from 1819, was this: "After dinner, the installation of officers took place. Baron Von Bell escorted into the room the new president, or Grand Krout, wearing a three-cocked hat, with a cabbage-leaf as a cockade, and a wreath of cabbage stumps around his neck."

I offer evidence below, from the same newspaper a week later, that Dr. Mitchill once again presided over the Krout Club at Hyer's Retreat in Broad-

Dr. Rich's Institute of Physical Education.

way. "Whether eaten raw or boiled, or after preparation in our excellent way of Sour Krout, the article is worthy of particular commendation." And this brings us back to William Wood's pillbox cap and the larger baseball story it tells.

In 2001, New York University librarian George Thompson hit the front page of the *New York Times* with his discovery of a newspaper reference to a game called baseball in New York City long before its presumed invention by the Knickerbockers ... and long before William Wood's offhand mention in his *Manual of Physical Exercises.* The *National Advocate* of April 25, 1823, contained this unsigned notice:

> I was last Saturday much pleased in witnessing a company of active young men playing the manly and athletic game of "base ball" at the Retreat in Broadway (Jones') [on the west side of Broadway between what now is Washington Place and Eighth Street]. I am informed they are an organized association, and that a very interesting game will be played on Saturday next at the above place, to commence at half past 3 o'clock, p.m.
>
> Any person fond of witnessing this game may avail himself of seeing it played with consummate skill and wonderful dexterity. It is surprising, and to be regretted that the young men of our city do not engage more in this manual sport; it is innocent amuse-

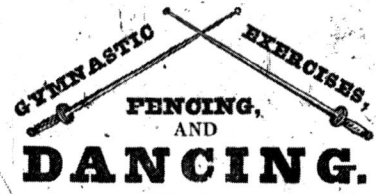

DANCING.

PROFESSOR COULON'S
GYMNASIUM

IS NOW OPEN DAILY, AT

169 Mott-street, 3 doors from Broome-st.

NEAR THE BOWERY.

DANCING SCHOOL

Every Wednesday and Saturday.

Ladies taught from 4 to 6—Boys' Class from 3 till 5—and
the Evening Class for Gentlemen is from
7 till 9, or from 8 till 10.

Mr. C. has the assistance of Mrs. Coulon in the Ladies'
Class; and also of Master Coulon in the Boys' Class.

FENCING.

The Manly Foils and Sword Exercises

Taught from 12 till 2, and in the Evening from 7 till 9,
EVERY TUESDAY AND THURSDAY.

GYMNASTICS.

The Excercises commence early every morning, also at 12
o'clock, and in the evening at 7.

☞ Private Lessons given at all hours to untaught or incomplete Pupils, of any age, wishing privacy and expedition. Card
of Terms can be had of Mr. Coulon, as above; of whom also can
be had, "THE DANCER'S GUIDE," price 25 Cents.

Professor Coulon's Gymnasium, advert in Longworth's City Directory for 1827.

"Hail, health-imparting, worth-inspiring KROUT!
Thy power benign let none presume to doubt;
For crowds can testify to thee belong,
The flow of humour, and the charm of song."

From Mitchill's paean to the noble cabbage, 1822.

ment, and healthy exercise, attended with but little expense, and has no demoralizing tendency.

The lease of the Retreat had transferred at some point in the spring of 1822 from the aforementioned W.B. Hyer to veteran innkeeper William Jones, just in time for the sudden flush of well-to-do New Yorkers fleeing that summer's yellow fever epidemic at the foot of the island. (The fever eased with cold weather and did not return in the spring of 1823.) Perhaps trying a novel idea to sustain a flagging business, Jones staged his baseball game on Saturday, April 19, of 1823, as mentioned in the *Advocate* of six days following.

The epidemic had created a stir for physical activity among New York's sallow clerks, whether it be in the form of fencing, gymnastics, or even baseball. Until yellow fever infected lower Manhattan in 1822, physical exercise taken for its own sake by those no longer in short pants brought scorn from

Dr. Mitchill as the Grand Krout.

puritanical souls and derision from men of business, who had long ago abandoned boyish things. City life was about amassing enough money to set up in business or return to country life enriched. Long hours spent in counting rooms left little time for fresh air, let alone sport.

Boating, gymnastics, baseball— all arose in New York in the 1820s as a response to medical emergency as well as to criticism from our ruddy-cheeked English cousins. A writer for London's *New Monthly Magazine* observed in 1829:

> There are several things in the first impression of New York which ought to be mentioned: amongst these, the dull complexion and expressionless physiognomy of the common people. Whether their sallow hue and the languor of their looks, so strikingly different from the fresh and ruddy animation of the English, are the effects of a local climate, and of influences peculiar to the situation of the city, I shall not undertake to determine; but unquestionably both the figure and countenance of the Americans improve as you proceed into the interior.

COMMUNICATION.

I was last Saturday much pleased in witnessing a company of active young men playing the manly and athletic game of "base ball" at the Retreat in Broadway (Jones') : I am informed they are an organized association, and that a very interesting game will be played on Saturday next at the above place, to commence at half past 3 o'clock, P. M. Any person fond of witnessing this game may avail himself of seeing it played with consummate skill and wonderful dexterity It is surprising, and to be regretted that the young men of our city do not engage more in this manual sport ; it is innocent amusement, and healthy exercise, attended with but little expense, and has no demoralising tendency.

A SPECTATOR.

National Advocate, April 25, 1823.

Merchant's mark inside cap.

The group of men who gathered for exercise at Madison Square in the early 1840s and would later become famous as baseball's Knickerbockers—for several years before 1845 the aggregation was nameless—might have tipped their caps (or straw hats, as they at first adopted) to William Wood, that pioneer in boating, gymnastics, and baseball.

An American Gothic Tale

Thomas B. Worth, a (Darktown) Life and Black Base Ball Forms

James E. Brunson III

Thomas Worth's monstrous black baseball images, derived in part from blackface minstrelsy's visual forms, illustrate the "Darktown Life" of baseball forms. They belong to a little understood phenomenon that art historian Henri Focillon calls "life of forms," the moment when an image undergoes a decisive evolutionary transformation. Within this context, Solomon Eytinge's "Blackville Comics Series" for Harper's Weekly influenced Worth's baseball imagery for "Darktown Comics" for Currier and Ives. Worth's postbellum "Gothic Tale" attempts to neutralize the monstrous black threat to the national pastime.

The shortstop [of the Alpines] … stood there with his eyes as big as saucers holding on to the ball like grim death and watching the man run in from third base and scoring his run.[1]

The burly legs of Batum, the captain of the Remsens, trembled with emotion as his men strode into the field chock full of watermelon and hope.[2]

It is probable that the popularity of minstrelsy was inspiration for the growth of comic scenarios involving blacks in print media.[3]

IN *WHAT DO PICTURES WANT? The Lives and Loves of Images*, W.J.T. Mitchell declares that negative racial stereotypes belong to an image-reper-

Base Ball 12, pp. 176–194
ISSN 1934-2802 (Print) / ISSN 1934-3167 (Online)
978-1-4766-7473-5 (Print) / 978-1-4766-4112-6 (ebook)

---

toire system that is despicable and worthy of destruction. However, Mitchell warns that they seem to have a life of their own. If the life of the baseball stereotype resides in the death of its model, who does the "image killing" and "image-resurrecting?"[4]

Now consider the Currier & Ives lithograph by the postbellum Gilded Age artist Thomas Worth known as *Foul Tip* (1882). To what extent does it bear out Mitchell's claims? More broadly, to what extent does it give the impression of having been made in something like the spirit of Mitchell's query? This article will explore Worth's artistic life and prodigious output, which captures perfectly the postbellum black image repertoire of baseball that circulated across print media, especially the impact of blackface on the "cooning" of the black baseballists.

On first glance, *Foul Tip* secures what literary critic Eric Lott calls a "public hearing," a cultural and economic valuation of the black body. Four baseball players yell at an umpire. One might instinctively feel—without thinking about it—that the figures are rendered naturalistically. Rich gray and black tonalities abound. They stain whitish paper, giving human form to muscled, outstretched limbs, clenched fists, and a resolute gaze that float atop its surface. This lithograph migrates uneasily between fine art and mass-produced

A FOUL TIP.

Thomas Worth's *Foul Tip*. Currier & Ives, 1882 (Library of Congress).

images. It caricatures Jacques-Louis David's *The Oath of the Horatii* (1784), a neoclassical painting that extols the antique virtues of stoicism, masculinity, and patriotism.[5]

Darktown haunts Thomas B. Worth. It conjures real and imagined spaces. Before and after the Civil War, segregated residential patterns sprang up systematically, blocking black access to middle-class communities. Social exclusion accelerated the emergence of districts and areas throughout the country, racialized as Africa, Stagg Town, Buck Town, Niggertown, Blackville, and Darktown. Partitioned communities also organized ball clubs. In 1858 Weeksville, a Brooklyn suburb, organized the Unknown B.B.C. In 1874, *Harper's Weekly* introduced the first caricatured black family, the Smallbreeds, who lived in a fictional town called Blackville. Blackville had two nines, the Black Legs and White Stockings. "A part of the Eighth Ward of city, comprising two or three blocks of Thompson street" reports the *New York Times*, "has long been known to the Police as Africa." In 1886 Ambrose Davis, of Bleecker and Thompson streets, organized the Gorham B.B.C. The imagined community of Darktown, and its baseball clubs, debuted in 1882.[6]

Worth, a Brooklynite, strolled public parks. From 1867 to 1882, he likely would have come upon a black baseball match. During the height of the production and circulation of Darktown Comics, 1882 to 1885, Brooklyn's Alpines, Remsens, and Maybees vied for "colored supremacy." As the epigraph shows, reporters mocked them, their narratives chock full of racial humor. They titillated readers with narratives reminiscent of Mark Twain's, which embraced the protocols of blackface minstrelsy: "Negro dialect, coal black hands and faces." Worth similarly donned the minstrel mask and projected his brand of comedy onto black bodies. While the virtues embodied in David's work had nothing to do with baseball, *Foul Tip* implied—for middle-class audiences conscious of the conspicuous relation between the painting and the lithograph—there was little fear that such qualities would land in the wrong hands.[7]

Foul Tip increases the desirability of Darktown Comics, brought on in part, by the rampant materialism of the postbellum Gilded Age, the period of economic ascendency in the United States following the Civil War. From the standpoint of this art historian, the differences between real and imaginary blackball images are less important than the continuities among them, the fact that all of them are "imaginary" in the other sense of the word—that is, that they are all constructed visible images. My visual analysis of Darktown Comics in general and blackball images in particular, extends to a valuation of their economic and cultural capital. This excessive commodification of black bodies is, it seems, symbolic surplus value measured in terms of "conspicuous consumption" and "sumptuary display."[8]

Unsurprisingly, *Foul Tip* turns "stoicism, masculinity and patriotism" on its head. Worth's reconstructed black bodies cram into a chaotic scene: four uniformed men confront the umpire. In the background, upper left, players clutching bats prepare to square off. In the upper right corner, embattled players roll on the ground. The central figures form a triangular composition anchored by shoes on the left; on the right, the base of the tilted barrel. Extended arms, striped britches and blouses, the umpire's posture, striped high-collar shirt, and striped pants, form right angles; the apex, the tip of the umpire's hat. The horizontal stripes on one players' pants suggest a prisoner's uniform. The angularity of the players' shadows, cadence of legs and arms, and right-side of the diamond draw attention to clenched fists directed at the umpire's cranium. This scene offers a droll preview of what transpires in the background.[9]

Foul Tip strolls the unrestrained wilderness of blackface images, a habitat or nesting space for Negroid grotesqueries. Beefsteak lips, as example, lend themselves to oral amusement. This leitmotif finds currency in Charles Winter's painting, *Minstrel Show* (1830s-1840s), nothing new. Superstitious beliefs burden blacking up in a makeup mirror. Masking the mouth in red paint or leaving it exposed as a circle of white flesh, requires perfection. Worth doesn't need cosmetics. He weaponizes lithograph pencil and liquid tusche, resurrecting monstrous forms that anticipate surrealism in early animated film.[10]

Here I want to introduce a primary context for Thomas Worth's baseball grotesqueries, namely, a particular Gothic tradition in nineteenth-century American art. That tradition is represented in a useful work by the art historian Sarah Burns entitled *Painting the Dark Side: Art and the Gothic Imagination in Nineteenth-Century America*, which poses three points of particular interest: (1) Gothic stories articulate the "horrors of history," often reanimated by unresolved issues involving race/gender, enslavement, emancipation, freedom, civil rights and disenfranchisement; (2) In such stories, these issues embody the form of a black monster, an abject figure that projects pollution, putrefaction, and defilement; and, (3) The monster—Frankenstein—"*unmistakably took on the character of the powerful, dreadful black giant whose awakening portended disaster for all (italics mine)*." Now I am neither suggesting that Worth viewed Darktown Comics as part of the "horrors of history" nor that he imagined the black baseballist as Frankenstein (though the artist likely relied on literary/artistic sources that reconstructed black bodies as an assemblage of mismatched pieces). But these points represent a current in literary criticism and visual culture that bears a close analogy with the very features of his lithographs—and for that matter, the works of artists that came before and after him—that I will emphasize in this article. And this means that they will be of help not only in enlarging and deepening our sense of Worth's enterprise but also, from my perspective equally important, in providing a kind of core justification for my approach and indeed for the critical vocabulary I will use (In discussing what I call Worth's "dark side," which weighs Darktown as an object of fascination and horror, I rely heavily on the work of literary critics and art historians, among them Sarah Burns, Toni Morrison, Elizabeth Young, Michael Rogin, David Roediger, Eric Lott, Umberto Ecco, W.J.T. Mitchell, Henri Focillon, Joshua Brown, Allan C. Braddock, Michael D. Harris, Richard Powell, Karen C.C. Dalton, Peter H. Wood, and Alexander Nemerov).[11]

Prologue to *Thomas Worth's (Darktown)* *Life in Base Ball Forms*

Thomas Worth "began his artistic career when quite young," reports the *Daily Saratogian*, "on blotters and hymn books and much against parental wishes." His rise to fame is compelling. Worth was born in 1834, and he was raised in Greenwich Village (a vacation destination, at the time, that also had a segregated community called "Little Africa"). He belonged to a banking family. His grandfather, father, and brother served as presidents for New York City's National Park Bank, founded in 1856, which did more commercial business than any other bank in the country. Worth was a bank teller. In 1867, he was victimized by the confidence man John Livingston "to the extent of a $30,000 check forged in the name of Commodore Vanderbilt." During the police inquiry, Worth sketched a pen and ink portrait—from memory—and it was photographed. He did it so well that detectives tracked Livingston to Chicago and made the arrest. Worth quit the banking industry and devoted himself entirely to art.[12]

Whether one attributes his success to artistic gifts or a privileged background, by the 1870s Worth is a hot commodity. An illustrator for *Harper's Weekly*, he creates the journal's masthead (since 1855, Worth had contributed to the journal). His commissions: Charles Dickens's *The Old Curiosity Shop*; *Wild Oats*, a humor/satirical paper; *Frank Leslie's Weekly*; and, a translation of the First and Fourth books of the *Virgil Aeneid*. In the 1880s, he works for *Judge Magazine*, and Currier and Ives.

An earlier work exposes a hidden meaning behind Darktown Comics. In 1868 *The Evening Post* notes: "Mr. Thomas Worth, a young artist who has become known by his drawings in wood, has a little picture in this gallery of a [N]egro boy, who stands before a broken looking glass, adjusting a flashy yellow tie." A crucial feature of the mirror's field of reflection is the ritual denial that there is a monster at all, its evolution traceable to illustrated sheet music, *Dandy Jim from Carolina* (1843)—countered by the endless repetition of the claim that blackness poses a real threat, as elegance infused with outrageousness, yet ruthless and corrupt. Worth's contemporary, the famed Eastman Johnson, painted "blacks as orderly, ambitious American citizens [were] ready to evolve socially and economically." While his blacks do not approach minstrel caricature, they do depict black social status as dominated by decay, disorder, and moment-by-moment activity. If Worth's class- and race-conscious recoil from blacks resonates, "it also reminds us that such consciousness, as in minstrelsy, often acknowledged the *lure* to be black, to use the mirror for self-protection or self-enlargement."[13]

Here, I want to say something about baseball forms. What are they? More precisely, how might we understand black baseball images as baseball forms? Baseball forms illustrate a little understood phenomenon examined by art historian Henri Focillon's "life in forms," the moment when an image undergoes a decisive evolutionary transformation. The progenitor of one image is another image, and the principle of life that links them is form. But as Mitchell explains, Focillon's theory does something more radical than simply model the evolution of artistic forms on the development of biological organisms. It turns the analogy upside down and it models biology on the evolution of images. "This may sound mystical or metaphysical," Mitchell muses, "but I think it is nothing more than a vivid intuition of a perfectly familiar and commonplace feature of the appearance of new images in the world."[14]

For sculptors and painters of the mid–1870s, baseball, then evolving into a professional sport, would have been an innovative subject for fine art. Isaac Broome (*Base Ball Vase*, 1876) and Thomas Eakins (*Baseball Players Practicing*, 1875) were two of the first artists to perceive its sculptural or pictorial potential. As baseball forms go, the pitcher, batter, and catcher are iconic (while the pitcher appears in Broome's work, that presence is inferred in Eakins' painting). There is in this regard a further point of resemblance between *Base Ball Vase* and *Baseball Players Playing*: the way in which the figures function as a metaphor of manly vigor, muscular bodies, and its effect—competitive spirit—represented through heroic gesture. These works capture perfectly the players in moments of abstraction, perhaps deep thought or reverie—absorption—but certainly unaware of being seen. While my observations pose more questions than are answerable here, these fine art pieces possess grace, dignity, and presence; wholly absent in Thomas Worth's black baseball lithographs.[15]

Baseball forms have genealogies: how is black baseball imagery produced, where does it come from, and how does it evolve? Black baseball imagery offers a reliable taxonomy, an art historical equivalent to "species" in natural history. A species is a basic classificatory unit or "taxon" for biological organisms. All members of a species share a family resemblance: at two levels, one visible and the other invisible. Not unlike human beings, black baseball imagery can look similar, then, and maintain this similarity "through successive generations."[16]

Base Ball Gothic: A Modern Black Frankenstein

> In dealing with the [N]egro, we should treat him not as a brute but as an infant, of larger growth, and if we turn him loose in the maturity of his physical strength, in the manhood of his passions, but in the childhood of his morals and intellect, we shall have before us a being not unlike that which is portrayed in a romance of recent date [Frankenstein], a man artificially compounded with the thews of a giant, with a mould more than mortal, into which is infused all of the power of doing mischief, but unto which its creator, failing to inspire a moral feeling, endangers his own safety in rash experiment.
> —*New York Herald*, November 7, 1859

> The closest symbolic descendants of Frankenstein in antebellum America are illegitimate black sons, debased from and by their white paternal foundations. Yet in real-life antebellum America, the voice of the master trumped that of the slave: Thomas Dew, a respected member of the Virginia elite, became President of the College of William and Mary, while Nat Turner was caught, tried and executed, and his body probably given to surgeons for dissection.
> —Elizabeth Young, *Black Frankenstein*

The *St. Louis Republican* published *Come in 'Yah* (1888), a baseball cartoon of the comical coacher. A portent or monstrous being, the sutured form is crafted by the visual protocols of blackface minstrelsy. Hastily sketched, but carefully designed, the body's mismatched pieces give pause. That the upraised, clenched fist could pass through the shirt sleeve seems improbable. Shoes envelope massive feet. That bony legs can carry, let alone lift them, is equally absurd. How does a scrawny neck support a cranium overdetermined by gargantuan mouth? Thick lips form around its impenetrable black space, threatening to gobble up the concealed head. *Come in Yah* evokes a modern Black Frankenstein.[17]

Blackball's gaping orifice again takes center stage, and a few journalistic specimens unleash its portentous effects. When the St. Louis Black Stockings defeat the Rockford Reds in 1883, the writer reporting on the game unleashes a monstrous spectacle: "The darkies gobbled everything that took the air; no matter how wildly it flew, they got there Eli! every time, and while apparently taking things easy, they were for all that punishing the home nine." The Black Stockings, it seems, have mouths large enough to gobble baseballs whole. Donning the minstrel mask, another sportswriter reconstructs black ineptitude as a toothy white grin. Following a muffed play in the colored championship of Brooklyn in 1884, the journalist jibes: "The pitcher of the Alpines showed his white teeth with a deprecatory grin as he let in a man on an error." The same writer reconstructs the catcher's gigantic hands as bestial: "[Alfred] Jupiter [Remsen catcher] put a wire mousetrap over his face … making his palms meet and part like alligator jaws." Metaphoric associations with gaping mouths are both economic and social. Black players threaten to gobble up gate receipts and jobs reserved for white players. Humor is serious business. "Laughing at black people amounts to a national pastime," Rae Beth Gordon declares, "and it defuses the threat represented by black virility."[18]

In Darktown Comics, art forms migrate between habitats of fine art, and the mass-produced copy, past and present. Worth's black baseball lithographs bear traces of these forms, among which they take their place. There is something appealing, even redeeming, about how they nest and thrive in Darktown Comics, because it implicates the fine arts for its dearth of black baseball imagery. It directs our attention to evidence unexplored and unexplained. Why look upon these lithographs and find

Come in' Yah, St. Louis Republic, **1888.**

social alienation amusing? Why adorn public or private spaces with them, knowing full well that racial exclusion operates as social custom? What fascination or horror lies behind them?[19]

In the course of my research, it became clear that black baseball's uncharted territory, visualized as Darktown, culminates in the reanimation of a monstrous figure. Literary critic Elizabeth Young has shown convincingly that the "African American Frankenstein monster" originates in the tension between two ideas: "a transatlantic understanding of the black slave as Frankenstein's monster who revolts against his white master and an American model of the United States as Frankenstein's monster that revolted against Britain." Frank Bellew, Worth's contemporary, created *Black Frankenstein*, for *Lantern Magazine* (1852). The woodcut illustration depicts an awakened curly-haired, barrel-chested, jagged toothed black giant, towering above its horrified white creator. In Mary Shelley's novel, Dr. Victor Frankenstein resurrects a living corpse from a smelly assemblage of body parts stolen from dissecting rooms. For art historian Alexander Nemerov, the living corpse evokes "the widespread fascination with seances, ghost stories, grave robbing, and dissection." According to Nemerov, dissection offers "a new kind of deathly identification, and created a form of self-representation through torment and extinction." The monster "had no name because its identity had been systematically denied to him, and he gave eloquent voice to that denial." The term Frankenstein became, in time, not a reference to the creator but to the monster.[20]

In his anti-slavery manifesto *David Walker's Appeal* (1829), David Walker compares the "wretched, degraded and abject condition" of blacks to living corpses: "What is the use of living when in fact I am dead." In baseball narratives and imagery, the living corpse is an elaboration of the dead metaphor: "once a living organism, like a human being, died and became a corpse." The black player, as living corpse—the "not me"—projects dark meanings; pollution, defilement, and social decay. Its metaphorical putrefaction, part of the baseball lexicon, evolving as to connote a peculiar odor. In 1867 at Rome, New York, a journalist voiced his dissatisfaction at a light-complexioned "Freedman" covering first base for the Useless Base Ball Club, an otherwise all-white organization: "Excuse us, from making strenuous exertion to reach first base upon a warm day when engaged in playing with that club … take my word for it, he would throw up his commission, and dinner also, and retire from the field in disgust." Here, the relation between monster and monster-maker is clear. Blackface minstrel performers, journalists/writers, and visual artists are monster-makers, that is, Frankensteins.[21]

The *Macon Telegraph* announces, "Sol Eytinge's inimitable Blackville

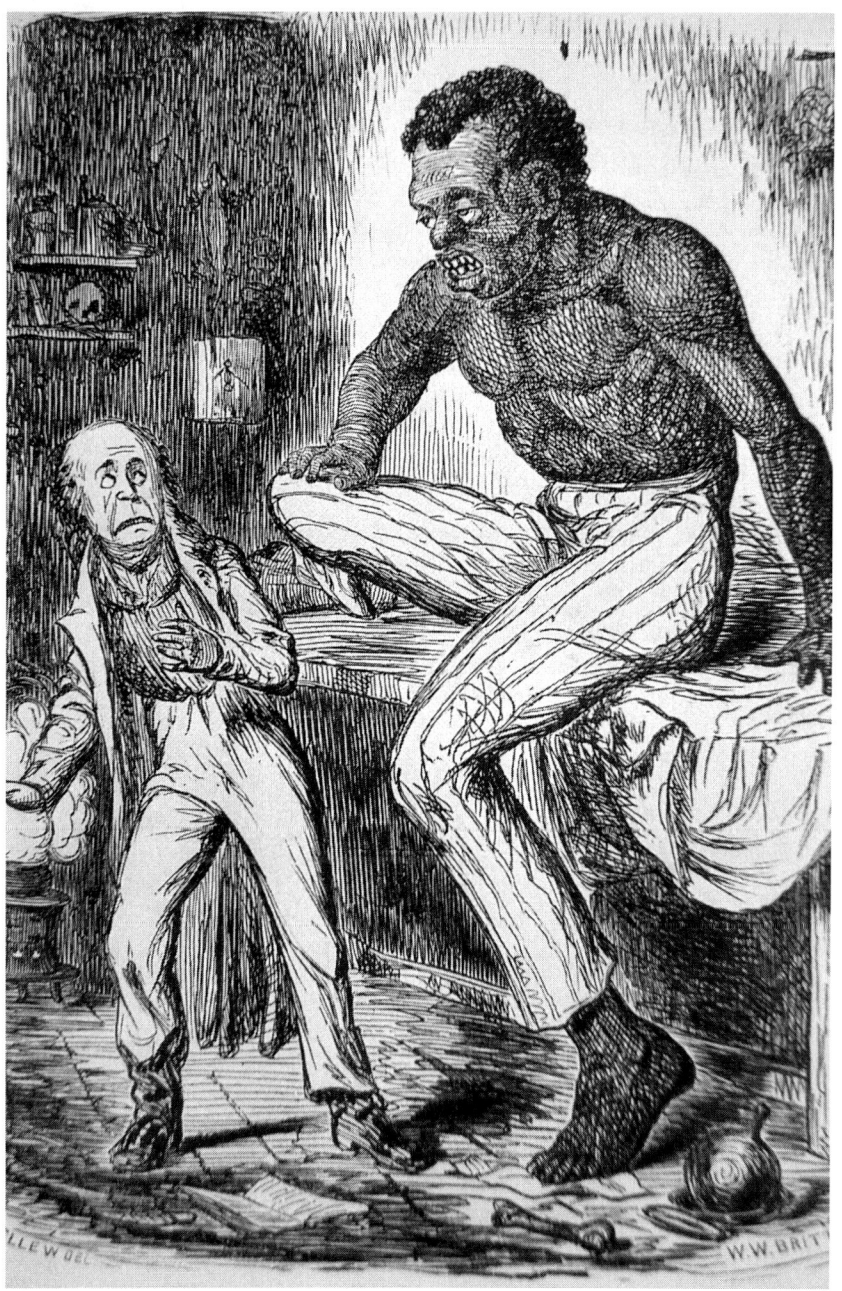

Frank Bellew's *Black Frankenstein, Lantern Magazine,* 1852.

Sketches, which have appeared in *Harper's Weekly* during the past dozen years, are to be published in book form." Between 1874 and 1885, Solomon Eytinge, Jr., illustrated Blackville Comics, named for Blackville, South Carolina. His illustrations—staggering in number—followed the exploits of the fictional community and the Smallbreeds, whose surname alludes to social discourses about genetic inferiority. Eytinge and Worth helped white middle-class society to mediate a world imagined as turned upside down. They colluded to reconstruct symbolic violence onto black bodies and depict them ludicrously in middle-class activities. If blackface minstrelsy signaled, as historian Alexander Saxton claims, the nationalization of North American theater, then both men found inspiration in blackface forms.[22]

Eytinge's *Base Ball at Blackville—The White Stockings against the Black Legs—First Blood for the Black Legs* spawns an imagined social upheaval (1878). Black rule dominates this wide, open wilderness. No enclosure restrains this crowd which contributes to the carnivalesque scene. Fashionable blacks, standing and sitting, congregate on a grassy knoll. Dandies, dandizettes, and players intermingle. Nothing restrains the former from interfering in the game. It is doubtful that the squat center fielder can shag skyscrapers or screaming liners in either direction. A mounted fan poses danger as well. Should the horse be spooked, it will trample the crowd. Everyone faces real danger.

BASE-BALL AT BLACKVILLE—THE "WHITE STOCKINGS" AGAINST THE "BLACK LEGS"—FIRST BLOOD FOR THE "BLACK LEGS"—[DRAWN BY SOL. EYTINGE, JR.]

Solomon Eytinge, Jr.'s *Base Ball at Blackville*, *Harper's Weekly*, 1878.

Both Eytinge and Worth are Bohemian artists. The association between bohemia and artistic life marks them as flaneurie (which means "way of see-ing"), the symbolic embodiment of the modern artist. The flaneur ("a stroller, lounger, saunterer, loafer") focuses on everyday urban experiences. For liter-ary critic Walter Benjamin, the relation of flaneurie to journalism defines the cultural identity of artist-reporters. Artist-reporters win public recognition for their self-proclaimed exploits. They are "dashing, theatricalized figures who constructed themselves as roving servants to the news." *Base Ball at Blackville* offers, not unlike *Foul Tip*, a stroll through a fictional black community.[23]

Base Ball at Blackville equates the *lure* of blackness with "bohemian thrillage." By this, I mean how the middle-class vogue for armchair slumming via the illustrated press becomes a titillating affair. Living corpses, unleashed on the green diamond, wreck unrestrained havoc: dominating the center of the composition, the White Stocking slugger takes a wild pitch from the Black Leg twirler to the face, clearly unprepared for the smashing blow to the nose and mouth. To his right squats the Black Leg's dumpy catcher. His grubby fingers brace to catch a ball that falls to reach its mark. In the foreground, to the left, the batter's amused teammate points to the action. Six teammates loll about in childlike stupor, transfixed by the scene. To middle-class view-ers—The House of Harper's core audience—*Base Ball at Blackville* is rooted in "species anxieties" that are endemic to modernity, from self-protection to self-enlargement.[24]

Doubling as minstrel show end-men, reclining players frame the ground plane which operates as the stage. In a sequence of figural gestures, right to left, arms and bat zero in on the umpire. The dandified umpire rests against a walking stick. Here, Eytinge doubles as interlocutor and monster-maker. While *Blackville* cartoons support this point, detailed analysis of this point is beyond the scope of this paper.

Whether seen as a cautionary tale against indolence or an allusion to the increasingly hostile territory that blacks tried to penetrate as Reconstruction began its social collapse, *Base Ball at Blackville* dismisses the childish attempts at playing the national pastime, with predictable results or violent effects.

A Monstrous Spectacle Totally Unleashed: "Gross illustrations unworthy of their place"

Finally, I want to examine Worth's *Champions of the Ball Racket; On the Diamond Field* (1885), and *Champions of the Ball Racket; End of Sea-son* (1885), both lithographs giving full-blown expression to the monstrous

THE CHAMPIONS OF THE BALL RACKET.
On the Diamond Field

Thomas Worth's *Champions of the Ball Racket; On the Diamond Field*, Currier & Ives, 1885 (Library of Congress).

spectacle of black baseball and the mirror's field of self-reflection as a form of "species" anxiety.

Champions of the Ball Racket; On the Diamond Field depicts a lively performance. No defensive player challenges the runner's move towards second base. Yet, the distance between first and second hardly merits the base stealer's dismay—given the twirler's inattentiveness—whose bulging eyes and upraised hands express horror. There is the catcher's odd position behind the right-handed batter, who stands on the wrong side of home plate. Targets abound. The catcher's mask, a bird cage, offers little protection. There is another mark. The defensive team's polka dot shirts conjure a bull's eye. Resembling baseballs, they subject the players' bodies to the batter's swing.

Darktown Comics relied heavily on Blackville Comics. Within this rectangular frame, the third baseman, catcher, and base runner form a triangular composition. On the left, the diagonal movement flows from third baseman to shortstop to pitcher to base runner. On the right, the movement flows from catcher to batter to base runner. Three figures in various states on repose form the base of this pyramid. These nesting figures, thoroughly recognizable, migrate from the habitat of *Baseball at Blackville*.

The trio finds debasement. According to *Cambridge Dictionary*, one of the references for "base" is "dishonorable or immoral; of inferior quality or value; debased; or counterfeit." Seemingly elevated above the fray, they relax in various states of repose. An obvious figure is the bare-headed player which also migrates from Eytinge's woodcut illustration. His figure kneels, its head juts upward from sloping shoulders. Worth's figure is prone, its head craning skyward. It recalls the iconic kneeling slave, found in fine art and mass-produced imagery. On the other hand, it intimates Eakin's *Whistling for Plover* (1874), a shot-gun toting black hunter melded to the earth, his legs effectively erased from the composition.[25]

The gestures of the third baseman, shortstop, and twirler share a family of iconic resemblance. Upturned hands are defensively positioned in front of the body—even though the pitcher holds an oversized-ball, his rounded shoulders and angularity, mimic crouching. The bodily stance, knees bent, is wide-open. From here, posture degenerates quickly. Hunched shoulders become stooped shoulders.

Looking more bewildered than heroic, these phantasmagoric figures devolve or evolve from minstrel grotesques to a ghastly primate. Eyes bulge from heads. Mouths agape with puckered lips offer perfect receptacles for catching baseballs. Two minstrelized faces then give way to that of a man-animal hybrid, a practically simian twirler: a sloped and receding forehead, flattened face, snout, and weak chin (another blackball form nesting in *Base Ball at Blackville*, a species of the lowest humanity, a monkey or "macao"). This monstrous spectacle reveals the moment when a blackball image undergoes a decisive evolutionary/devolutionary transformation.

The central modern myth of scientific resurrection, Frankenstein, is itself resurrected in *Champions of the Ball Racket*, in which the monster-maker reanimates a new kind of living corpse. But the idea of reconstructing the black baseballist as an image of Negro caricature doesn't originate with Darktown Comics. Worth's sources derive not just from illustrated almanacs, sheet music illustration, cheap pamphlet novels, humor/satirical journals, but also from pseudo-scientific inquiry, social sciences, and art history. The Negroid stereotype is central to the public display of the black baseballist from the first, and it depends, not just on woodcuts and lithography, but on the original objects created for the fine arts as well. Eakins's *Baseball Players Playing* and Broome's *Base Ball Vase* "simply illustrate some of the common ways in which whites historically maintained hegemony; through tacit assertions of social and spatial privilege and outward claims about democracy, science, and order."[26]

The mulatto ballplayer exemplifies how that hegemony might be maintained. Baseballists of mixed-racial parentage—a national threat of racial amalgamation—raised uncomfortable questions about what whiteness actually meant. Early baseball history is rife with stories of the seeming counterfeit; not white blackface minstrels, in this case, but blacks caught passing for white or mulattos (light-skinned or nearly white in complexion). When an astonished sportswriter encounters the New Orleans Pickwick ball club in 1881, he declares that all of them possess "bright skins" and "several were so fair as to pass for white." Mulatto ballplayers are hardly confined to Louisiana. New York had its share as well—excluding the "public hearing" secured for black bodies by Eytinge and Worth. The horror of discovering a white Negro player among teammates, or the thought of having to play mulatto players/teams prompts ominous predictions of social decay, as demonstrated above.[27]

The Champions of the Ball Racket: At the Close of the Season parodies a team photograph, by arranging uniformed players and baseball props in a recognizable scene. In the immediate foreground, two crossed bats and three balls are artistically arranged. To the far left, the seated player conjures a phallic emblem: long arms and hands cradle his head, and the light vertical space between the darkened arms and the oval formation

THE CHAMPIONS OF THE BALL RACKET.
At the close of the Season.

Thomas Worth's *The Champions of the Ball Racket: At the Close of the Season*, Currier & Ives, 1885 (Library of Congress).

of the lips, summons sexual demeanor. As Lott explains, "Bold swagger, ir-repressible desire, sheer bodily display: in a real sense the minstrel man was the penis, that organ returning in a variety of contexts, at times ludicrous, at others rather less so."[28]

The Champions of the Ball Racket: At the Close of the Season vividly il-lustrates how armchair slumming sought to maintain some symbolic con-trol over an imagined social threat. The monster-maker's portrayal of the anatomically, racially, and socially unfit forces a lack of manly vitality back onto the battered ball club. Worth's baseball lithographs—too many to cover here—indulge both in symbolic violence and mask the seeming counterfeit of engaging in racial pleasure.

"What does it mean to protest suffering?"

Darktown Comics has gained in value, enhancing Thomas Worth's star status, if not notoriety. Currier and Ives increased its output from four in 1880 to ten in 1881, seventeen in 1882, eighteen in 1883, and peaked in 1884 with thirty prints. In 1884, his lithographs accounted for more than one-third of the firm's output. At the height of his success in 1887, the *Daily Saratogian* observes: "Thomas Worth [is] representative of the old school of caricature. [It] takes us back to Vanity Fair and Yankee Doodle days. [Worth] treats of life somewhat in the name of [George] Cruikshank." Art critic Fred Weiten-kampf reminisces, "An especially favorite subject is found in the [N]egro. The late Thomas Worth seemed to have touched the existence of conventional caricature in his Darktown lithographs, laughable despite their exaggeration. But [Eugene] Zimmerman has since then completely outdone him in hideous distortion."[29]

While there are aspects of Darktown Comics that remain a mystery—how did growing up near "Little Africa" impact Worth's perception of the blacks?—these prints stir strong feelings, affect tastes, and perceptions widely. In 1915, Worth recalls mocking a "well-dressed darky" who expresses outrage, in a large crowd of whites guffawing at a public display of Darktown Com-ics. The Duke of Newcastle, accompanying the Prince of Wales in the United States, in another instance views a display of Darktown prints in a Currier and Ives store. He buys a full set (one hundred prints). Darktown enters Americana as part of the "Golden Age of American Illustration." In 1931, the *Brooklyn Eagle* declares, "The greatest number known to have been cir-culated of any of the old Currier and Ives prints was one of the Darktown Comics, the amusing ancestor of the present-day funny page strip, of which

73,000 copies were sold." In 1939, the Brooklyn Museum displayed Darktown lithographs in the exhibition "Popular Art in America."[30]

"What does it mean to protest suffering," Susan Sontag queries, "as distinct from acknowledging it?" Art historian Alexandra Bonfante-Warren's response reflects bewilderment as to Worth's insensitivity and downright malice toward black people. Perhaps the satisfaction of ridiculing them is the pleasure of being personally recognized and confirmed as the author of the Darktown Comics. When Currier & Ives was liquidated in 1907, the drawings were removed from all the lithographic stones, except the Darktown Comics, which were sold along with the publishing rights. Worth's highly popular and unabashedly racist images not only ridicule black folk, but their economic and cultural value validates his relentless visual attacks against them. The monster-maker, it seems, is never vanquished.[31]

NOTES

1. "The Colored Clubs Amuse a Small Crowd at the Polo Grounds," New York (NY) *Herald*, May 30, 1884.

2. "The Colored Championship of Brooklyn Settled," New York (NY) *Times*, October 1, 1884.

3. Michael D. Harris, *Colored Pictures, Race and Visual Representation* (Chapel Hill: University of North Carolina Press, 2003), 63.

4. W.J.T. Mitchell, *What Do Pictures Want?* (Chicago: University of Chicago Press, 2005), 13–30.

5. Eric Lott, *Love and Theft: Blackface Minstrelsy and the American Working Class* (Oxford: Oxford University Press, 1995), 116. David's painting picks as its narrative the Roman Horatii, male triplets destined to wage war against the Curiatti. Wholly supported by their father the Horatii brothers express their fidelity and solidarity with Rome before battle.

6. "Big Africa Vanishing," New York (NY) *The Times*, September 24, 1877; "A Serious Discussion," New York (NY) *Globe*, September 1, 1883; Harris, *Colored Pictures*, 57–58.

7. "If I could have the Nigger show back again, in its pristine purity, and perfection, I should have but little further use for opera…. The minstrel used a very broad Negro dialect; he used it competently, and with easy facility, and *it* was funny—delightfully and satisfyingly funny." Mark Twain, *Autobiography of Mark Twain*. ed. Benjamin Griffin and Harriet Elinor Smith, Vol. 2 (Berkeley: University of California Press, 2013), 294.

8. W.J.T. Mitchell, *The Last Dinosaur Books, The Life and Times of a Cultural Icon* (Chicago: University of Chicago Press, 1998), 53; Thorstein Veblen, *The Theory of the Leisure Class* (New York: Macmillan, 1899; Reprint New York: Penguin Books, 1994).

9. Guy C. McElroy, Jr., and Henry Louis Gates, Jr., *Facing History: The Black Image in American Art, 1710-1940* (San Francisco: Bedford Arts, Publishers, 1991), xxxii. "Reconstruction also signifies the manner in which a thing is artificially constructed or naturally formed; structure, conformation, disposition. This definition, coupled with the bitter experience of political Reconstruction, helped shape the two antithetical images of African-Americans that still inflect the ways black people are perceived in this country. I speak specifically of the

curious heritage of the New Negro and his doppelganger, the black Sambo, and their complex antithetical relationship as surrogates in a simmering but undeclared race war."

10. McElroy, Jr., and Gates, *Facing History*, 28–29.

11. Sarah Burns, *Painting the Dark Side; Art and the Gothic Imagination in Nineteenth-Century America* (Berkeley: University of California Press, 2004), xvii–xix; 109–115; Mitchell, *The Last Dinosaur Books*, 65. The word "monster" is linked to "demonstration," the showing of visible evidence in a scientific argument. In Catholic ritual, the "monstrance" is the vehicle in which the sacred host is held up for display to the congregation.

12. "Extraordinary Forgery," New Orleans (LA) *Times-Picayune*, September 20, 1867; "Livingston's Big Forgery," New York (NY) *Sun*, October 14, 1875

13. "Fine Arts," New York (NY) *Evening Post*, June 15, 1868; Harris, *Colored Pictures*, 44–45; Richard J. Powell, *Cutting a Figure, Fashioning Black Portraiture* (Chicago: University of Chicago Press, 2008), 63; Alan C. Braddock, *Thomas Eakins and the Culture of Modernity* (Berkeley: University of California Press, 2009), 20–21; Eric Lott, *Black Mirror: The Cultural Contradictions of American Racism* (Cambridge, MA: Belknap Press, 2017), 20–21; 34.

14. Henri Focillon, *The Life of Forms in Art* (New York: Zone Books, 1992); Mitchell, *The Last Dinosaur Books*, 54.

15. James E. Brunson III, "The American Ideal of Manly Beauty: Isaac Broome's Base Ball Vase, 1875–1876," *Base Ball 10: New Research on the Early Game*, Don Jensen, ed. (Jefferson, NC: McFarland, 2018), 167–189; I am not unaware of the Currier and Ives 1860 lithograph, *The National Game: Three Outs and One Run*, or the 1866 lithograph, *The American National Games of Baseball-Grand Match*. Currier and Ives never intended to create or promote fine art, or even to produce expensive prints.

16. W.J.T. Mitchell, *The Last Dinosaur Book* (Chicago: University of Chicago Press, 1998).

17. Umberto Ecco, *The Infinity of Lists* (New York: Rizzoli, 2009), 155–156.

18. "The Coons Carry Off the Cake," Rockford (IL) *Register-Gazette*, June 20, 1883; "When Greek Meets Greek," New York (NY) *Herald*, October 4, 1884; Rae Beth Gordon, "Natural Rhythm: La Parisienne Dances with Darwin: 1875–1910," *Modernism/Modernity 10*, No. 4 (2003), 634.

19. I am not unaware of an 1874 illustration, derived from a photograph, of the Hampton College Base Ball Club, of Hampton, Virginia, which appeared in *Harper's Monthly Magazine*. It is a dignified portrait of black middle-class aspirations and upward social mobility.

20. Elizabeth Young, *Black Frankenstein* (New York: New York University Press, 2008), 19–57; Alexander Nemerov, *The Body of Raphaelle Peale* (Berkeley: University of California Press, 2001), 125–128.

21. Peter P. Hinks, *David Walker's Appeal to the Colored Citizens of the World* (University Park: Penn State Press, 2000), 75; "Rome Matters," Utica (NY) *Observer*, August 2, 1867; "Defines His Position," Rome (NY) *Citizen*, August 9, 1867.

22. Alexander Saxton, *The Rise and Fall of the White Republic* (London: Verso, 1996), 166; Henry Clay Lukens, "American Literary Comedians," *Harper's New Monthly Magazine*, April 1890; 783–797; Albert Bigelow Paine, *Thomas Nast: His Period and His Pictures* (New York: Macmillan, 1904); William Winter, *Old Friends; Being Literary Recollections of Other Days* (New York: Moffat, Yard and Company, 1909); Albert Parry, *Garrets and Pretenders: A History of Bohemianism in America* (New York: Covici, Friede, 1933); "Literary Notes," *Telegraph* (Macon, GA), Jan. 28, 1884.

23. "True Bohemians were artistic professionals whose products were recognizable in the market and able to command a price comparable to other commodities…. Every man who enters an artistic career without any other means of livelihood than art itself, will be forced to walk the paths of Bohemia … we repeat as an axiom: bohemia is a stage in artistic life…" Mary Gluck, *Popular Bohemia* (Cambridge: Harvard University Press, 2008), 18, 65–68; Brown, *Beyond the Lines*, 51–2.

24. Chad Heap, *Slumming: Sexual and Racial Encounters in American Nightlife, 1885–1940* (Chicago: University of Chicago Press, 2009), 154–161.

25. Thomas Ball's *Emancipation* (1876), a monumental bronze sculpture, commemorates the formerly enslaved. While living in Florence, Italy, and looking for a suitable black model, Ball recalled that the "only one available was not good enough." Ball complained that as he conducted the model through his apartment, the latter posed himself in front of several mirrors. Here, self-reflection and self-enlargement again rears its ugly head. Nonetheless, Ball's black figure represents not the "emancipated slave" but the "ideal slave," still knelling in the pose of the eighteenth-century English abolitionist emblem. The question posed by Worth's figure is whether it depicts the "ideal slave" or an emancipated black man. Worth, versed in contemporary art and art history, would have known the distinction.

26. Braddock, *Thomas Eakins and the Culture of Modernity*, 130; *The Great National Game* (*Punchinello Magazine*, 1870) offers an allegorical representation of the black baseballist, an image that depicts the figure preparing to take a whack at citizenship. The illustration meditates on post-Civil Wat trauma, that is, how the baseball forms reconstruct the black body for changing political projects and circumstances.

27. Eastman Johnson's *The Freedom Ring* (1860) depicts Rose Ward, formerly enslaved in New Orleans, gazing upon a newly acquired ring. White in appearance, the "little mulatto child" is a cautionary tale about how not to depict black people. Teresa A. Carbone and Patricia Hills, *Eastman Johnson: Painting America* (Brooklyn: Brooklyn Museum of Art, 1999), 152–153; "Base Ball," New Orleans (LA) *Picayune*. August 29, 1881.

28. Lott, *Love and Theft*, 25.

29. "Noted Cartoonists," Saratoga Springs (NY) *Saratogian*, January 5, 1887; "Currier and Ives," St. Johnsville (NY) *Enterprise and News*, April 23, 1941; Frank Weitenkampf, *The Critic: An Illustrated Monthly Review of Literature, Art, and Life*, Volume 47, New York (NY), 1905, 142–143.

30. "Old Prints Once 25c Now $3000," Brooklyn (NY) *Eagle*, February 8, 1931; "At the Art Galleries," *Brooklyn Eagle*, June 4, 1939; Donald A. Petesch, *A Spy in the Enemy's Country: The Emergence of Modern Black Literature* (Iowa City: University of Iowa Press, 1989), 244.

31. Alexandra Bonfante-Warren, *Currier & Ives: Portraits Of a Nation* (New York: MetroBooks, 1998), 94; Susan Sontag, *Regarding the Pain of Others* (New York: Farrar, Straus, and Giroux, 2003), 22.

The Minor Leagues and a Major Conflict

Canadian Professional Baseball and the Great War

Craig G. Greenham

Research has shown Canadian troops during World War I demonstrated the country's affinity for American sport. An investigation into the home front provides further evidence of Canada's athletic consistency with its neighbors to the south. Minor league baseball in Canada did not follow the British example with soccer and suspend play but, instead, continued in a manner that mirrored the neutral United States, despite Canada's heavy involvement in the war effort. Continuance of professional baseball, whether in wholly Canadian circuits or leagues with cross-border membership, resulted in a battle of attrition. In an era rife with league instability, the extra pressures of the war ultimately proved too much for all but one club, the Toronto Maple Leafs. This examination enhances our understanding of baseball during times of military conflict and how the strains and stresses of wartime society shaped the sport in Canada.

Many Canadian historians acknowledge the First World War as a turning point in the young country's history.[1] The success and tenacity of its soldiers in battle caused an outpouring of nationalistic fervor previously unknown in Canada. The conflict was an environment that also afforded Canadians, particularly English Canadians, an opportunity to demonstrate imperial pride.

Base Ball 12, pp. 195–220
ISSN 1934-2802 (Print) / ISSN 1934-3167 (Online)
978-1-4766-7473-5 (Print) / 978-1-4766-4112-6 (ebook)

Their love of baseball, however, set the Canadian soldiers apart from other countries and colonies fighting under the British flag.[2] An affinity for the game not only culturally distanced Canadian troops from Britain, but playing baseball, given the game's intrinsic link to American culture,[3] also demonstrated a cultural harmony with the United States. Despite the seriousness of battle and, in some ways, because of it, baseball played on the battlefront was a critical aspect of the war experience for many Canadian soldiers. It provided troops with a game that developed desirable mental and physical characteristics as well as an activity that proved a welcome mental distraction and alleviated homesickness. The sport was the showcase event for many of the sporting days in which Canadian soldiers took part—particularly Dominion Day and Empire Day—occasions that were intended for nationalist and imperialist pursuits, respectively. German military offensives, the Spanish flu pandemic, old-fashioned attitudes toward military drill held by some officers in the CEF, and sporting equipment shortages proved to be formidable foes of baseball in Europe, but the Canadian troops' desire for baseball ensured its success and incorporation into the soldier's experience.[4]

The challenges of playing baseball were not confined to war-torn Europe. Professional baseball in Canada, played at the minor league level, survived the Great War, but barely. On the home front, other obstacles confronted the sport's success. With a citizenry drastically divided on crucial issues regarding military spending, homeland security, manpower deficiencies and Canada's role in and obligation to the British Empire, sport on the home front was not foremost on many minds. The game struggled in these conditions and professional baseball teams across the embattled country either folded or were on the verge of ruin under the weight of the war. Rosters were left depleted as players enlisted to serve their country in the struggle, while money became scarce for club owners who absorbed financial losses as spectators either volunteered for military service or could not justify the time and money spent in a ballpark. In an era rife with league instability, the extra pressures of the war ultimately proved too much for all Canadian clubs but one, the Toronto Maple Leafs.

Research has shown Canadian troops during World War I demonstrated the country's affinity for American sport. This investigation into the home front provides further evidence of athletic alignment with its neighbors to the south. Professional baseball in Canada did not follow Britain's example with soccer and suspend play but, instead, continued in a manner that mirrored the approach of the neutral United States despite Canada's heavy involvement in the war effort. Continuance of professional baseball, whether in wholly Canadian circuits or leagues with cross-border membership, resulted in attrition that left the landscape almost barren by war's end. Additional strain was placed on professional baseball's survival in Canada with American entry into the war in 1917. There were no assurances that the plucky Toronto Maple Leafs could have endured much longer had the Allies not been victorious in the autumn of 1918.

This examination of professional baseball in Canada during the Great War is intended to enhance our awareness of Canada's cultural links to the United States, even as Canada fought under the British flag, as it explores the arduous path to survival amid a depleted society. This study also fills a gap in the historiography as no comprehensive account of Canadian professional baseball during the Great War exists and an improved understanding of this tumultuous period illuminates its importance during times of military conflict

Britain's Example

Canada emerged from colonial status to become a country in 1867, but its independence from Britain was gradual. The Statute of Westminster in 1931 and the Constitution Act of 1982, for example, were critical political steps that enhanced Canada's autonomy. Beyond the political, British influence helped to shape Canadian pre-war society.[5]

Britain's heavy commitment to the war effort and proximity to the enemy meant the gravity of the conflict directly challenged its sport traditions. The First World War marked an obvious disruption in the history of soccer and most other forms of social recreation in Britain. When war erupted in the summer of 1914, public officials in Britain called for the soccer[6] season to be cancelled.[7] The English professional league continued, however, until May the following year and tried to avoid public scrutiny as professional soccer teams donated money indiscriminately to various war charities, provided storage room for army supplies and an agreement to host drill sessions for troops in their stadiums.[8]

Most importantly, soccer was employed as a recruitment tool for the war. Elite soccer players frequently enlisted in front of fans at the stadium. Of 5,000 professional soccer players, 2,000 signed up for military duty. The league, at the behest of the War Office, adorned British pitches with recruitment posters that asked fans to follow the lead of the league's star players. By November 1914, *The Times* claimed that 100,000 men had already volunteered for military service via soccer events.[9] So effective were the recruitment campaigns that attendance at soccer games fell by almost half and it was only a matter of time before the sport was halted for the duration of the war.

The last match was played on April 24, 1915, between Sheffield United and Chelsea. After the match, Lord Derby, Chairman of the Football League and soon to be the architect of Britain's conscription laws, proclaimed at the trophy presentation that the competitors had played with and against each other for the Cup, but the time had come to compete alongside each other for Britain. The English League echoed those sentiments when it asked that every eligible man respond to a calling higher than soccer and join the war effort. Soccer's response to the call-to-arms was immense and it was an innovative effort to solicit fans' involvement in the military.[10]

In Canada, by contrast, a debate over the continuation of elite level sport that ultimately spelled the end of soccer in Britain for the war's duration never took place. Indeed, while the odd newspaper cast a critical eye at the sport from time to time, it did not ask readers to reject organized competition. Thomas Boyd, president of the Amateur Athletic Union of Canada (AAUC), called for the dissolution of competitive leagues in mid–1915, but his words carried little weight, particularly when applied to Canadian professional baseball.[11] The Maple Leafs and the Montreal Royals, for example, played lengthy seasons of 139 and 137 games respectively in 1915.[12]

Minor League Baseball

Before this article delves into the Canadian professional minor league clubs, it is crucial to revisit the system under which they operated. The *raison d'etre* for minor league baseball was different in the 1910s than it is today. Branch Rickey, general manager of the St. Louis Cardinals, was largely responsible for the reorganization of the minors in the late 1920s.[13] Disappointed continuously that the minor league players he scouted were sold by their teams to his richer competitors, like the Chicago Cubs and New York Giants, Rickey changed the face of the minors when he started to purchase minor league teams from D classification all the way up to Double-A, the highest rating outside the major leagues in that era.[14] This method became known as the farm system because it gave major league franchises a chance to *grow* their own talent. The system proved successful, as the Cardinals won nine National League pennants and six World Series crowns between 1926 and 1946. Before the creation of farm systems in the 1920s, players' contracts were bought and sold, and the minor league clubs were not affiliated with any major league team. This independence allowed minor league teams to make substantial money, in some instances, as they could sell players to the highest bidder from the major leagues. These minor league clubs had no wealthy, senior partner in the majors to assist them through lean years. This was the case during the Great War.

Canadian Clubs

At the outbreak of war, there were two entirely Canadian professional baseball leagues in the country—the Western Canada League (WCL) and the Canadian League (CL). Their pre-war existence, rife with team collapse and relocation, demonstrates the fragility and transient nature of minor league baseball in Canada, even when the country was at peace. The WCL, classified at D-level, began in Alberta in 1907 with four provincial teams: the Edmonton Grays, Calgary Bronchos, Medicine Hat Hatters, and the Lethbridge Miners. The league went on hiatus in 1908 but reappeared in 1909 in an expanded eight-team format in the other two prairie provinces (Saskatchewan and Manitoba) when it added the Moose Jaw Robin Hoods, Regina Bonepilers, Winnipeg Maroons, and the Brandon Angels. League clubs came and went throughout the years to service areas eager for professional baseball and to leave those that proved unsupportive and unfeasible—a trend typical in minor league baseball elsewhere. The Saskatoon Quakers replaced Medicine Hat in 1910 and the Lethbridge and Regina clubs ceased operations in 1911. By the 1912 season, the league had shrunk back to its original size as a four-team league in Alberta as the Red Deer Eskimos and Bassano Boosters[15] joined the teams in Calgary and Edmonton before expanding again for the 1913–1914 seasons to six clubs—three from Alberta (Calgary, Edmonton, and Medicine Hat) and three from Saskatchewan (Regina, Saskatoon, and Moose Jaw).

The CL was the other pre-war baseball league that was wholly contained in Canada. The circuit began in 1885 but instability saw it vanish and reappear several times until it was resurrected in 1911 as a C-level circuit. Its teams included the Brantford Red Sox, Guelph Maple Leafs, London Tecumsehs, Hamilton Kolts/Hams, Ottawa Senators, St. Thomas Saints, Peterborough Whitecaps/Petes, and the Berlin Busy Bees.[16] The CL's classification rose to B in time for the 1914 season that also included the Erie Yankees and Toronto Beavers, but without the Berlin club. Erie and Toronto, however, proved short-lived as they, along with Peterborough, folded after the 1914 season, perhaps fearful of committing to the next season if the nation was at war.

The differences between the 1914 and the 1915 seasons were considerable for Canadian baseball. The grim reality of the Great War quickly revealed

Opening day of the 1915 season in Northwestern League. The Vancouver Beavers hosted the Victoria Bees at Athletic Park in Vancouver. The Bees folded after that season but the Beavers played on for two more campaigns (*City of Vancouver Archives on Flickr, Archives item# PAN N14B. Photographer W.J. Moore*).

itself and the sport suffered, particularly on the prairies. Overwhelmed by the demands of wartime society in the conflict's early days, minor league baseball's organizational structure, the National Association of Professional Baseball Leagues (often referred to as the National Association or NA), extended an offer to the two wholly Canadian leagues. The NA's proposal allowed for protected territorial rights until after the war. This privilege irked baseball executives in competing leagues that wanted unfettered access to the players of any suspended league.[17] The WCL found it necessary to accept the option put forth by the NA and folded for the war's duration before the 1915 season. The CL refused to yield to the pressures of wartime society that included dwindling fan support and player availability due to enlistment. It played the 1915 season. Although the league exhausted its reserve funds in the effort, the CL valiantly completed the season with its association intact and *The Sporting News* suggested the league should be awarded the "Golden Cross of Gameness from Organized Baseball."[18] This accomplishment took an immense financial toll on the league and despite a desire from most clubs to play a season in 1916, the CL followed the path taken by the WCL and ceased operations until peace was restored in Europe.[19]

Under the circumstances of such a massive commitment to the war effort, these two Canadian professional leagues stood little chance of surviving the war. The resources and manpower required for the European struggle were unimaginable before the conflict. Gripped by the severity of the war, Prime Minister Robert Borden continued to raise enlistment goals. By the end of 1914, 56,584 enlisted, a significant total given the war was not even six months old. Borden was convinced more support was required, however, and pledged a military force of 500,000 troops at the beginning of 1916—a considerable sum given the country's population hovered around eight million.[20] Borden's promise was undertaken with not only an Allied victory in mind but to ensure Canada's representation reflected what he believed was its prominent place within the British Empire.[21]

In addition to the teams that played in the two wholly Canadian circuits, eight other Canadian baseball teams participated internationally in leagues—the Northwestern League, the Northern League, and the International League—against American cities. The neutrality of the United States

Team photograph of the 1914 Saskatoon Quakers in the Western Canada League. The league ceased operations after that season. Back row (left to right): William "Chief" Cadreau RHP, Rudy Kallio RHP, Alex Harper SS, Lester "Tug" Wilson OF, Fred Chick 2B, Joseph Collins 2B/OF/RHP, Russell Northrup RHP. Front row: Bill Hurley 1B/MGR, Jimmy Flanagan OF, Alfred "Roxy" Walters C, Roy Mills OF, Roy Grover 3B. In front: unknown mascot (courtesy David Eskenazi).

buoyed the success of these leagues, at least until the spring of 1917 when the Americans joined the war on the side of the Allies.

The Northwestern League, which was B classification, had two Canadian entrants—Vancouver and Victoria. Like the divisions mentioned above, relocation and frequent name changes add confusion to this league's history. The Northwestern League began in 1905 and among its founding clubs were the Vancouver Horse Doctors and the Victoria Legislators. The Legislators did not even finish the season before resuming operations as the Spokane Indians. Another team came to Victoria in 1911, known as the Bees, and lasted until 1915. While Vancouver's team had more stability, their club underwent several changes in moniker: Horse Doctors (1905, 1907), Beavers (1908–1911, 1916–17), Champions (1912, 1915) and Bees (1913). In the Northwestern League, the Vancouver Beavers were among the strongest teams on the diamond and in 1916 *The Sporting News*, which served as the baseball bible on either side of the border and had an extensive network of local correspondents,[22] reported that "Vancouver fans are according [*sic*] baseball with a good support, notwithstanding the abnormal conditions brought on by the war, and there is every likelihood of attendance increasing as the season progresses."[23]

In March 1917, with the season quickly approaching, thoughts of war and club collapse were common occurrences in baseball, but positive press persisted. The Vancouver Beavers were set to start their season in the Northwestern League with high hopes under the guidance of manager Bob Brown, who drew comparisons with such fabled bench bosses as Connie Mack and John McGraw of the major leagues. After some gloomy comments about the shape of baseball in Canada in 1917, *TSN* waxed optimistically that "conditions were never more promising in Vancouver for the game. Notwithstanding war conditions and the departure of thousands of fans for that 'somewhere in France,' those of the loyal band of rooters remaining on the job have set about their work in an enthusiastic manner."[24] *The Sporting News*, it must be remembered, was a baseball newspaper whose very existence relied on reporting on the professional version of the game, so its contributors and editorial staff remained sanguine despite the enormous threat the war posed to baseball's continued play in Canada.

The publication's optimism seemed to have merit as the 1917 May home opener was played in front of a larger crowd than the previous two seasons. *The Sporting News* lauded Vancouver fans and used their support for their ballclub as examples to Americans, whose country just entered the war in April, on how to support the local club through difficult times. Of the spectators, *TSN* commented: "Fans are more optimistic, business is picking up after two years of depression and this town is taking to the diamond game with renewed vigor."[25] Even into mid-season, the Beavers attracted good crowds and the feeling was that this trend would continue because British Columbia's enlistment totals were favorable compared to other provinces.[26] British Columbia fans had seen the worst, the reasoning went, and weathered it.[27] Despite Vancouver's resilience, the league fell onto hard times with America's entry into the war and suspended operations in July 1918.

The Northern League, at one time or another, had participation from four Canadian cities. Its existence, similar to other leagues of the period, was turbulent and there were three incarnations of the circuit from 1902 to 1917. It began as Class D baseball with the Winnipeg Maroons being the sole Canadian entrant. The Brandon Angels joined them for the 1908 season but quit after just one campaign. The St. Boniface Bonnies became league members for the 1915 season but also folded after a single season. The Fort William-Port Arthur Canucks[28] entered the Northern League from 1913 to 1916 when the circuit's classification was boosted to C but left the league midway through the 1916 season.

The Maroons, who played in the 4,000-seat Happyland Park, remained the constant club in the league.[29] They were successful at the box office and the diamond, winning five Northern League pennants between 1902 and 1916, and an invitation to join the elite Class AA American Association (AA) was

Team photograph of the 1916 Winnipeg Maroons, the final season before the Northern League folded in 1917. The Maroons were a very successful team, capturing five league pennants between 1902 and 1916 (courtesy David Eskenazi).

predicted in Winnipeg sporting circles. However, the Great War was a foe far greater than anything the Maroons confronted on the diamond. The summons from the higher league never materialized and the league disbanded in 1917 due to a lack of players—the result of military enlistments on both sides of the border. A baseball correspondent for *TSN* that covered the Northern League bemoaned that in Canada, all anyone could talk about was the war and that there was little room for baseball in the conversation. "'War talk' is the absorbing thing ... baseball is temporarily in collapse."[30]

The International League

While Canadian clubs in leagues of lesser rank collapsed, the possibility for survival at the most prestigious level of the minor leagues persisted. The eight-team IL, one of only three Double-A baseball leagues of the time,[31] had two Canadian franchises and their health was vital to the IL since they combined for one-quarter of the league's membership. These two clubs, the Toronto Maple Leafs and the Montreal Royals of the International League (IL) were the crown jewels of Canadian baseball. They assured league president Edward Barrow that they were able to play the 1915 season. James McCaffery and Sam Lichtenhein, owners and presidents for the Maple Leafs and Royals respectively, were reported by the *New York Times* to have "come out strongly last night against the supposition that the war had affected the conditions in the sport world in Canada."[32] Whatever the health of the two Canadian teams, it was resolved at the meeting in New York's Hotel Imperial that players' salaries were to be reduced for the upcoming season since many of them made as much money per season, stated Barrow, as their colleagues in the major leagues.[33]

Despite the challenges the Great War placed on the Canadian economy and society, speculation swirled that the upstart Federal League (1914–1915), which planned on challenging the two major leagues, the National the American League (AL), as a third major league by pilfering its rosters, wanted to establish a franchise in Toronto. Montreal, however, was considered too remote and not financially desirable for the Federal League moguls.[34] Ultimately, the two established major leagues strong-armed the Federal League out of operation but talk of big-league baseball in Toronto never entirely dissipated.[35]

The Maple Leafs and Royals played through the 1916 season but with different results. In mid-season, Toronto was celebrated in *TSN* for standing by baseball during a difficult period in the history of the city and country. It proclaimed, "No city on the continent can show greater loyalty to baseball."[36] A month later, the attendance for Maple Leafs games continued to astonish the baseball press when its Dominion Day crowd of 12,000 surpassed the Independence Day total of 11,000 in Buffalo, despite the benefit of American neutrality in the war. Toronto's gate was all the more impressive when the specifics of their ballpark are taken into account. The location of Maple Leaf Park on Hanlan's Point[37] lacked convenience, as *TSN* remarked. "One had to take a street car, then cross over street level railroad crossings which sometimes hold you up long enough to miss the boat, which means a wait. Next you have to jump a ferry for a 15-minute ride on the bay to the park, which is situated in the amusement section of the island."[38] Attendance in Toronto had been steady during the season and the final homestand that coincided with the "big fair"[39] promised to put the Maple Leafs in good financial stead; the turnout delivered on expectations. Despite tens of thousands of Torontonians absent from the city due to the war, the additional economic burden on the patriotic citizenry, and the middling performance of the Maple Leafs on the diamond, Toronto led the IL in attendance in 1916.[40]

After the season, baseball gossip hinted that Toronto was not long for the IL. The Maple Leafs, along with the Richmond Virginians, were the only profitable IL clubs in 1916 and Toronto's market was lauded as ripe for a major league team.[41] The Washington Senators of the AL were in financial trouble and Toronto was the rumored relocation destination for the troubled franchise. To quash the speculation and preserve the Toronto market for the Maple Leafs, IL president Barrow told *TSN* that Toronto was one of the best baseball towns, but the circumstances of the war precluded any discussion of the major leagues. Barrow painted a dire picture of the city. He spoke of the tens of thousands of Toronto's young men at the front or on their way there, many of whom had already been killed or wounded in battle:

> Those 50,000 consisted of the young blood, the kind that patronized baseball. Take 50,000 of the young men out of any half-million city and it makes a big hole in its sport loving population. Those boys would have whooped it up for a big league club under different conditions.... The city is very patriotic and now there is talk of compulsory military service.... Ban Johnson [president of the AL] is as familiar with Toronto baseball conditions as I am and he is not likely to move a franchise to a city were war is the sole topic.[42]

Though praise for Toronto as a baseball city was commonplace, Montreal was regarded by those who followed the IL as one of the circuit's weak links. While the Maple Leafs packed the stands, the Royals gate suffered. The club's front office was reported to be pessimistic when it referred to the attendance at Montreal IL games as "rotten."[43] The Royals tended to lose money, whether they played in war or in peace, and 1916 was no exception.[44]

Speculation swirled about the club's future in Montreal, and relocation to an American market seemed likely.[45] In the Royals favor throughout the difficulties, however, was that it boasted one of the most supportive owners in the IL. Lichtenhein, who also owned the Montreal Wanderers hockey club in the National Hockey Association and National Hockey League, was constantly praised by the baseball press for his patience with the Royals.[46]

Anxiety over the fate of Canadian professional baseball was not restricted to baseball fans on Canadian soil. Baseball backers in the United States kept a watchful eye on the state of baseball in their northern neighbor during the Great War and praised Canadian soldiers for playing the game overseas and introducing it to a European audience.[47] Baseball was painstakingly promoted globally as an example of authentic American culture and interest its international appeal was evident in the era.[48] *The Sporting News* published a column in December 1916 with the lengthy headline, "Baseball Will Come Back in Canada After the War: When Dominion's Young Men Pour Out of the Trenches and Return Home Then Will Game Boom as in States After the Civil War."[49] The piece highlighted the plight of the game in Canada for its mostly American readership—many of whom were unaware of the toll the war in Europe exacted on society. It must be remembered that in 1916, the United States was not yet involved in the fighting thus there was no additional strain on baseball there. The article highlighted the growth of the game in pre-war Canada and tried to forecast baseball's future in some of the country's larger cities, like Toronto. The writer prophesied: "Baseball will come back with a vengeance. The boys that have carried it over to and played it in England and on the battle fields of France and Belgium will most certainly bring it back in Canada to a success eclipsing all previous records."[50] The article predicted that baseball would be used as a national healer in the same manner as it was used in the United States after the American Civil War.[51] It further suggested that if the Civil War was any measure, many returning players from the Canadian forces should have baseball skills superior to when they enlisted. The column concluded by saying, "Godspeed the day when the slaughter ends and baseball comes into its own again in Canada, more gloriously than ever. And then—Toronto a major league city, of course."[52]

The Sporting News claimed that the survival of the Maple Leafs in 1917 was tied to their success in the standings. The club's collapse was possible, the argument went, given the impact of the war on Canadian society without a pennant-competitive club.[53] With so much on the line, the Maple Leafs hired former major league star Napoleon Lajoie, then 41 years old, to manage and play for the team. This acquisition gave Toronto not only its biggest attraction but also a personality with a broad appeal in the minor leagues.[54] Lajoie's signing was more than a publicity stunt. Followers of the circuit believed his addition was a meaningful step towards the capture of the IL crown, as well as a move that would provide fans with, as *TSN* reported, "amusement worthy enough to lift their minds from more serious things for an hour or two each day."[55]

The Maple Leafs fans were supportive, but frosty weather in Toronto limited the size of the opening day crowd despite Lajoie's appeal.[56] The cold did not dampen Torontonians' enthusiasm for baseball long. In June, a well-attended exhibition was staged between the St. Louis Browns and Boston Braves of the major leagues. In August, more than 10,000 spectators turned out for another exhibition game, this time between the Chicago Cubs and Detroit Tigers. *The Sporting News* reported that for those in attendance, baseball was the discussion, not the war. Again, as was the case throughout the entire conflict, Toronto was held up as the standard of a city that loved baseball and an example to be followed by American fans, whose country joined the war in Europe on April 6, 1917. "Probably no town outside of Europe has had the horrors of war brought more forcibly before it than Toronto. Thousands of crippled, maimed, and blinded Canadians are cared for in that city.... Despite these conditions, the people there want to see sports to relieve tension."[57]

Praise of the dedicated Canadian baseball fans was not only doled out by *The Sporting News*. The part-owner and president of the Chicago Cubs, Charlie Weegham,[58] was quoted as saying, "No better proof that baseball is needed in this country could be had than that game in Toronto. Canada is head over heels in war yet it is turning out to see ball games. That crowd at Toronto was an eye opener to me."[59] While it is true that Weegham, involved in the management of the Cubs, had a commercial interest in the continued success of baseball in the United States as well as Canada, his words were indicative of the rhetoric that championed baseball as an activity that alleviated societal tension during the Great War. The Lajoie–led Maple Leafs provided entertainment home and abroad with a blend of baseball excellence and patriotism. The Union Jack, then Canada's flag, along with the American stars and stripes, were hoisted up a flagpole in Buffalo in May 1917 as part of a doubleheader. Lajoie and Major W.H. Grant, a veteran of the battle of St. Julien, led the Maple Leafs in military drill to the delight of the American fans.[60] The turnout and excitement in the stands resurrected earlier the possibility that Toronto, one day, would join the ranks of the major leagues. The Maple Leafs' capture of the 1917 IL pennant only boosted the city's reputation for baseball excellence.

The situation in Montreal was more difficult. The Royals were focused on payroll, not pennants. Inspired by a group of disgruntled MLB players that felt unfairly compensated, a contingent of players within the IL threatened to withhold their playing services unless they were paid more. The already financially strapped Montreal Royals refused to give into their demands and president Lichtenhein publicly lambasted players that even entertained the notion of a holdout:

> The minor league ballplayers are lucky to have jobs the coming season. Many leagues are thinking seriously of closing up shop. I lose money annually without a chance of getting it back and who gets the money? The player. Does he want me to still dig deeper? Supposing we turned around and asked the players to whack up profits on a 50–50 basis? Fultz's[61] talk is all nonsense, and I would rather shut up my park than have him dictate to me. The baseball players have it much softer even than actors. Ball players are paid their hotel and travelling expenses away from home, while the actor pays his own. Most of the magnates are in the game for the love of the sport. I do not believe that 10 per cent of the clubs have made a dollar in years, but the players all get their money, and if the clubs do not pay this same frightful National Commission[62] makes them come through.[63]

Although the players eventually fell into line, the 1917 season was not guaranteed for the Royals. Its status as a club in the International League remained in serious jeopardy. *The Sporting News'* Montreal correspondent claimed that despite Toronto's boasts of hardship, Montreal was more negatively affected by the war and the mere fact that baseball was still a consideration in the city was a testament to its enormous appeal. The Royals played the 1917 season and to prepare for it, management suggested holding training camp in the United States to remove players from the military atmosphere of Montreal, or, if the players appeared soft, have them train under returned sergeant major drill instructors "who would make drilling players sweat blood."[64]

Whatever the strategy, the 1917 season for the Royals was a disaster. They finished 56–94, just barely ahead of the last place Virginians. The IL, in general, was pleased with its teams' local draws, except for the Royals and the once-profitable but now inept Richmond club.[65] Both teams were the subject of newspaper reports that hinted at their demise after the 1917 season, which Lichtenhein did little to dissuade. The *New York Times* reported: "Sam Lichtenhein, the progressive little owner of the Montreal club, has never made much money out of baseball, but he has always been one of the staunchest supporters of Barrow's circuit. He had an unusually bad season last year and does not deem it advisable to try it again under present conditions."[66] Significant changes to the IL, based on American entry into the war, seemed to be a certainty as the off-season unfolded.

Clubs other than Montreal appeared to have considerable obstacles in their path as 1917 came to a close. On top of the financial concerns, player enlistments in the military decimated the rosters of several teams. Speculation suggested the fabled IL would not see a 1918 season. President Barrow advised that the league disband as challenges continued to mount. To worsen matters for Toronto baseball fans whose loyalty throughout the war demonstrated their desire for elite baseball in 1918, the courtship of the city as a relocation destination for a major league franchise ceased.[67] Seemingly the Maple Leafs had two options for survival: join the struggling the AA, or be part of a new league that combined the four best franchises each from the IL and AA.[68] The Maple Leafs chose the latter and McCaffery traveled to Louisville, Kentucky, to pitch the idea of the new circuit to key clubs from the AA. His proposal fell on deaf ears, however, and a new league would not be formed. *The Sporting News* referred to the situation:

> It does seem a shame, however, that a few intelligent magnates should be held up because of a bunch of thick-bearded, short-sighted gentlemen who are not capable of grasping opportunity and refuse to be shown how. The magnates who at present form the progressives are keen-sighted businessmen who in spite of obstacles have been able as a whole to make the game a success artistically and can stand their losses financially, and so they will be able to continue a few more seasons if necessary until their fellow magnates of duller intellect realize that a reorganization of the baseball map is inevitable and an absolute necessity for the real success of the game.[69]

With the failure to reach an agreement for the formation of a new league, the prospects of professional baseball in Toronto for the 1918 season grew grimmer. Still, McCaffery was optimistic of the IL's survival and worked tirelessly to that effect.[70]

McCaffery's dedication was clear but some club owners doubted Barrow's desire to find a solution since rumors linked the IL president to a managerial position with the Boston Red Sox in the majors.[71] Beyond leadership issues, the Montreal Royals were unlikely to continue play in 1918, even if a league could be salvaged or created. The 1917 season was particularly poor for the club and Lichtenhein's patience as an owner had its limits. *The Sporting News* wrote that situations in both Montreal and Richmond seemed hopeless and it might be better for the health of the league if those clubs quit and perhaps a leaner, six-team IL might be able to survive. Richmond was said to be a decent baseball town, but its southern location placed it far from other clubs, meaning that whatever money it made at the ballpark went to pay expensive railway fares. The Royals, meanwhile, had good ownership, but the club "has always been a white elephant so far as the financial end was concerned."[72]

The New International League

The closer the 1918 season came, the farther away the chances for another IL season seemed. Montreal and Richmond announced withdrawal from the league in the winter of 1918 and the president of the Buffalo Bisons declared bankruptcy.[73] The vote to suspend league play for 1918 was scheduled for December 1917 but was postponed by owners in anticipation that the future would somehow brighten. Optimists held a glimmer of hope that the Great War might end, a generous benefactor would emerge, or that the IL might continue as a six-team league. By February 1918, however, the war was still being fought, and no benefactor was prepared to relieve owners of their mounting bills—least of all the major leagues, which had financial issues of its own and refused to bail out the minor leagues. To add to the instability of the International League, Barrow quit as league president after it was announced that his pay was to be reduced by two-thirds (from $7,500 to $2,500 a year).[74]

In Canada, other off-field factors created problems for the IL. The Military Service Act, which was the official name of Canada's conscription bill, became law in July 1917. Initially, this law likely had a limited impact on baseball's health in Canada since implementation was delayed. By the start of 1918, however, the federal government began to draft men, thereby depleting rosters and fan bases. While this bill's most noted legacy was the discord it created between the French and English Canadians, it no doubt decreased the pool of baseball fans from which Canadian-based clubs could draw.

Conscription was not the only legal obstacle that faced the IL. Blue laws meant that the Maple Leafs could not host sporting events on Sunday. After New York State decided to allow play on Sundays, Toronto was now the only city in the defunct IL that had that avenue closed to them due to its strict Sabbatarianism. This restriction might have limited Toronto's ability to join or create another league. *The Sporting News* did not see the lack of Sunday baseball as harmful to Toronto's chances, however, when it remarked, "Toronto does not need Sunday baseball nor does the public wish it at present, this city as is well known is the best ball town on the circuit, in spite of war and a closed town on Sunday."[75] Still, Sunday baseball might have been helpful for the financial fortunes of the Maple Leafs during these lean years.

But it was not just Toronto's bottom line that was a concern. With American involvement in the war as of 1917, all clubs in the IL faced immense challenges for a 1918 season. Overcome with the pressures associated with minor league baseball during the Great War, the IL folded. Montreal and Richmond both were allowed to cast votes to decide the league's fate for 1918, despite their announced intention to withdraw. Buffalo, whose team was in forfeiture, had its ballot cast by acting league president and president of the Rochester club, Charles Chapin. The result of the vote was 6–2 in favor of dissolution. The specifics of the ballot, however, were surprising. The two clubs that had expressed a desire to continue were Newark and Richmond—the latter the club that had attendance problems and had expressed a desire to leave the league in the months that led up to the vote.[76] The *New York Times* reported, "B.W. Wilson of the Richmond club then offered an amendment to the motion asking for the league to continue and made an attempt to persuade the club owners to hold the league together."[77] Wilson did not find anyone to second his amendment and the original motion to disband was carried.

What was equally unforeseen was Maple Leafs owner McCaffery's vote to disband, given his effort to keep professional baseball in Toronto for the 1918 season.[78] In Toronto, where professional baseball's success despite the ravages of war impressed observers, the search for a new circuit intensified. In April, a new league, unimaginatively named the New International League was formed, composed of five healthy teams from the original IL, including Toronto, and rounded out with three teams from the New York State League.[79] As mentioned, the league was referred to as the New International League initially. However, the "New" was dropped from the name over time. *The Sporting News* wrote: "the brand of ball may not be all this city (Toronto) has had in the past, or what it hoped for, still it will do as a war diet and the fans will accept it as loyally as they have other war retrenchments."[80]

While Toronto fans were praised for their loyalty throughout the war years, the most celebrated individual on the roster was chastised, perhaps unfairly, by the press for disloyalty over his lack of trust in the IL and the Maple Leafs. Napoleon Lajoie began unauthorized negotiations in the off-season with the Indianapolis Indians of the rival AA to serve as the team's player-manager. The player-manager feared the dissolution of the IL was imminent and that he would be left jobless, despite McCaffery's reassurances that there would be professional baseball in Toronto and that the Maple Leafs would honor his contract in any event. *The Sporting News* criticized Lajoie for being unfaithful to McCaffery, whom it lavished with praise and called the fairest of all owners, and contended that Lajoie's ill temper, feuds with players, and poor managerial style were overlooked in 1917 because he hit .380 and was the most dangerous bat in the pennant-winning lineup.[81] To complicate matters, once Lajoie made it known that he was interested in playing elsewhere, the Maple Leafs sold his contract to the Brooklyn Dodgers in the majors.

In an unexpected twist, however, Lajoie had no interest in rejoining the majors. He was more than 40 years old, and he was only interested in the player-manager role that he had been allowed to perform in the minors, so his preference was to join Indianapolis in the AA. There was no chance of him assuming a managerial role in Brooklyn. The Dodgers had had Wilbert Robinson in that position since 1914 and they had no plans of replacing him with Lajoie.[82] Lajoie rejected this transaction and took his case to the National Commission, baseball's highest court.[83] Several clauses in the Fraternity of Baseball Players of America Agreement, which bound all players in professional baseball, suggested that Lajoie, given his years of experience in the majors and minors, might be considered a free agent after the dissolution of the IL. Despite McCaffery's reported honest intentions with Lajoie and the payment to him of a $1,000 bonus for winning the IL pennant, an amount not stipulated in Lajoie's contract, the National Commission sided with Lajoie and granted him free agent status, thus denying the Maple Leafs compensation from Brooklyn. Three other Maple Leafs also were awarded free agency as well based on clauses in the Fraternity of Baseball Players of America Agreement.[84]

Since McCaffery claimed the National Commission had no jurisdiction to rule on this matter, he launched an appeal via new IL president John Ferrell. The appeal was not granted, much to his dismay and that of *The Sporting News*, a publication that never missed an opportunity to praise and defend the Toronto owner.[85] Later that summer *TSN* referred to McCaffery as the "gamest and pluckiest magnate in Organized Baseball,"[86] and invited the members of the National Commission to Toronto to watch an exhibition game between the Cincinnati Reds and New York Yankees. The writer quipped that there would no doubt be "bloodthirsty fans" who want to get their hands on the "illustrious guests," so McCaffery should procure hundreds of soldiers to keep them from harm.[87] The *Globe*, a Toronto newspaper, also seemed gleeful to report that Lajoie's tenure in the AA as player-manager for the Indianapolis Indians was, thus far, unsuccessful. Under the headline, "Call Lajoie Bad Failure," the newspaper reported that attendance in Indianapolis had dwindled because Lajoie was "not delivering the goods."[88]

The absence of Lajoie in the Maple Leafs batting order was only part of the challenge to the season. American entry into the war created other issues, particularly with border crossing restrictions to prevent draft dodging. The Maple Leafs were scheduled to open the season on the road in the United States, but the Canadian authorities did not allow the Canadian players and personnel to cross the border into the United States. Similarly, the Maple Leafs experienced more difficulties on their way back to Toronto for their home opener against the Binghamton Bingoes in front of more than 10,000 fans. American authorities detained all of Toronto's American-born players until they proved their army draft status, which delayed the team by one day. The Bingoes, coincidentally, exited the United States at a different crossing and did not experience any problems.[89]

The Maple Leafs rose above these challenges and edged the Bingoes for the IL's pennant on the last day of the season.[90] McCaffery was championed for his determination as the chief architect of the recreated IL and a man whose dedication to baseball in Canada was unsurpassed. *The Sporting News* continued to heap praise: "This gentleman from Toronto comes of good stock, the kind of stock which has made Canada famous in the front line of the battle fields of Europe.... He has kept a baseball team going despite extraordinary adverse conditions.... McCaffery repeatedly gave his word to local fans that if within human power this city would have a team in a good baseball league in 1918."[91] McCaffery's creation was also suggested to be more "wieldy" from a travelling standpoint, despite the occasional trouble at the border, and in time would prove better caliber than the original IL.[92]

Thus, the Maple Leafs, because of a solid fan base and a determined owner, were able to survive 1918. Perhaps inspired by McCaffery's triumph in forming a league out of the ashes of the IL, George "Knotty" Lee had designs for resurrecting the CL in 1918 after two dormant seasons. A former player and one of the parties responsible for the initial success of the CL, Lee managed the Hamilton, Toronto, and Guelph clubs throughout the league's earlier existence. What convinced Lee that it was possible to restart the CL was not a hunch that the war might soon end or a reserve of money that would enable him to operate the league with a minimal fan base. Instead, he believed the key to the resurgence of the CL had to do with the clock. The Canadian government had just instituted daylight savings time and Lee thought the shift in clocks would allow fans to finish their workday and still catch a baseball game that started at twilight.[93] Lee was quoted in the pages of *TSN*: "Had the daylight saving bill not been brought into effect it would have been useless even to attempt to make the league pay. So many of the fans have gone to the front, and so many of those at home are working all day, that there would be few who could turn out to games."[94] Ultimately, Lee's plan did not materialize into a league. Still, his efforts demonstrated the types of creative solutions necessary to ensure professional baseball's survival in wartime Canada and the willingness of baseball boosters to entertain such notions.

Aside from daylight saving time, other war measures also had an impact on Canadian professional baseball as the 1918 season progressed—including policies crafted in the United States. Although they were the lone Canadian-based team in the recreated IL, many players on the Maple Leafs were American-born, or spent their off-seasons in the United States, and, thus, were subject to its rules. In June 1918, the NL approached the United States War Department to try to secure draft exemptions for its players, similar to that achieved by movie and theater actors. Neither the AL nor the minor leagues indicated plans to make a similar pitch.[95] Perhaps those circuits waited for the NL to set a precedent or to observe where its attempt failed and remedy that point when it came time for their own request.

In the end, President Woodrow Wilson and his Secretary of War Newton Baker denied special draft exemptions for ballplayers.[96] Baker mandated that all men had to be in an essential war industry or pick up a rifle, a decision which drew the ire of the baseball press. Sportswriters alleged that North Americans at home, as well as those overseas in the trenches, delighted in knowing the baseball scores. To conscript players in large numbers threatened baseball and a continent's morale.[97] The fact that neither politician was openly a big baseball booster only proved more irksome for some in the media that championed the game. *The Sporting News* remarked that "the only persons the writer has met who seem strongly opposed to baseball in times of war are persons who know little or nothing about the sport.... The ignorance of some of these persons on the subject of baseball is lamentable."[98] The question surrounding the future of the majors, let alone the minors, became a pressing issue.[99] Vocal opposition to Baker's "work or fight" instructions and what they meant for baseball's future convinced the war secretary to meet with the National Commission.[100] Instead of waiting for the outcome of the meeting, the American Association immediately cancelled the remainder of its season and was criticized by *TSN* for its hasty actions.[101] In an ironic twist given Lajoie's departure from Toronto, the IL vowed to play out the season if at all possible; it was the only minor league to do so.[102]

The 1918 major and International League seasons were shortened but both were able to crown champions. As mentioned, the Maple Leafs were the victors in the new IL's first season while the Boston Red Sox beat the Chicago Cubs four games to two in the World Series.[103] While Baker seemed immovable in his stance against exemptions for ballplayers, he slightly acquiesced in his position in late-August. The War Department granted special draft exemptions for members of the Boston Red Sox and Chicago Cubs—the two teams that were to meet in the World Series set to begin in early September. The reason for Baker's change of heart was the tremendous interest these games held overseas for the troops. The National Commission agreed to explore ways to deliver game accounts to Canadian and American troops overseas as quickly as possible after each game.[104] From what is known about Canadian and American soldiers' appetite for baseball, the troops were certainly pleased that the leagues were able to complete their seasons and enjoyed the game summaries.[105]

Conclusion

Professional baseball in Canada during the Great War endured a brutal ordeal and had the scars to prove it. The country was peppered with professional clubs before the outbreak of hostilities in 1914 but when peace for finally achieved in November 1918, only the Maple Leafs remained. The list of casualties, to borrow from military parlance, was extensive. Minor league baseball across the country was resuscitated once peace was restored but in the vast majority of cases, it lasted only a short while and then vanished for decades—sometimes forever.

It is difficult to say, of course, that had Canadian baseball promoters followed the template put forth by British soccer in suspending play during the hostilities that all would have been well for professional baseball in the postwar years. What can be said with certainty, however, that maintaining professional baseball, consistent with the neutral Americans, came with a cost. The decision to continue play through the conflict might have been born from the realization that Canadians, at least athletically, were more similar to their southern neighbors than the head of an Empire an ocean away. The truth, however, was that its war commitments distorted Canada's resemblance to the United States. Baseball promoters in the United States, represented so aptly by *The Sporting News*, kept a watchful eye over the state of professional minor league baseball in Canada and praised its owners and organizers profusely throughout the conflict. Its commitment to professional baseball gave hope to American baseball magnates that questioned baseball's future in the United States once it joined the war in the spring of 1917.

NOTES

1. This claim is common in university survey textbooks on Canadian history. It also serves as the foundation for monographs written by academic historians like Desmond Morton and popular historians such as Pierre Berton.

2. Readers interested in learning more about Canadian soldiers' use of baseball during the First World War should consult Craig Greenham, "On the Battlefront: Canadian Soldiers, an Imperial War and America's National Pastime," *American Review of Canadian Studies* 42, No. 1 (2012), 34–50, and Andrew Horrall "'Keep-a-Fighting! Play the Game!' Baseball and the Canadian Forces During the First World War," *Canadian Military History* 10, No. 2 (2001), 27–40.

3. Porter's *Spirit of the Times* declared that baseball was America's national pastime in 1857. Celebrated American writer Walt Whitman was one of the first of the literati to promote the game as national institution. "Base-ball is our game: the American game: I connect it to the national character." This quotation appeared in Horace Traubel, *With Walt Whitman in Camden* (New York: D. Appleton & Company, 1908), 330. Traubel, in 1888, began chronicling his daily conversations with Whitman, which continued until Whitman's death in 1892. The quotation came from Sunday September 18, 1885.

4. Greenham, "On the Battlefront," 34–50.

5. Much has been written on Britain's influence on pre-Great War Canada. Readers are directed to Carl Berger's two classics *Imperialism and Nationalism, 1884–1914: A Conflict in Canadian Thought* (Toronto: Copp Clark, 1969), and *The Sense of Power: Studies in the Ideas of Canadian Imperialism, 1967–1914* (University of Toronto Press, 1970) for an enhanced understanding of Britain's role in early Canaday.

6. Elite level rugby had suspended operations in Britain at the start of the war.

7. Elsewhere in the British Empire, the Australian press, church, and parliament successfully rallied around the notion of postponing sport until peace was restored.

8. Ross J. Wilson, "It Still Goes On: Football and the Heritage of the Great War in Britain," *Journal of Heritage Tourism* 9, No. 3 (2014), 198.

9. James Walvin, *The People's Game: A History of Soccer Revisited* (Edinburgh: Mainstream, 1994), 92–95.

10. *Ibid.*

11. "Urges Sportsman to Enlist in Army," *Toronto World*, July 23, 1915.

12. The standings for the 1915 season can be found at: https://www.baseball-reference.com/bullpen/1915_International_League_season. The potential length of a baseball schedule makes the decision to continue the professional game all the more impressive. Professional hockey's schedule, for example, was considerably shorter. The National Hockey Association, the forerunner to the National Hockey League, played a 24-game schedule and the Pacific Coast Hockey Association played an 18-game schedule in 1915–1916.

13. Richard Puerzer, "Engineering Baseball: Branch Rickey's Innovative Approach to Baseball Management," *Nine* 12, No. 1 (2003), 77–78.

14. The minor leagues were reorganized in 1912 and the new top classification of Double-A was regarded as the highest level of minor league baseball. The Triple-A classification that currently exists as the best level in the minors was established in 1946.

15. Bassano, Alberta, seems like an odd choice to include in this loop given its small population of the settlement (even today, Bassano has less than 2,000 residents) and its geography (140 kilometers east of Calgary), which would have made more sense if Medicine Hat was in the league but at this point it was not. The Boosters folded after just one season.

16. In 1916 Berlin changed its named to Kitchener. The city was renamed based on anti-German sentiment that was commonly held in Canada during the First World War. The Earl of Kitchener was the British Secretary of State for War and his surname was seen as favorable to the German capital of Berlin.

17. R.W. Kent, "Kent Has Crow to Pick with Board," *The Sporting News,* December 10, 1917, 8.

18. Gordon Belyea, "Baseball Will Come Back in Canada After the War," *The Sporting News*, November 9, 1916, 6.

19. *Ibid.*

20. Desmond Morton and J.L. Granatstein, *Marching to Armageddon: Canadians and the Great War, 1914–1919* (Toronto: Lester & Orpen Dennys Limited, 1989), 30.

21. Readers interested in the history of Canada's attempt to raise an army during the First World War should read "Doing Your Bit: Volunteers and Conscripts" which is the third chapter in Desmond Morton's *When Your Number's Up: The Canadian Solider in the First World War* (Toronto: Random House, 1993).

22. *TSN* was published out of St. Louis but had an extensive network of correspondents, including in the many Canadian markets. In the publication's nameplate

it made three claims: "Base Ball Year 'Round"; "Base Ball Latest and Best"; and "The Base Ball Paper of the World." Its position as baseball's publication of record is unchallenged and equally apt in Canada due to its comprehensive coverage.

23. A.P. Garvey "Great Race in the Northwestern," *The Sporting News*, June 8, 1916, 2.

24. A.P. Garvey, "Not All the Macks Are in the Majors," *The Sporting News*, March 8, 1917, 5.

25. A.P. Garvey, "War Alarmists, Take Note from Canada," *The Sporting News*, May 10, 1917, 2.

26. A.P. Garvey, "Bob Brown's Beavers Just Beginning Drive," *The Sporting News*, June 7, 1917, 1.

27. *Ibid.*

28. Fort William and Port Arthur were the twin cities that merged to form Thunder Bay, Ontario in 1970.

29. Lewis Stubbs, *Shoestring Glory: Semi-Pro Ball on the Prairies* (Winnipeg: Turnstone Press, 1996), 40.

30. (No first name provided) Newman, "War Has the Call in Canada," *The Sporting News*, December 7, 1916.

31. The International League, American Association, and Pacific Coast League were the three Double-A leagues.

32. "Future of League Hangs in Balance," *New York Times*, February 15, 1915.

33. *Ibid.*

34. "Sporting News in Brief," *New York Times*, September 11, 1915.

35. When the Federal League collapsed, largely due to MLB influence, owners of Federal League clubs were bought out by owners in the AL and NL or, in some situations, offered other incentives—like the opportunity to purchase an existing MLB club that was for sale. The owners of the Baltimore Terrapins were offered no financial compensation or ability to join MLB and, feeling abandoned by fellow Federal Leaguers and excluded by the existing leagues, decided to grieve MLB's interference over their league under existing antitrust laws. Although successful in district courts, the Terrapins saw their victory overturned on appeal. The Terrapins ownership then escalated matters to the United Supreme Court where, in 1922, the appeal was upheld and MLB was found exempt from the Sherman Antitrust Act. The decision was written by Justice Oliver Wendell Holmes, Jr.

36. George Diggers, "Toronto Making One Record to Be Proud Of," *The Sporting News*, August 24, 1916, 2.

37. Hanlan's Point Stadium was the home to the Maple Leafs from 1897–1899 and then again from 1908–1926 when it was replaced by Maple Leaf Park which was also on Hanlan's Point. In 1900, the team was sold by the Toronto Ferry Company to 52 buyers who moved the team off the island and to Diamond Park at the corner of Dufferin and King Streets where the Maple Leafs played until the end of the 1907 season. James McCaffery bought the Maple Leafs in 1908 and remained owner and president until his death in 1922. The other pre-war home to the Maple Leafs was Sunlight Park (1896–1897).

38. Gordon Belyea, "Fans Want Birmingham to Put Up a Little Fight," *The Sporting News*, July 20, 1916, 3.

39. The "big fair" refers to the Canadian National Exhibition. It first became a permanent fixture in Toronto's social scene in 1879 when it was called the Toronto Industrial Exhibition at what is now known as the grounds of the Exhibition Place.

40. Gordon Belyea, "Baseball Will Come Back in Canada After the War," *The Sporting News*, November 9, 1916, 6.

41. Harry Sandage, "Bound That Barrow Shall Have No Peace," *The Sporting News*, October 26, 1916, 2.

42. *Ibid.*

43. Diggers, "Toronto Making One Record to Be Proud Of."

44. From 1900–1917, the Montreal Royals finished higher than fifth place in the stand-

ings only once—a third-place finish in 1916. Perhaps the team's financial line would have improved with a better on-field product.

45. (No first name provided) Newman, "War Has the Call in Canada," *The Sporting News*, December 7, 1916, 2.

46. The NHL began in 1917 and was formed from the dissolved NHA.

47. Greenham, "On the Battlefront," 39.

48. Sporting goods magnate and former professional pitcher Albert G. Spalding made a concerted effort to spread the sport outside of American borders. When the United States was in its adolescence and without fully developed and distinctive national traditions, some believed, like Spalding, that baseball represented one of the first genuine forms of authentic American culture and was an ideal cultural export. He spearheaded a global baseball tour in 1888–1889 in an attempt to grow baseball's popularity and to expose the world to American cultural imperialism. While baseball was offered to the global community as a gift from the American people, as well as a means through which Americans could effectively boast about their athletic creation, the sport did not enchant people the world-over. America's national pastime failed to make meaningful in-roads in many of the foreign lands Spalding visited with his all-star cast (tour stops included the American West, Hawaii, New Zealand, Australia, Ceylon, Egypt, Italy, France, and England). Spalding's vast sporting goods empire was already in existence, so of course, he stood to gain financially from baseball's global expansion. For more information on these tours, the reader should consult Mark Lamster, *Spalding's World Tour: The Epic Adventure That Took Baseball Around the Globe—and Made It America's Game* (New York: Public Affairs, 2006), and James Elfer's *The Tour to End All Tours: The Story of Major League Baseball's 1913–1914 World Tour* (Lincoln: University of Nebraska Press, 2003). For information on the tour's brief impact in Britain, please consult Andrew Horrall, *Popular Culture in London, 1890–1918* (Manchester: Manchester University Press, 2001).

49. Belyea, "Baseball Will Come Back in Canada After the War."

50. *Ibid.*

51. Baseball's first military experience occurred during the American Civil War. George Kirsch's *Baseball in Blue and Gray: The National Pastime During the Civil War* (Princeton, NJ: Princeton University Press, 2007) provides an informative account of baseball in this period.

52. Belyea, "Baseball Will Come Back in Canada After the War."

53. Gordon Belyea, "Outlook Not Overly Bright in Toronto," *The Sporting News*, January 18, 1917, 1.

54. Gordon Belyea, "Lajoie Successor to Great Line of Leaders," *The Sporting News*, February 1, 1917, 2.

55. *Ibid.*

56. Gordon Belyea, "Toronto Enthusiastic If Not Very Numerous," *The Sporting News*, May 10, 1917, 2.

57. George Robbins, "War Really Aid to Baseball Interest," *The Sporting News*, August 23, 1917, 1.

58. Weegham, along with William Wrigley, Jr., and nine other investors purchased the Chicago Cubs after a failed stint with the renegade Federal League. Under Weegham's direction, the Cubs moved into Weegham Park, which was renamed Wrigley Field in 1926 when Wrigley bought out his partners. For more information, consult the fourth and fifth chapters of Glenn Stout, *The Cubs: the Complete Story of Chicago Cubs Baseball* (Boston: Houghton Mifflin, 2007).

59. Robbins, "War Really Aid to Baseball Interest."

60. "Bisons Take Pair from Larry's Leafs," *The (Toronto) Globe*, May 31, 1917, 9

61. Dave Fultz was an outfielder for the Philadelphia Athletics. In 1912 he was able to unionize major league ballplayers in an organization called the Players Fraternity. The group threatened a strike in 1917 but such a drastic measure was prevented when Fultz was able to obtain several concessions from the owners. The union disbanded during the Great War. For more information on the labor relations between players and management from this period,

the reader is urged to consult the fifth chapter of Lee Lowenfish, *The Imperfect Diamond: A History of Baseball's Labor Wars* (Da Capo Press: New York, 1980).

62. The National Commission was a three-man panel consisting of the presidents of the American and National Leagues as well as the commission chairman whose job it was to mediate disputes. The National Commission was in place before MLB appointed its first ever commissioner, Judge Kennesaw Mountain Landis, who was installed to settle problems and scandals quickly and decisively. The move towards a commissioner was motivated by the throwing of the 1919 World Series by the Chicago White Sox. Accounts of the National Commission can be found in numerous books on baseball history, including Lee Lowenfish's *The Imperfect Diamond: A History of Baseball's Labor Wars* (New York: Da Capo Press, 1980).

63. "Jennings Predicts Champions in 1917," *New York Times*, January 28, 1917.

64. (No first name provided) Allerton, "Montreal Emerges to Say Game Still Lives," *The Sporting News*, March 22, 1917, 7.

65. Harry Sandager, "This Dope May Cheer Gloomy A.A. Moguls," *The Sporting News*, June 7, 1917, 1.

66. "Barrow May Form Six-Club Circuit," *New York Times*, December 10, 1917.

67. The rumor mill throughout the Great War suggested that Toronto and Baltimore were the front-runners to acquire a major league team if an established club wished to relocate. *The Sporting News* argued that Toronto was the better of the two options, given the fan support afforded to the Maple Leafs during the Great War. Whenever a major league team appeared to be on shaky ground, rumors swirled about a possible relocation to Toronto. Perhaps the option of moving a team to Toronto was used by certain major league owners as leverage to an apathetic fan base. In any event, these rumors were more fiction than fact. No team changed cities during the Great War.

68. Gordon Belyea, "Toronto Gulps Down Another Bitter Pill," *The Sporting News*, December 6, 1917, 5.

69. *Ibid.*

70. Gordon Belyea, "Toronto Resentful Over Barrow Deal," *The Sporting News*, December 27, 1917, 7.

71. In December 1917, team owners voted 5–3 to drop Barrow's annual salary to $2,500 from $7,500. The owners from Toronto, Montreal and Newark proposed a salary of $4,000 but were defeated. The account can be found in *The Sporting News* (December 27, 1917). Out of principle, Barrow left the IL and managed the Boston Red Sox in 1918 to a World Series title. His managerial duties in Boston lasted until 1920. He was then hired by the New York Yankees as their general manager and was the architect of the team from 1920–1945, a span that saw the Yankees win 10 World Series crowns. He has since been enshrined in the Baseball Hall of Fame in Cooperstown.

72. Gordon Belyea, "Jim McCaffery Says Lajoie's Not Going," *The Sporting News*, January 31, 1918, 1.

73. "Big Minor League May Retire Today," *New York Times*, February 11, 1918.

74. *Ibid.*

75. Belyea, "Jim McCaffery Says Lajoie's Not Going."

76. "Big Minor League Votes to Disband," *New York Times*, March 29, 1918.

77. *Ibid.*

78. Perhaps the IL's financial woes forced McCaffery to cast his ballot for dissolution, despite his desire for the Maple Leafs to play the 1918 season. As well, he might have had an alternate arrangement with other clubs in mind or tentatively in place prior to the vote.

79. Teams from the IL that joined the newer version of the IL in 1918 were Baltimore, Toronto, Rochester, Buffalo, and Newark. Clubs from Jersey City, Binghamton, and Syracuse/Hamilton joined them for the 1918 season.

80. Gordon Belyea, "Lajoie Dispute as Toronto Views It," *The Sporting News*, April 4, 1918, 6.

81. *Ibid.*

82. Wilbert Robinson managed the Brooklyn Dodgers from 1914 to 1931 and was inducted into the Baseball Hall of Fame in 1945.

83. Gordon Belyea, "Faith in McCaffery Was Not Misplaced," *The Sporting News*, April 11, 1918, 5.

84. "Commission Unties Knots in Tangled International Case," *The Sporting News*, April 18, 1918, 3.

85. "Minors May Take Up International Fight," *The Sporting News*, May 9, 1918, 1.

86. Gordon Belyea "War Delays But Can't Kill Game in Toronto," *The Sporting News*, May 23, 1918, 3.

87. *Ibid.*

88. "Call Lajoie Bad Failure," *The Globe*, July 16, 1918, 6.

89. Belyea, "War Delays But Can't Kill Game in Toronto."

90. The Maple Leafs finished with an 88–39 record, one game better than the Bingoes. The Binghamton Bingoes, Jersey City Skeeters, and the Syracuse Stars replaced the Montreal Royals, Richmond Virginians, and Providence Grays. The Stars only lasted until August in Syracuse when they were relocated to Hamilton, Ontario. The team did not play the 1919 season and the Reading Coal Barons replaced them.

91. Belyea, "Faith in McCaffery Was Not Misplaced."

92. *Ibid.*

93. It must be remembered that night games were still more than a decade away. The first lit night game occurred in 1930 and was the brainchild of the Negro Leagues. Five years later, the Cincinnati Reds brought it to the majors. For more information, consult David Pietrusza, *Lights On! The Wild Century-Long Saga of Night Baseball* (Lanham, MD: Scarecrow, 1997).

94. (No first name provided) Pyke, "Talk of Canadian Revival," *The Sporting News*, April 18, 1918, 2.

95. "National Leaguers to Consider Draft," *The Sporting News*, June 6, 1918, 1.

96. Readers that would like to learn more about baseball's American experience during the First World War are encouraged to consult Jim Leeke's *From the Dugouts to the Trenches: Baseball During the Great War* (Lincoln: University of Nebraska Press, 2017)

97. George Robbins, "Baker Rule a Blow to Nation's Morale," *The Sporting News*, July 25, 1918, 1.

98. *Ibid.*

99. "Plays Right into Hands of Stealers," *The Sporting News*, July 25, 1918, 1.

100. "Baker May Yet See Baseball Side of It," *The Sporting News*, July 25, 1918, 1.

101. "Association Rather Hasty," *The Sporting News*, July 25, 1918, 1.

102. "International May Stick," *The Sporting News*, July 25, 1918, 1.

103. The World Series was almost cancelled after the fourth game because word had spread that the owners were not going to award players on the Red Sox and Cubs with their World Series bonuses ($2,000 for each player on the winning team, $1,400 for each player on the losing team). With 25,000 fans in Boston's Fenway Park awaiting Game Four, Boston Mayor Fitzgerald appealed to the players' patriotism who ultimately compromised by proposing that their World Series shares be donated to a war charity. The World Series was completed but, somehow, the owners escaped making the donations. Lowenfish's *The Imperfect Diamond*, 96–98.

104. "Baker Approves World's Series," *New York Times*, August 23, 1918.

105. Greenham, "On the Battlefront," 34–50.

The Typewriter Boys of Summer (1887–1920)

PETER WEIL

The combination of typewriter companies and baseball was a part of the larger creation of an American culture in which the game became a vital part of the lives of workers in the burgeoning factories of the 1880–1920 period and beyond. Predictability was the central goal of factory managers. Employees worked on highly regimented production lines that embodied repetitive activities day after day. Baseball, with its emphasis on the interplay of individual skills, recognition of individual achievement, and the possibility of changing and unpredictable outcomes, became a positive embodiment of the values of the workers that stood in stark contrast to their factory lives. In the early post–Civil War period, factory owners were reluctant even to hire workers who played baseball. However, starting in the late 1880s, the owners changed their views, adopting much of the workers' subcultural ideas about baseball as they attempted to mediate laborers' demands, to control laborers' free time, and to advertise their companies that manufactured the new technologies. A more general goal was to assert in the public arena that factories deeply cared about the welfare of their employees. Notwithstanding these mixed, often conflicting motivations and goals, the creation and sporting play of typewriter factory baseball teams were important for the players, their employers, and their communities. This article provides an overview of these developments in the sport in the context of the typewriter industry.

THE COMBINATION OF TYPEWRITERS and baseball was one of the true grand slams in industrial history.[1] The Olivers (established in 1902), seen within

Base Ball 12, pp. 221–238
ISSN 1934-2802 (Print) / ISSN 1934-3167 (Online)
978-1-4766-7473-5 (Print) / 978-1-4766-4112-6 (ebook)

practicing near their factory at the Woodstock fairgrounds field in Wood-stock, Illinois (1906–07), were only one of several, albeit the most famous, of the writing machine teams that played from the late nineteenth century to the first half of the twentieth century.[2] Other official factory teams, with their earliest documented dates, included Caligraph (American Writing Machine, 1888), Wagner (maker of Underwood, 1900), Remington (1904), Underwood (1904), Smith Premier (1907), Royal (1908), Yost (1908), Secor (1909), El-liott-Fisher (1910–11), Noiseless (1910), Monarch (1913), Standard (Corona, 1913),[3] and Molle (1920). These teams are generally categorized as semipro because, whether the members were paid or not for playing baseball, their activity on the team usually was linked to their compensation as employees at a factory. Contemporary media reported the existence of Caligraph, Secor, Elliott-Fisher, Noiseless, and Molle squads only once, and then only briefly. The discussion here will feature especially those noted more frequently, in-cluding Oliver and the Union Trust teams (Remington, Smith Premier, Yost, and Monarch), and, more briefly, Underwood, Corona, and Royal.

I discuss here the beginnings of this happy synthesis of typewriters and baseball, drawing upon published sources, especially period newspapers and magazines. My use of such sources restricts my discussion to typewriter company teams that made the news. Even then, media coverage during this period was uneven and happenstance, often lacking final scores and other de-tails. There may have been other official company teams and, also, unofficial ones organized by employees on their own that were never reported, or that I missed in my searching of several news media databases.

Typewriter Companies Accept Baseball

Before discussing specific typewriter factory teams, a bit of general his-tory concerning the development of industries and the sport of baseball is needed to understand better the specifics concerning writing machine fac-tory teams. Before the end of the Civil War (1861–65) in the United States, baseball already was becoming a popular American pastime, but industrial companies tended to resist hiring men who regularly participated in the sport. They saw baseball as a distraction that made employees less attentive to their jobs. These firms blamed early-morning weekday practice sessions required by amateur and semipro teams.

However, in the post–Civil War period, the number and size of factories greatly expanded, requiring far more workers. Owners could ill afford seeing playing baseball as a mark against the skilled and semi-skilled employees they sought to hire. Factories began sponsoring teams, and that number increased later on, after—as companies responded to employee pressure—factory owners shrank the workweek from 65 hours in 1865 to between 50 and 56 hours by the 1890s. Company owners and factory managers, worried that this increased leisure time would result in heavy drinking and other work and family problems for employees, came to see factory- and sales office-sponsored baseball teams as means to control employees' new freedom, to the good of the companies and the employees.

Another set of factors that brought about a change in industrialists' perspectives, especially those managing the much larger factories of the 1890s and beyond, was the increased competition they faced for skilled labor. In the case of companies like Remington, Underwood, and Royal, for example, their strong emphasis on marketing to Europe required hiring employees who were literate in German, French, Russian, and other languages. Often they were the very same laborers who had been reared in European industrial apprentice systems.

In addition, some companies saw baseball teams as a form of advertising in a culture where baseball had become the most popular local and national sport.

The final stimulus for the willingness—even, for some companies, the desire—to create factory teams was the growing labor unrest after 1890. Companies came to see participation by employees in company-related leisure activities to solidify their identity with the interests of the company and to create an esprit de corps among their workers. It was in this historical context that factory baseball teams, paralleling those of sales offices, multiplied and developed.

During the next decade, the first of what became numerous national and local distribution and sales office writing machine company teams were formed. Ironically, the earliest of these were reported for the United Kingdom, home of cricket, not baseball. There, the Wyckoff, Seamans, and Benedict Remington team was organized no later than 1895 by the UK national and British Empire main office in London. In that year, they played the Derby city team and lost badly, 34–17, but later in the season persisted to become the London Baseball Association champions.

In the U.S., major sales office baseball teams were formed in the first decade of the twentieth century, including those for the main offices in New York City of Underwood (1905) and WSB Remington (1907). For example, the central office's Underwood team, the "Utes," in April 1910. The Utes had their own field in Brooklyn, New York (52nd St. and 20th Ave.), where they played the New York City Remington office team on July 15, 1907, and won

13–8 in what was called a "lively batting contest." Branch offices and smaller, local agencies of typewriter companies formed teams in the first half of the last century in much of the U.S., but especially in New England and the Midwest. While interesting and important in the history of typewriter companies, these marketing-based baseball organizations are not the focus of this article.[4] Instead, I will present here an overview of typewriter factory teams.

Typewriter Factory Baseball Team Histories

Caligraph

The Caligraph team was the first documented typewriter factory team, but it was mentioned only once in the media, in 1888. At that point, the company had already moved production in 1885 from Corry, Pennsylvania, to Hartford, Connecticut, a city that was later to become a major nexus for typewriter and other industrial baseball activity. The Caligraphs played the Hartford Machine Screw Co. at a game sponsored by that company's employees association.

Oliver

The earliest substantial info on an American typewriter factory team is about the Olivers in 1902. The team was composed of workers from the Oliver Typewriter factory in Woodstock, Illinois. While this statement is accurate, it ignores a reality that was to become common concerning the creation and operation of such teams. Oliver, in 1902, followed by other typewriter companies, began recruiting some workers whose primary qualification was their known skills as baseball players on semipro, collegiate, and pro teams. In the first documented instance of this practice, Oliver that year recruited George Moriarty, who had played on a non-industrial semi-pro team and was subsequently recruited by the nearby Chicago Cubs the very next year.

The Olivers first year and much of the second year were so successful that the Chicago Cubs agreed to play the typewriter team in a demonstration game. As to be expected, the Cubs triumphed, 12–0. But the 19-year-old Moriarty's stellar performance in the game resulted in his being hired by the Cubs and becoming the youngest player on a major league team. Making a poor showing, the next year he was sent down to the minors, but later he reentered the majors, ending up on the Detroit Tigers, where he finished his playing career.

Over the years, the strength of the Olivers, matched by their cockiness,

1902 Oliver Typewriter team practiced at Woodstock Fairgrounds.

Sign announced a 1902 Chicago Cubs World Series win to Oliver assemblers.

earned them the enmity of many of their opponents. This began early in their first season when the Olivers defeated the Chicago Athletes 8–0, and, when the winners left the field, the Olivers gave each Athletes player a goose egg.

The Olivers' first uniform used the original company logo, "The Oliver." Around 1906, the logo on the jerseys was changed to an early form of the combined "OTCO" symbol. The workers' enthusiasm for their own team probably stemmed from their love of the sport itself, as can be seen in the photo from the Oliver assembly room in October 1907, where the workers made note of a Cubs win over the Detroit Tigers in the World Series that year.

The creation of the Oliver team in 1902 took place at the same time as other efforts to engage the company's employees in company-organized activities outside the Woodstock factory. For example, a baseball (not softball) team was set up for women who worked at the factory, and a brass band made up of factory men was organized to support the Olivers—and, some years later, to play concerts in a bandstand built by the company in the center of the town. The band marched and played through the streets of any location where the Olivers had a game and blared away to welcome the team on and off the field and to celebrate any on-field successes, much as today's home runs are marked by music. The band also played in holiday parades of the Olivers' hometown, Woodstock. It often marched with the team to the fairgrounds, where the community had built a small baseball stadium for them to play in. The popularity of the Oliver Company factory team and the factory band and the importance of both to the community are indicated by the fans' regular monetary contributions, which helped pay for equipment and travel. In addition to constructing a baseball field, community support included the purchase of tickets for attendance, which guaranteed the existence of this and other typewriter factories' teams and bands. At the end of the season, any extra funds were commonly used by the Olivers and by other typewriter factory squads to reward players for making the most runs, the most home runs, and the most runs batted in, and stealing the most bases. In the case of the Olivers, the company's attempts to engage employees in activities external to their work in the factory were not initially adequate to avoid a 1903 strike, but subsequently, labor relations did improve.

Remington

Two years after Oliver's team began, the Remington Typewriter Company, the most powerful component of the Union Trust, decided to form their own baseball team in 1904, naming it "the Remington Works." Remington was the dominant component of the Union Writing Machine Company, generally referred to as the "Union Trust."[5] All the Trust's surviving smaller members, except American Writing Machine, subsequently formed teams as well, but their typewriter factory competitors were limited to those within the Trust. Enmity between the Union Trust and other typewriter factories thus affected typewriter company baseball.

The decision to organize a baseball team was a part of the Remington management's response to strikes in 1903 at two of the major typewriter manufacturers, Underwood and Oliver. Remington also was concerned about its own labor relations problems, which had developed that same year in Remington's alignment department, concerning extra pay for the special language skills required to install Cyrillic types on machines being exported to Russia properly. Remington's first response was to introduce an employee loyalty program in May 1903, in which employees with 10 or more years of service whom the company judged as loyal and obedient, would be given gold and enamel badges and an annual bonus of $100.[6]

By 1904, factory-organized baseball teams were organized at Remington and the Smith Premier factory in Syracuse, New York. While the Remingtons did play two typewriter-related teams, the Smith Premier factory one and the Typewriter Exchange (Boston, Massachusetts) marketing team that year, the Remingtons primarily played against community teams from the area.[7] By 1905, Remingtons factory managers initiated new ways of relating to and controlling their employees. The company organized the intramural Typewriter Baseball League within the Ilion factory. The regular production-line male employees were placed on teams representing the seven departments of the factory and competed in a regular schedule both to select the champion department and to discover the best players to assign to the Remington Works nine who represented the factory in games with external baseball teams. The factory's foremen, the immediate supervisors of the workers, were excluded from these workers baseball teams. However, they were instructed to organize cricket teams for themselves.

Originally, the company paid for baseball uniforms and some equipment. But much of the funding for the Remington (and other) baseball squads came from the players themselves, members of the Ilion community where the factory was located, and admission charges, which were originally a dime, but by 1910 were raised to a quarter. These funding arrangements were like those we have seen for the Olivers and paralleled those for other typewriter factory teams. The Remington and other typewriter factory teams also raised additional funds though sponsoring entrance fee dances and musical performances. Practice for the internal factory teams took place during the lunch hour and at least one evening after work per week, and games originally were played on Saturday afternoon. For the Works team, these activities were expanded to include Sunday, and then at least one weekday game. Moreover, the employee reward ceremony and the Works baseball team were brought together for the first time in 1905 at the first Remington Field Day, which was held on a large sports field at a company-supplied stadium.

The Remington Typewriter Band was also launched as an employee-staffed organization to increase participation by workers after work. The band first played at the Field Day in 1905, and then regularly performed at the Remingtons' games. By 1909, the now well-known band also played concerts at non-sporting venues, as below at Cooperstown, New York. That first Field Day in 1905 included a baseball game between the Remingtons and the Savage Arms team from Westfield, Massachusetts, who won the game. The 1905 Field Day also included other sports competitions, such as tugs of war, and more of these were added by 1906, including an indoor foot race that was held the same week as the actual Field Day. The Remington Works team played the neighboring Remington Arms nine at the 1906 event in a major grudge game. The Remington Works won in a close game, 7–6, in five innings. Across is a photograph of the 1906 Remingtons. Vital to their win that day and their successful season was the speed of Paul Risedorf, who had won the 220-yard indoor race in 24 seconds. He is shown in the team picture (front row, second from the left).

The Remington Typewriters again played the Remington Arms team at the 1908 Field Day. The game was so important to the typewriter company that it organized a special squad named the "All Typewriters" that included members of teams from Remington, Smith Premier, and Monarch. To prepare this hybrid lineup for the competition, they trained together every day for three weeks and were primarily fed raw beef supplied, most probably, by the Remington factory. To further strengthen the All-Typewriters, the team

1909 Remington Typewriter band played at Cooperstown.

1906 Remington Typewriter Co. team.

managers recruited "Johnny" Clark, a pitcher from a nearby (but unnamed) college team, just for this game. Clark's arm was compared favorably in the media to that of Leon "Red" Ames of the New York Giants. Even with a red protein-enriched hybrid team and a stellar ringer battery, the All-Typewriters lost. The unbeaten Arms nine triumphed over the All-Typewriters, 18–15.

During the 1904–1908 seasons, the Remington Works team played a wide array of local and regional non-industrial and industrial teams. None of these competitions were under any league organization, but in 1909, the club joined the Commercial Athletic League and became the 1909 Central New York Champions.

This League included the Underwood factory team. For the first time Remington might have played a typewriter team outside the Union Trust. However, any games between the squads of these two companies were not reported in the media I researched. Remington's joining of this League made season management more efficient, but it did not preclude the Remington squad from scheduling games with non-league teams. When Remington and other typewriter factory teams played outside their leagues, the competitions were often referred to as "practice games." However, these non-league games

1912–15 Yost Typewriter Co. team with their products.

were an essential part of a team's reputation and their ability to attract strong competitors and large, entrance fee-paying crowds.

Remington continued to play in this manner over the next several years and used its Field Day to feature baseball competitions with two other Union Trust teams, Yost in 1913 and Smith Premier in 1912 and 1914–17. The Yost nine trampled the Remington squad, 10–1, to win the "Typewriter Baseball Championship" at the 1913 Field Day. Workers from the Smith Premier and Monarch factories participated in other sports at that Field Day, but the year before, in the first of a series of hotly contested Field Day baseball games between Remington and Smith Premier, Remington won. The Remington Types further embarrassed the Smith Premiers on the Field Day in 1916, trouncing them 9–0. McCoy, the Remington pitcher, threw a no-hitter. As one reporter sarcastically said about this defeat, "The fact is that the Smith Premier boys made a clean score, such as it was, for a score of no runs, no hits, and no errors and nine additional ciphers for each inning was their portion."

Smith Premier

Notwithstanding such disdain based on a single game, the Smith Premier team was not a weak one, and over several years often triumphed over its rivals. One instance of this team's power included its strong win, 9–2, over its cross-town Syracuse nemesis, the Monarch factory squad, on their shared

1915 Field Day, in front of a crowd of 3,000 at Longbranch Park in Syracuse. That success was due, in part, to the pitching of Orrin Day. He was not an employee of Smith Premier and had recently played for a Central New York Amateur League team. The ringer arrangement was common by this time in factory team baseball and semipro baseball in general. The shared field day included the wearing of the same badge by members and supporters of both teams.[8]

Yost

Yost, with its factory at Bridgeport, Connecticut, was part of the same holding company as Smith Premier. This business fact resulted in the team's often being referred to as the "Union Typewriters," a name not used for others in the Trust. The Yost squad is first reported to have played games in 1907, and in 1908, they competed in their city's Industrial Baseball League and won the league's championship. This community league, which included some teams from outside the city, specifically required all members of competing teams to be working in the factory of a member team. Not all semipro industrial leagues had such a rule, and, if they did, the rule was generally not enforced. However, this league did apply it. Yost, by July of 1909, was by far the strongest team in the league and was expected to win the championship again.

But the Yost nine became involved in a major controversy concerning the full-time factory employee requirement that threatened to cost them wins in four games, virtually eliminating any chance to achieve the championship. One opponent, the second-place Crane Valve Co. squad from Stamford, Connecticut, protested Yost's win in a game where the Yosts included an employee, Bill Regenery, who the Cranes claimed no longer worked at the factory. Three other teams joined the Cranes, asking that Yost's wins be negated for all games played by Regenery. Yost admitted that the player was absent from the factory but asserted that he was only temporarily assigned to the Yost sales and repair office in New York City. In August, the League managers met and took all four wins and an additional fifth one away from Yost. The decision was a hotly contested one, even among the managers of the league teams. This was primarily because the Yosts were a strong, successful team, who drew large numbers of paying fans wherever they went, earning more than $1000 alone for the League's pool in 1910. The decision against the Yosts resulted in their picking up their equipment and abandoning the league. The squad then played out the season against far less competitive non-league teams, such as the Brooklawn Country Club (Fairfield County, Connecticut), triumphing with a win of 11–1.

By 1913, the Yosts, now often referred to as the "Remington-Yost" team, had rejoined the Bridgeport Industrial League, and played other teams outside it. As an example, the Yosts played the Black Rocks in the league one day in May, and, the next day, a Norwalk (Connecticut) team outside the organization. They also played in demonstration games, the most famous of which were the 1913 and 1914 contests in Bridgeport against an all-Chinese team from the University of Hawaii. The Remington-Yost team lost both contests. But, as we have seen, they won the Typewriter Factory championship in 1913 when they met the Remington Types at the Field Day that same year.

The Yost factory at Bridgeport, Connecticut, was manufacturing the nos. 15 and 20 frontstrike machines the year Remington played the Yosts. The Yost team that triumphed looked like the one in the photograph included herein, posing with examples of the devices they made. The Yost nine, labeled the "Rem-Yosts," played in the 1915 season, and the media articles focus exclusively on a series of grudge games with the Remington Arms nine. I found nothing reported on the Yosts after 1915, though most sources indicate that production at the Yost factory continued until 1924.

Underwood

The Underwood Typewriter Company factory baseball team is first documented in 1904, the same year that the Remington Types began. The Wagner factory moved in 1901 from Bayonne, New Jersey, to Hartford, Connecticut. While Wagner-Underwood had a team in its old home, I found no evidence this team continued after the move to Hartford. The new facility officially became an Underwood one in 1903, with the dissolution of Wagner as the managing manufacturer. The next year, the new team was formed by recruiting men from all the departments.

In their initial year, the Underwoods played local squads from both smaller and larger non-typewriter companies and the Boston Typewriter Exchange. But they did not join any roundball leagues until 1909, the year Underwood joined other factories in the Hartford area (Royal Typewriter, Pope Manufacturing Co., Electric Vehicle, Billings and Spencer, and some smaller factories, such as TATA) to form the Commercial Athletics Association (CAA). The CAA divided their teams into letter-designated leagues, and Underwood was in "B." The Underwoods became the Association's Champions, winning its Spalding Trophy that first year by vanquishing the TATA nine 14–1. In 1910, the Underwoods continued to play well, but the new Association appears to have collapsed, and the team made its own arrangements for games. I found nothing more on the team until 1916, when they played the Sing Sing Correctional Facility (Ossining, New York) team in a demonstration game, for which no score was reported. In 1917, the Hartford factory company left the Association and joined the Commercial Athletic League, a larger organization in which it competed during the next decade.

Royal

The Royal Typewriter Co. factory team was the next one formed. It was organized in 1908, the year the company began manufacturing in Hartford. Formally, the squad was called the "Royal Typewriter Baseball Association." Its financial arrangements and need to raise money from players' own pockets were like those described for the Oliver team. However, the Royal Association paid each player $75 per year; payment for seasonal achievements, such as the most home runs, was the highest documented for any pre–1920 team, at $45 for each feat. Throughout their long history, the Royals were well-known and somewhat resented because of their recruiting the best players from their opponents' teams. The Royals' manager, A.A. McKay, was experienced and had managed the 1900 Wagner factory team in New Jersey.

From the beginning, Royal was serious about baseball, not only hiring a seasoned coach but also fully outfitting the team in handsome, dark royal blue uniforms. Their players practiced three nights per week after work, instead of the usual one, and were expected to play in scrub games the other two. The next year the Royals joined the Commercial Association, but they also regularly played teams outside the league. For example, that year they met on the diamond with squads from towns like Unionville and New Britain and with those from institutions, e.g., Middletown Hospital and even with private clubs like the Bushnell Athletic Club.

In 1910, the Royal company reportedly built the finest of the baseball fields constructed by any of the typewriter companies in Connecticut, with bleachers that held 400 fans. It was far enough away from the factory that the company's management offered a reward to any player who hit a home run that broke a factory window. This outstanding diamond helped them attract highly competitive opponents who wanted to play on such a beautiful field. That year they played the first-year team from Middletown, Connecticut's, Noiseless Typewriter, but the rest of the Royals' opponents did not manufacture typewriters.

Sometimes towns with several baseball squads challenged the powerful Royals, assembling a single team from two or more local teams to represent the town, as when an "All-Hartfords" semi-pro team was assembled for that purpose in 1911. The Royal squad joined the Hartford City League the next year.

Shifting leagues, participating in the games of two leagues at once, and playing additional non-league games were all part of the behavior of the industrial teams like the Royals. The point is they wanted to play baseball and wanted to play against tough teams. In 1914, the Royals joined the Connecticut State Baseball League, but, in 1915, they joined the Connecticut Independent Baseball League and continued playing in the State League and non-league games. Joining multiple leagues and shifting from one league to another were not practices unique to the Royals. Rather, they were common practices for many typewriter factory teams. Also by 1915, the Hartford management assembled a Royal Fife and Drum Corps to support the Royals nine and to perform in parades and other venues.

Standard and Corona

The new Groton, New York, factory of the Standard Typewriter Company, a far smaller manufacturer than Remington, Underwood, and Royal, began producing Standard Folding machines in late 1909, with only about 200 employees. I found no published information on a Standards team.[9] However, what is clear is the evidence that Standard Typewriter had organized a team playing as the "Coronas" in the 1913 season, just after the new Corona model 3 had replaced the Standard Folding 2.

In 1913, the Standard company organized the "Corona Baseball Club." Play was encouraged but voluntary, and each member had to pay an annual fee to support the team. The amount for that first year is not known, but by 1918, it was about $5 per year. The Coronas had such a strong reputation by the beginning of 1915 that, for an early season demonstration game, a hybrid All-Auburn team to oppose them was made up of the strongest players from the Auburn (New York) town team, the All-Collegiates (i.e., Ithaca's Cornell University and Ithaca College squads playing together), and the Midnight Sons. The results were not discovered. At some point between 1913 and 1917, the factory built the Corona Athletic Field in Groton for their team and established the Corona Typewriter Band, which played roles like those in support of the baseball teams of other writing machine factories. The Coronas played ball for at least the next thirty years.

Factory Support for Major League Baseball

While many typewriter factories never fielded a baseball team, the companies and their workers and the typewriter company's customers usually

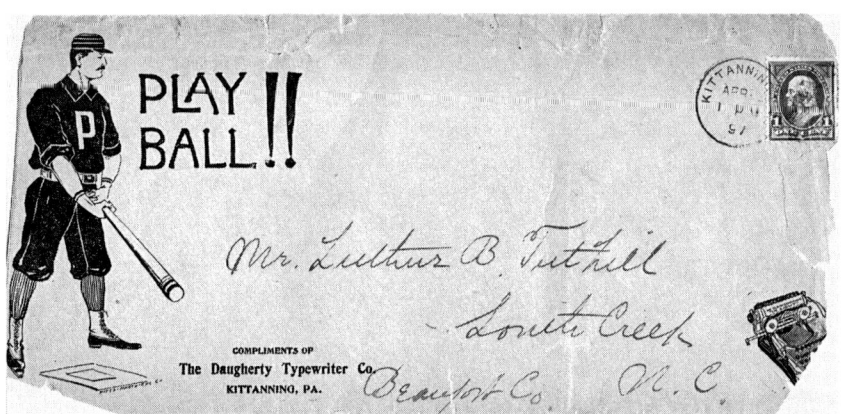

Daugherty Typewriter supported the Allegheny (Pittsburgh) Pirates in 1897.

were big baseball fans. For example, in 1897, Daugherty Typewriter Company of Kittanning, Pennsylvania, used envelopes with a baseball theme to seek customers and to send bills. The companies that only later created teams also saw in baseball an effective means to reach their potential customers. Monarch, for example, issued a series of baseball trade cards in 1911, two years before it had a team. The cards featured star players, such as one of Eddie Collins, star second baseman of the Philadelphia Athletics.

Conclusion

At first glance, typewriters and baseball appear to be no more connected than bicycles and fish, but they did come together. And this divine combination did so in a manner that generated immense fun for factory workers and their fans. The typewriter and its manufacturing developed while baseball became a central part of the lives of workers who were working on highly regimented production lines in the growing American factories for more hours, more and more intensely, than at any other time in American history. The subculture of factory workers developed during rapid industrial growth and changes in relationships between factory owners and their employees. Baseball, with its emphasis on the interplay of individual skills and the recognition of individual achievement, team identity, and the possibility of changing outcomes, became a positive embodiment of the values of the workers. This was in a world in which, otherwise, much of their lives was controlled by others and daily results at the factory were highly predictable, itself a goal of the factory owners. Ironically, it was just that aspect of worker identity that was adopted by typewriter factory owners and by other industrial managers to attempt to mediate laborers' demands, to control laborers' free time, and to advertise the companies that made the new technologies. A more general goal was to assert in the public arena that factories deeply cared about the welfare of their employees. Notwithstanding these mixed, often conflicting motivations and goals, the creation and sporting play of typewriter factory baseball teams were necessary for the players, their employers, their communities. Let's remember and celebrate the typewriter boys of summer. Play Ball!

Acknowledgments

I greatly appreciate the assistance of Tyler Anderson, Mike Brown, Greg Fudacz, Bert Kerschbaumer, Jos Legrand, and Paul Robert in writing this article. I also appreciate the assistance of the Stamford (Connecticut) Historical Society concerning my questions about the possible existence of a Blickensderfer Typewriter factory baseball team. Special thanks goes to Lee Lowenfish for his encouragement to send this to Donald Jensen, and to Anne Sloan for her thoughtful and vital editorial suggestions.

Notes

1. An earlier version of this article appeared in *ETCetera*, No. 125 (2019): 8–16. The data herein are from many sources, especially numerous newspapers and magazines. Please note that, in order to conserve space, if the same newspaper is sourced from multiple dates, the dates of the articles will follow the name of the publication. Sources include: *American Machinist* Vol. 28, no; 1 (1905), 245; Nancy L. Baker, *Images of America: Woodstock*. (Chicago: Arcadia Publishing Co., 2006); "Baseball: Derby vs; Remingtons." *Reynolds (London, England) Newspaper*, May 12, 1895; *Bridgeport (CT) Times and Evening Farmer*, 2/12/1909, 4/23/1909, 7/14/1909, 8/20/1909, 8/26/1909; 3/22/1910, 6/17/1910, 5/19/1912, 10/25/1912, 3 /23/1913, 5/1913; 6/23/13; and 9/23/1915; *Buffalo (NY) Evening News*, 6/7/1905 and 5/1/1909; "Underwood Typewriter Outing" *Buffalo (NY) Courier*, August 1904; *Chicago Daily Tribune*, May 31, 1903; "Commercial A.A. Games." *Sunday [Brooklyn, NY] Daily Eagle*, September 12, 1909; "Corona Team Wants Games." *Rochester Democrat and Chronicle*, June 26, 1920; "Exchange 6, Underwood 3." *Boston Sunday Globe*, June 19, 1904; "Factory Costs and Business Methods: Encouragement of Employees by Wyckoff, Seamans and Benedict," *Iron Age* (April 24, 1905): 509; "Industrial League Games." *Oshkosh (WI) Daily Northwestern*, June 4, 1920; *Ithaca (NY) News*, 10/13/20 and 5/19/21; R.G. Knowles and Richard Morton. *Baseball*. (New York: George Rutledge and Co, Ltd, 1896); "Molle to Play Tustin." *Oshkosh (WI) Daily Northwestern*, June 17, 1921; *New Haven Morning Journal Courier*, August 18, 1888; Clarence Vernon Noble, "The Cost of Living in a Small Factory Town [Groton, New York]" (Ph. D., Cornell University, 1925); "Old Rivals to Meet." *Washington Herald*, May 29, 1911; "Oliver Baseball Team: Players Nearly All Selected and First

Game Arranged." *The Woodstock Sentinel* May 8, 1902; "Opening of Remington Typewriter Baseball Park," *The Remington Budget* Vol. IV, No. 9 (1905), 1; "Premium on Faithfulness." *New York Times,* May 22, 1903, "Realization of Ideals in Industrial Engineering," *Transactions of the American Society of Industrial Engineering* Vol. 27 (1906): 363–372; "Remington 17, Monroes 1." *Rochester Democrat and Chronicle,* May 22, 1905; "Remington Typewriter Annual Field Day," *Journal of Commercial Education* Vol. 32 (1908): 150–151; "Remington Field Day," *New York (NY) Tribune,* June 28, 1909; "Remington Typewriter Field Day," *The Typewriter World* Vol. 40, No; 1 (1912): 94; Paul Robert and Peter Weil; *Typewriter: A Celebration of the Ultimate Writing Machine.* (New York: Sterling, 2016); Harold Seymour. *Baseball: The People's Game.* (New York: Oxford University Press, 1990); "Strikes at Typewriter Factories" *Syracuse Post-Standard,* September 24, 1906; *The Typewriter and Phonographic World* (1903): 470–476; *Thompsonville (CT) Press,* September 8, 1910; "3000 Attend Employees Annual Outing"; *Syracuse (NY) Herald,* June 27, 1915; "Trophy for Calafin Team." *New York Daily Tribune,* July 31, 1910; *Typewriter Topics* (September 1915); "Twelfth Annual Remington Field Day," *Typewriter Topics* (August 1916): 47; "Typewriter Day in Ilion," *Remington Notes* vol. 1 (1906): 1–2; "Typewriter Visibility No Longer Talking Point," *Printers' Ink* (1909): 10–12; "Typewriting Notes," *The Phonetic Journal,* (1895): 610;Peter Weil, "Ephemera: Remington Field Day," *ETCetera* No; 90, (2010): 8–10; Peter Weil, "New Information on the First Remington Field Day," *ETCetera* No; 91 (2010), 16; "What's Going On," *Typewriter Topics* Vol. 6 (1907): 156; "Win Fifth Straight Game"; *Austin Daily Statesman,* May 1, 1915; http://herkimer.nygenweb. net/ilion/ilionsocial.html;http://www.ilionalumni.com/maincovers/2016_03_cw_seamans. html;https://www.madeinchicagomuseum.com;https://oztypewriter.blogspot.com/2012/03/ from-oliver-typewriter-factory-floor-to.html;http://www.baseball-reference.com/minors/ team.cgi?id=ae7e00bc; http://www.covehurst.net/ddyte/brooklyn/otherparks.html.

2. This photograph and ephemera used in this article are from the author's collection.

3. Based on a photograph, the Corona team was preceded by an earlier one from the original parent firm, Standard Typewriter Co. The date of the possible Standard nine photo, which is displayed in the discussion of the Corona team, is not marked on it. However, it dates from the 1910–1912 period, after the Standard factory became fully operational in early 1910. The introduction of Standard's third model, the Corona 3, apparently was the basis for the changing of the team's name in 1913, the first baseball season that followed the new identity for the factory's product. Lastly, no mention of the Standard Typewriter team was found in published sources.

4. These sales office teams are far too numerous to discuss within this article, but one reason for excluding them here is that the cultures of factory workers and sales staffs were somewhat different ones. The greatest difference was the emphasis in sales offices on the strong values of highly individualistic competition to reach both personal and company goals, and the American concepts of this pre–1920 period that sales staffs were members of a social class superior to that of factory workers. Thus, while these corporate bases have similarities and are linked, they are different enough for them to be addressed separately.

5. The Union Trust was created in 1892 as the Union Writing Machine Co. and renamed in 1908 as the Union Typewriter Company. That was dissolved in 1913, with Remington Typewriter Co. taking over direct control of all the products formerly produced within the Trust. The Trust ultimately included Smith Premier, Yost, Monarch, American Writing Machine, and Densmore. For discussion of the context concerning baseball at Remington and its related Trust affiliates, see Weil, June 2010, 8–10 and September 2010, 16.

6. The average pay of the workers in the Remington Factory in 1903 was around 27 cents per hour or $750 per year ($19,950 in 2018 dollars). Thus the $100 ($2,850 in 2018 dollars) bonus represented a significant addition, more than 13 percent, to the pay of employees who were judged to be loyal and competent throughout their employment, starting in their eleventh year as employees. To be considered "loyal," an employee could not participate in labor organizing.

7. Between 1901 and 1905, Ilion was home to a semipro mid–New York State Baseball League team, the Typewriters. It was not affiliated with the Remington Co. Thus, in the early years of the Remington team, it was not called the "Remington Typewriters." Instead, it usually

was referred to as the "Remingtons" and the "Remington Works" team. However, by 1908 and later, the Works team was often also called the "Typewriters." To complicate matters further, the separate and independent Remington Arms Co. created its own baseball team, but on their uniforms and in media stories it was regularly identified as the "Remington Arms" team to distinguish it from its neighboring factory's squad.

8. In 1915, both organizations had been fully absorbed into the Remington Typewriter Co.

9. The Standard Typewriter Co. became the Corona Typewriter Co. in 1914, thus aligning its name with its product, the Corona typewriter.

Unfamiliar Side of the Coin

Mutual vs. Atlantic, August 1863

Eric Miklich

Realizing the public was willing to pay to witness high quality base-ball, which began in 1858, the more talented clubs attempted to improve continuously. Those efforts resulted in more fierce competition on the playing field, which probably occurred more than the print media cared to report. The August 3, 1863, meeting between the Mutual Club of New York and the Atlantic Club of Brooklyn, in fact, was so robust that the newspapers were forced to reveal to their readers the harsh level base-ball could reach. This match demonstrated that America's pastime was not always the romantically friendly competition many proclaim it to have been during this period.

The Atlantics

On August 4, 1863, the *Brooklyn Daily Eagle* proclaimed: "From the period of the organization of the Atlantic Base Ball Club, of this city, up to the close of the season of 1861, that club was invariably successful against every other one they encountered. Occasionally, of course, they would lose a single game, but from 1856 to 1862, they were successful in every series of home-and-home contests they were engaged in."[1] Whether in the nineteenth, twentieth, or twenty-first century, however, facts are forbidden to interfere when heartfelt moments are being conveyed.

Since their formation in 1855, the Atlantics had maintained top-tier

Base Ball 12, pp. 239–249
ISSN 1934-2802 (Print) / ISSN 1934-3167 (Online)
978-1-4766-7473-5 (Print) / 978-1-4766-4112-6 (ebook)

status. However, 1863 was the second year in a row that they were not the best. The Atlantics were defeated in a championship series by the Eckfords of Brooklyn BBC in 1862, which resulted in the Eckfords capturing the Silver Ball Trophy as well as the season's championship. The press did what they could to elevate the Atlantics to the pinnacle of baseball. Heartbroken, the *Eagle* stated that by "courtesy," the Eckfords, "who were also their warmest friends,"[2] were anointed the champion in 1862. It was in the *Eagle's* opinion that "in reality, there can be no champion club in base ball, as the rules are now."[3] In actuality, a club other than the *Eagle's* favorite was better and that was very difficult for the newspaper to accept.

Strong competition, the introduction of a championship trophy, large crowds, and fanatical betting could come together to produce immense emotions on the field. The Atlantics seemed to be the one entity to evoke such results and trouble historically surrounded the club and its supporters. Some of that trouble was self-imposed by the ball club. Known for being notoriously bad winners by running-up scores on clubs, regardless of their talent level as well having a reputation for being sore losers, by 1863 the Atlantics had had problems with several clubs: the Excelsiors, Eckfords, Enterprise, and Mutuals. Coupled with the ruffians, pickpockets, and gamblers who religiously followed the Atlantics, it was a reputation that developed continuously.

The August 1863 meeting was the first of the season between the Mutuals and Atlantics. Each club was considered a contender for the Silver Ball trophy, presented to the top club in the country. The Mutuals looked to continue their success against the Atlantics, having defeated the home club in their only meeting in 1862 by the score of 15–10 and in two of the previous three matches.

The Match Takes Shape

The Mutual Club arrived at the Capitoline Grounds at 2:30 p.m. in a handsome four horse carriage.[4] Despite the stifling heat, thousands of spectators had congregated hours before in and around the new home of the Atlantics in Bedford, Brooklyn. The "Mutes" pushed their way through the crowd and arrived at the Atlantics' club room in preparation for their 3 p.m. contest.

"The weather was oppressively hot, the thermometer ranging up to ninety-five in the shade at the time the game commenced; yet in spite of the broiling sun, 4,000 spectators stood patiently beneath its scorching rays for over nearly four hours," reported the *New York Sunday Mercury*.[5] The heat was one of the factors that contributed to the events that were to unfold.

The other was the playing surface. "As for the ground, a rougher one, or one more unfit in condition for the locale of an important contest like that of Monday, would be hard to find," proclaimed the *New York Clipper*. " It being common ground, carts drive over every part of it, and the in-field, owning to the miserable manner in which the sods were laid, when the ground was made, and the neglect to remedy the evil in the spring by a proper rolling and leveling, made it impossible for either party to field a ball with any degree of success, it being chance work throughout."[6]

Striking first in the match, the Atlantics scored four runs. The Mutuals immediately answered with four runs of their own. In the second and third innings, both clubs scored two and four runs, respectively, leaving the contest tied at 10 runs apiece. In the opinion of the *New York Sunday Mercury*, the large number of runs scored was due to poor fielding: "the fact was, the ball was not only an unusually hard one, but the perspiration that poured from the players made their hands greasy, and it was difficult to hold a ball at all."[7]

An intentional misplay by Mutuals second baseman Ed Brown in the fourth inning was specifically cited by the *Mercury*. "Start hit a high ball for Brown to take on the fly—Chapman having previously gone out on the fly. Ticknor, who runs his bases well, watched Brown closely, and running the chances of his dropping the ball and picking it up on the bound, which Brown often does to get two out instead of one...."[8] Until the 1865 season, a fair batted ball caught on the fly or the first bounce retired the batter. When this occurred, base runners had to watch the actions of the infielder to determine if they should return to their base or attempt to advance. The infield fly rule did not technically become a written rule until the *Players' National League Guide*, printed in 1890.

The heat and intensity of the match caused some words to be exchanged between the opposing players during the fourth and fifth innings, an uncommon occurrence, and appeared to agitate the supporters for each side. The Mutuals took a 12–11 lead after five innings. The next three innings saw the Atlantics score 15 runs to the Mutuals' six, vaulting the Atlantics to a seemingly unsurmountable 26–18 lead. Some of the Atlantics supporters were so certain of a victory that they headed home.

The Mutuals' Final Strike

The Mutuals came to bat in their ninth inning eight runs behind. Many of the spectators remaining probably felt that this final turn at bat was simply a formality. After stringing a few hits together, the Mutuals scored two quick runs. Following a single by catcher William Wansley, Mutuals pitcher Billy McKeever took his turn at striker's line. McKeever stood at the line to allow Wansley the chance to move to second base on an errant pitch or a misplay by the catcher. However, the Atlantic battery committed no errors. McKeever reportedly took at least 50 pitches without attempting to swing his bat.[9]

It would not be until the 1864 season that the rules makers empowered the umpire to warn and then call balls on the pitcher for delivering unhittable balls. Since strikes could be called on the batter starting with the 1858 season, it is difficult to understand why the umpire allowed McKeever to stand at home base for so long. To further irritate the Atlantics, McKeever spoke aggressively to Atlantics pitcher Al Smith and catcher Dickie Pearce as they passed the ball back and forth. McKeever eventually singled, moving Wansley to third base.

The next batter, third baseman William McMahon, reached first base which loaded the bases for left fielder John Zeller. Zeller cleared them with a triple, bringing the Mutuals to within three runs of tying the game. The remaining Atlantic supporters became more vocally aggressive and were countered by fans of the Mutuals. As the crowd shouted and cursed among themselves, right fielder Mott singled home Zeller and scored himself, reducing the Atlantics lead to one run.

The intensity escalated on the field as the members of the contesting clubs again began to hurl insults at each other—the Atlantics out of despair and the Mutuals out of confidence. Mutuals center fielder Harris promptly tipped out to catcher Dickie Pearce for the first out of the ninth inning. Some of the Atlantic players began to badger the umpire, hoping John Grum of the Eckford BBC would call the game "for the frivolous reason of its 'getting dark.'"[10] Grum refused the protest and quickly decided that the match game should continue.

First baseman John Goldie hit a long fly ball to center field which was caught by the Atlantics' John Chapman. Relief more than confidence overcame the Atlantics backers as they were one out from a victory. But second baseman Ed Brown doubled to quell the Atlantic rowdies and reignite the Mutual fanatics. With a boisterous crowd not far from either foul line, shortstop John Beard stepped to the striker's line. The Atlantics' usually calm pitcher Al Smith unleashed a wild pitch allowing Brown to score from second base to tie the game. The Mutual supporters exploded with excitement, adding fuel to the Atlantics and their backers' anger. The *Mercury* wrote:

> It was now that that the evil results of high betting, that these Championship contests lead to, began to be manifested. During the obtaining of the last few runs, there had been considerable "chaffing" among the members of the two clubs, and as this style of

talk is not safe or advisable among quick tempered men, it was not long before personalities began to be introduced, and anything but friendly remarks made by both parties, one to the other.[11]

The *Eagle* reported that one of the Atlantics explained Pearce's lack of effort because he was having trouble seeing the ball.[12] Other Atlantics agreed and once again the Atlantic players began to "discuss" the issue of low light with Grum. This discussion reportedly lasted 25 minutes.[13] During the meeting, the crowd stationed at home base and near the first and third base foul lines pressed onto the field and had to be pushed back.

Grum failed to give in to the Atlantic protest for the second time and the game continued. However, another delay ensued as the ball had to be located before play resumed.[14] Pearce, whether due to fatigue, disinterest, or a pay-off, exhibited odd behavior once the game restarted. He again failed to hold the third strike, this time against Beard, who swung at "three high ones"[15] after seeing numerous unhittable pitches. Pearce made no attempt to put Beard out at first base, or any base for that matter, and watched the Mutuals shortstop quickly make his way back home, scoring the 27th and winning run. Bedlam broke out in Bedford as the Mutual supporters went wild. Shouts, curses, hoots, and hollers could be heard quite a distance away.

Because only two hands were retired, the Mutuals sent Wansley to the line. (Not until the start of the 1880 National League season would a game end immediately when the winning run was scored in the bottom half of the ninth inning.) He swung at the first three hittable pitches he saw, after receiving an abundance of bad ones. Pearce purposely did not corral the third strike. Wansley began walking around the bases, literally, before he was tagged out near third base by Atlantic third baseman Charlie Smith to end the match.

Print Reactions

Since their inception, the Atlantics showed no mercy for their opponents. A review of their final scores preceding this match reveals that they regularly scored 20 and 30 runs and some times as many as 40, 50, and 60 runs in defeating their challengers. These facts make it laughable that the *Mercury* would print the following regarding the game:

> The Mutuals ought to have remembered that it was a trying position for the Atlantics
> to be placed in; and had their members kept cool and silent, attending only to their
> game, and gone on with their play, leaving to the umpire, whose sole duty it was,
> to decide any disputed questions, all would have been well, and the Atlantics would
> not have been led into the committal of the actions they were, but in-as much as

the Mutuals did not act in this manner, but, on the contrary, allowed themselves to become as excited as the Atlantics were, and without the same excuse, they became, in a measure, responsible for a great deal of the trouble that occurred.[16]

The *Mercury* continued to admonish the Mutuals:

We think, from the action of Beard, when he stood up to the bat, that the Mutuals would have closed the game as a draw one, under the circumstances, seeing that it was their old friends, the Atlantics, who were their opponents; but when it was seen that Pearce, after missing the ball on the third strike of Beard, made no exertions to get it to put Beard out at first base—his action, in this respect, being unaccountable to us—the Mutuals determined to have the game played out to a close, and to win if possible. So they at once hurried up Beard around the bases, and he came home without difficulty, thus scoring the winning run, amidst the wildest applause and the greatest excitement.[17]

In reporting on the Atlantics' protest of the limited light, the *Mercury* stated, "The plea of its being 'too dark to play,' which was put in by some of the most excited Atlantic players, was one that had not the slightest reasonable foundation."[18]

The Clipper reluctantly printed the results. "In view of the many well fought and fairly played contests that we have seen on the Atlantic grounds, in cases of worse defeat than they met with yesterday, we feel deep regret in being obliged to record the proceedings of Monday last, and have no doubt that all of the best members of the club feel just the same regret at what took place."[19] The article praised the play of Atlantics pitcher Al Smith and catcher Dickie Pearce as well as third baseman Charlie Smith. The Mutuals were not so fortunate and received the following remark: "On the Mutuals side there were fewer instances of good fielding."[20] The *Clipper* had this to say of the Atlantics' behavior as the lead slipped away. "They began to lose control of themselves, and finally resorted to a course of proceedings that caused one of the manliest and fairest players of their club to charge them with bringing disgrace upon it by their actions."[21] The *Eagle*, however, made it clear that after the Mutuals pulled to within one run and heated exchanges occurred between the clubs, "all of the Atlantics are not angels in regard to good temper."[22]

Even *The Philadelphia City Item,* published by former National Association of Base Ball Players President Col. Thomas Fitzgerald of the Athletic club, had an opinion on the match. In summarizing the contest, the *City Item* wrote, "Truly a great victory. Where was the 'bully little pitcher, Pratt,' all this time?"[23] As mentioned earlier, Athletics would have their disagreements with the Atlantics in 1866.

Umpire John Grum received only high marks from the newspapers covering the match. He was commended for standing on the field, not allowing himself to be intimidated by the unruly Atlantic supporters and Atlantic players who aggressively urged him to call the game due to darkness, as the Mutuals mounted their comeback.

A total of six home runs were hit in the game, which lasted four hours and fifteen minutes. Elements that would soon be more commonplace in higher-profile matches were apparent during this match. For the players, baseball had undoubtedly become a competitive event as opposed to a social event.

It was the Atlantics' greatest collapse to date and mimicked what the Mutuals had been long accused of: throwing matches. The Brooklyn club would not forget this contest. It was the last time the Mutuals would defeat the Atlantics until October 12 of the 1868 season, a span of 11 meetings.

Below is the box score for the game, compiled from information published in the August 9 *New York Sunday Mercury* and the August 15 *Wilkes' Spirit of the Times* and *New York Clipper*.[24]

Mutual

	H.L.	Runs
Goldie, 1B	4	3
Brown, 2B	2	4
Beard, SS	5	2
Wansley, C	2	3
McKever, P	3	3
McMahon, 3B	3	3
Zeller, LF	2	3
Mott, RF	2	3
Harris, CF	3	3
Total		27

Atlantic

	H.L.	Runs
Pearce, C	1	6
P. O'Brien, RF	1	5
C. Smith, 3B	2	3
Crane, 2B	3	3
A. Smith, P	6	1
Ticknor, SS	2	3
Chapman, LF	4	2
Start, 1B	3	1
Galpin, CF	5	2
Total		26

Runs Made in Each Inning

	1st.	2nd.	3rd.	4th.	5th.	6th.	7th.	8th.	9th.
Mutual	4	2	4	0	2	2	2	2	9–27
Atlantic	4	2	4	1	0	9	1	5	0–26

Scores—For Mutual, James McConnell; For Atlantic, G. Moore.

Umpire—J.J. Grum, of the Eckford Club.

Passed Balls—Wansley, 2; McMahon, 1; Pearce, 6

Home Runs—Wansley, 1; Goldie, 1; P. O'Brien, 1; Pearce, 1; C. Smith, 1; Crane, 1

Fly-Catches Made—Beard, 1; Brown, 4; Zeller, 1; Goldie, 1; Harris, 1-Total 8. C. Smith, 2; Crane, 2; Start, 3; Galpin, 3; Pearce, 1; Chapman, 1—Total 12.

Catches Missed—Wansley, 2; McMahon, 2; Goldie, 3; Mott, 1, Zeller, 1; Harris, 1; Brown, 2, McKever, 1-Total 13. Pearce, 2; Crane, 2; Ticknor, 2; Chapman, 1; A. Smith 1—Total 8.
Put Out On Foul Balls—Mutuals, 5 times; Atlantics, 1 time.
Put Out At First Base—Mutuals, 5 times; Atlantics, 7 times.
Struck Out—A. Smith, 1; Galpin, 1.
Left on Bases—Mutuals, 4 times; Atlantics, 7 times.
Time of Game—4 hours, 15 minutes.

The previous day pitted a horse McKeever was part-owner of named *General Butler* against another named *Cooley* piloted by William Riley in a one-on-one winner-take-all harness race series. The showdown began at three o'clock at the Chicago Driving Park.[25] "The attendance at the race was immense, thousands of people were in attendance."[26] A purse of $5,000 was to be awarded to the victor.[27]

Cooley won the first two races by a neck and then by 15 lengths.[28] In the second race, *Butler* was very unsteady and broke every few strides.[29] McKeever had enough of his driver, aptly named Sam Crooks.[30] With no reported extensive racing experience, McKeever took the reins for the third race and won by 20 lengths.[31] This confirmed his suspicion that Crooks was in on a fix. Before the fourth race commencing six false starts occurred in addition to jockeying, swearing, and an altercation between Riley and McKeever.[32] The crowd cheered and hissed, the shenanigans consuming half an hour as darkness began to overtake the course.

Eventually, the race got under way and "within two hundred yards of the winning post *Butler* made a sudden movement toward the inside track, coming in front of *Cooley* so that the wheel touched the horse's nose."[33] *Butler* won the fourth race by half a length. The bad blood between the drivers continued, fueled by the throngs of those with money on the outcome, which nearly led to an uncontrollable situation.

The contestants and the crowd eventually settled down and preparations began for a fifth race, but in complete darkness. The two drivers had words again and the crowd voiced their opinions between those wanting to postpone the contest and those wanting it to continue. The park was on the brink of eruption again, further delaying the final race.

Once under way, *Butler* took the lead by a length before the horses and drivers melted into the darkness. As it was impossible to follow the contestants, the crowd waited anxiously at the post. *Cooley* emerged first and crossed the line, with *General Butler* close behind. McKeever, however, was nowhere to be seen. *Butler* circled the track two more times before "a blanket was thrown over him, and he passed into the stable."[34]

What the darkness did conceal were two planks extending from the rail into the path of the drivers which were held by two men, as reported by a patrol stationed near the fatal blow.[35] The 12-foot-long planks were heard hitting the ground as the assailants ran.[36] The wood was discovered to have come from a lumber pile near the stands.[37] One was intended for *Butler* and the other for McKeever.

McKeever was found "on the back stretch, about twenty rods from the half mile post"[38] barely alive and initially reported as dead. The plank that struck him above and slightly in front of the left ear before glancing back and breaking his skull, was found with blood and a tuft of hair at its end.[39]

Riley was immediately a suspect and would provide a variety of stories as to what happened. Initially, "Riley went up to the Judges' stand, and amid such a din that it was difficult to hear, and in so much agitation that it was equally difficult to understand, he told that McKeaver [sic] had run into the fence and capsized his sulky, and that he (Riley) had stopped Cooley to avoid running over him, being behind the fallen man at the time of the accident."[40] With little hesitation, he was taken into custody by Assistant Superintendent Nelson.[41]

The judges announced that McKeever was lying dead at the backstretch. The crowd was in a frenzy, less over the announcement of McKeever's death than over a lack of decision for the outcome of the final race. The crowd pressed the judges, who repeated that a driver was killed, but the crowd demanded a ruling on the race itself. The judges decided to postpone their decision which further angered the throng. The judges then decided that all bets were off, sending the crowd on its way.

McKeever was not dead, but his skull was crushed. Once located, he was moved "with all possible speed to the residence of J.H. Gore, county physician, No. 887 Michigan avenue, but a few blocks distant from the spot where he fell."[42] After an examination, Gore concluded that McKeever had been struck on the left temple by a some hard substance which had fractured the skull extensively.[43] Dr. Gore extracted three pieces of the cranium, one piece about one inch by one and a quarter, and the other perhaps half an inch square each, the patient all the time remaining insensible. It was hoped that when the pressure was taken from the brain, consciousness would return, but such was not the case, and this fact proved what was afterwards ascertained by examination—that the brain itself had been contused.[44] McKeever's friends in New York were telegraphed about his condition. He passed away at 4:30 p.m. on September 23.

Two brothers named Hickey who owned a saloon on Sherman Street[45] were arrested later that night after a fight with authorities. They were "charged with fastening a projecting board to the fence, which they knew would upset McKeever, as he had the inside track and very near the fence."[46] The following

A FATAL RACE.

Trot Between Cooley and General Butler--McKeaver, the Driver of the Latter, Killed.

AN EXCITING CONTEST AND NO WINNER—THE BETS DECLARED OFF.

McKeaver Struck Down on the Back Stretch — His Skull Broken — He Expired Yesterday—Excitement — Arrest.

The *Chicago Tribune*'s September 24, 1866, announcement of Billy McKeever's brutal demise.

day "seven other men were arrested, some of whom, it was said, declared they would knock McKeaver [*sic*] out before he should win."[47]

McKeever's body was transported back to New York and delivered to his brother John at 19 Gay Street.[48] Services were held at Grace Church on the corner of Fifth Ave and Tenth Street on December 31 at one o'clock.[49] He was laid to rest in Green-Wood Cemetery in Brooklyn with many members of the Mutual Base Ball Club present.[50] Billy McKeever's final stop found him in the company of numerous past and future nineteenth century baseball players.

The Chicago Driving Park, which opened in August of 1863, closed on November 10, 1866. The *Chicago Tribune* wrote, "The public well enough understands the reasons which have prompted this course, it was found impossible to keep this place free from blacklegs, and the gentlemen who compose the Association have wisely decided to discontinue that...."[51]

NOTES

1. *Brooklyn Daily Eagle*, August 4, 1863, 2.
2. *Brooklyn Daily Eagle*, August 4, 1863, 2.
3. *Brooklyn Daily Eagle*, August 4, 1863, 2.
4. *New York Sunday Mercury*, August 9, 1863.
5. *New York Sunday Mercury*, August 9, 1863.
6. *The New York Clipper*, August 15, 1863.
7. *New York Sunday Mercury*, August 9, 1863.

8. *New York Sunday Mercury*, August 9, 1863.
9. *Mears Base Ball Scrapbooks—Vol.1*, 1862–1863.
10. *Mears Base Ball Scrapbooks—Vol.1*, 1862 1863.
11. *New York Sunday Mercury*, August 9, 1863.
12. *Brooklyn Daily Eagle*, August 4, 1863, 2.
13. *Wilkes's Spirit of the Times*, August 15, 1863.
14. *Brooklyn Daily Eagle*, August 4, 1863, 2.
15. *Wilkes's Spirit of the Times*, August 15, 1863.
16. *New York Sunday Mercury*, August 9, 1863.
17. *New York Sunday Mercury*, August 9, 1863.
18. *New York Sunday Mercury*, August 9, 1863.
19. *The New York Clipper*, August 15, 1863.
20. *The New York Clipper*, August 15, 1863.
21. *The New York Clipper*, August 15, 1863.
22. *Brooklyn Daily Eagle*, August 4, 1863, 2.
23. *The Philadelphia City Item*, August 8, 1863.
24. Substantial editing, organizing and punctuation was added to produce a more easily readable box score. The *Wilkes' Spirit of the Times* article listed Sadler as the first batter, playing first base for the Mutuals.
25. *Chicago Tribune*, September 2, 1866.
26. *New York Herald*, September 24, 1866, 5.
27. *Chicago Tribune*, September 2, 1866.
28. *New York Herald*, September 24, 1866, 5.
29. *Wilkes' Spirit of the Times*, September 29, 1866.
30. William Ryczek, *When Johnny Came Sliding Home* (Jefferson, NC: McFarland, 1998), 77.
31. *New York Herald*, September 24, 1866, 5.
32. *New York Herald*, September 24, 1866, 5.
33. *New York Herald*, September 24, 1866, 5.
34. *New York Herald*, September 24, 1866, 5.
35. *Turf, Field & Far*, December 27, 1902.
36. *Turf, Field & Far*, December 27, 1902.
37. *Turf, Field & Far*, December 27, 1902.
38. *Chicago Tribune*, September 2, 1866.
39. *Turf, Field & Farm*, December 27, 1902.
40. *Chicago Tribune*, September 2, 1866.
41. *Chicago Tribune*, September 2, 1866.
42. *Chicago Tribune*, September 2, 1866.
43. *Chicago Tribune*, September 2, 1866.
44. *Chicago Tribune*, September 2, 1866.
45. Ryczek, 77.
46. *New York Herald*, September 24, 1866, 5.
47. *Turf, Field & Farm*, December 27, 1902.
48. *New York Herald*, September 29, 1866, 4.
49. *New York Herald*, September 29, 1866, 4.
50. *New York Herald*, September 29, 1866, 4.
51. *Chicago Tribune*, November 6, 1866.

Book Reviews

Hardly a Humble History

Pastime Lost: The Humble, Original, and Now Completely Forgotten Game of English Baseball. David Block. Lincoln: University of Nebraska Press, 2019, illus., 298 pages.

For readers of this publication and others devoted to early baseball history, there should be instant name recognition when it comes to David Block. After all, his first and only other book-length effort to date, *Baseball Before We Knew It: A Search for the Roots of the Early Game,* published in 2005, is a seminal work on the origins of America's National Pastime.

Albert Goodwill Spalding and his Mills Commission of the early twentieth century did their best to convince America that baseball was purely an American game invented in 1839 in Cooperstown, New York, by Abner Doubleday, then (at the time of the Commission) a late military hero. It took nearly four decades before a substantive argument would be advanced for an alternate theory, first put forth by nineteenth century pioneer baseball journalist Henry Chadwick, that baseball had descended from the English bat and ball game of rounders.

This second origins story was given new steam in 1947 by a librarian of the New York Public Library, Robert W. Henderson, with the publication of his book, *Ball, Bat and Bishop: The Origin of Ball Games.* The book sparked a rise in interest in rounders and the giving of an increased importance to the 1840s New York Knickerbocker Base Ball Club and one of its members, Alexander J. Cartwright. Author Monica Nucciarone placed Cartwright (who had acquired the title, "The Father of Baseball") in a more proper, albeit less important, perspective with her biography, *Alexander Cartwright: The Life Behind the Baseball Legend,* in 2009.

Many historians clung to the "Rounders/Knickerbocker/Cartwright" centric view of American baseball origins into the early years of this century. A surprising number of ordinary fans still are fixated on the central role

Base Ball 12, pp. 252–255
ISSN 1934-2802 (Print) / ISSN 1934-3167 (Online)
978-1-4766-7473-5 (Print) / 978-1-4766-4112-6 (ebook)

played by Doubleday and Cooperstown in 1839. But with impeccable research David Block brought forth a very different and distinct origins story in the pages of *Baseball Before We Knew It*. Block discovered that rounders as well as another game played in England, distinctly referred to as "base ball," were, in fact, distinct from each other. Furthermore, it was base ball that clearly preceded rounders chronologically in the written record. It remained distinct from rounders throughout the decades in which the two games overlapped.

Block found that for approximately two centuries, from the early 18th through the early 20th, the game of "base ball" stood apart from rounders in the historical record in England. It was played by either gender, separate or together, by children and adults, indoors or outdoors, and most often involved striking the ball with the palm of the hand. Furthermore, given its more than century-long history while North America was being colonized by English families and post-revolution English immigrants, "base ball" was an already engrained recreation among children and adults on this side of the pond.

So, with this being a review of Block's *Pastime Lost,* why should I spend this time tracing through past writing and research on baseball's origins? The answer is twofold.

First, this newest book by Block is painstakingly researched—the result of fourteen years work and eight trips to the U.K. by the author. *Pastime Lost* starts us off precisely at the point where *Baseball Before We Knew It* concluded. English "base ball," begun in the early eighteenth century and, more than any other game, was the ancestor of what would become America's National Pastime. This new book is all about that ancestor game.

Second, Block, or his publisher, chose to use the descriptor "Humble" as an adjective for "English Baseball" in the book's title. I would prefer that readers know that "English Baseball" is hardly "Humble" in terms of its historical importance to baseball's origins story. The use of the term "Humble" will become evident to readers as they become aware of how ubiquitous base ball was for nearly two centuries as a "peoples' game" in populated southeastern England and later with its eventual spread into other regions of the United Kingdom. If anything, "Humble," in Block's usage, simply implies non-professional play and does not imply unimportance.

Block, if he intended it or not, truly takes his readers on a journey—three journeys told simultaneously. First, there is the journey of English base ball from its first appearances in the written record: diary and journal entries; personal letters; newspaper announcements and reports; and in book prose. This written record, beginning in the early eighteenth century, concludes in the first decades of the twentieth century when it becomes comprised of mostly firsthand reminiscences.

There is no wanting for documentation in the book that the game was played frequently by both genders, sometimes separately but also together, and by children and adults. It was played casually but sometimes competitively, where prizes were awarded or when bragging rights of a town or village were at stake.

Less frequent but most precious, as the author points out, are descriptions of how English base ball was played. The game was played outdoors and indoors, often with the open palm of the hand striking a small soft ball and running to predetermined stations, usually posts or, perhaps, specified furnishings within a room if indoors.

English base ball was played by all classes of people. Block has made an incredible discovery—of a newspaper report from 1749 of Frederick, Prince of Wales, the estranged son of King George II and father of King George III, playing a game of "base ball" on what is now Ashley Park, Walton-on-Thames, Surrey. The land was then the estate belonging to the wife of Charles Sackville, Earl of Middlesex, who also played in the match which took place despite inclement weather.

Then, there is, of course, Jane Austen's relatively well-known mention of the term "base ball" in her novel *Northanger Abbey,* which she penned in 1798 (but which was not published until 1818 after her death). Block devotes considerable time to Jane Austen and her family, particularly her favorite brother, Francis, and his daughter Catherine Anne. When Catherine Anne's mother died suddenly after the birth of her eleventh child, Catherine was fortunate to have a devoted aunt, Cassandra, who read to her and her siblings the works of their late Aunt Jane. Catherine would eventually keep the "base ball" connection to the Austen legacy alive when she completed a partial manuscript of Jane Austen and successfully brought it to publication. This is only part of Block's discussion of the Austen family. But I found it fascinating and his account left me longing to learn more.

The second journey that Block charts is that depicted by his research. His three-hundred pages of prose and notes reflect this relentless determination to track down what may or may not become another brush stroke in the overall picture of base ball as it was played for two centuries in England. Block visits scores of locations, indoors and outdoors, thousands of miles from his home, on his journeys to the United Kingdom. Scores of people—archivists, librarians, antiquarians, historians, and ordinary folks—share his journeys of discovery. The length and breadth of the author's search for clues as to where, when, and how the game was played will leave readers impressed. It will also serve as a model of what exhaustive research looks like, not just in digital form but on-site, where the "smell of old paper and ink can be intoxicating."

Finally, but hardly least, there is a third journey, one certainly not intended by the author: his personal journey as a researcher and writer. Block expresses much joy in this book, a certain lightness and relaxation (even when nearly missing the last train from a relatively remote town) that enhances the story. Block even concedes to twice allowing himself to accept secondary sources in *Pastime Lost*, something he fervently refrained from doing in *Baseball Before we Knew It*. His reasons for allowing for these two "concessions" are, however, meticulously dissected and explained by Block, leaving the most critical reader or researcher convinced of the necessity and the validity of both sources.

The art of how to tell the story of a "…Now Completely Forgotten Game…" has been mastered by David Block. It will leave readers of *Pastime Lost* not just glad they may have learned nearly all there is to know about baseball's truest ancestor game, but it will give them a deeper appreciation for historical research in general and a deeper understanding of their own journeys as researchers and writers as well.

—**Peter Mancuso** chairs SABR's Nineteenth Century Committee. While his research has focused on Staten Islanders associated with nineteenth-century major leagues, he seeks opportunities to promote the study of all nineteenth-century baseball.

"Who's Ty Cobb—And Why?"

Ty Cobb Unleashed: The Definitive Counter-Biography of the Chastened Racist. Howard W. Rosenberg. Tile Books, 2018 illus., 544 pages.

With the regularity of biographies of Hunter S. Thompson or accounts of *The National Lampoon*'s heyday, another new Ty Cobb book appeared in 2018. Howard W. Rosenberg, known for his four-volume study of Cap Anson, has self-published *Ty Cobb Unleashed*, which is less of a birth-to-death recounting of Cobb's life than a repudiation of the most recent Cobb scholarship. Rosenberg's book is not anti–Cobb so much as it is against such kneejerk Cobb defenders as Charles Leerhsen. "If (Al) Stump is Cobb's worst dream, Leerhsen is Cobb's best one," Rosenberg proclaims. "The truth is no doubt closer to Leerhsen, but Leerhsen assumed too much on the pro–Cobb side of some key issues."

Ty Cobb Unleashed is at once impressively researched *and* poorly organized and written. Rosenberg has marshaled compelling evidence to establish that Cobb was, contrary to revisionists, indeed violent and racist. Unfortunately for the reader, he presents these details in a haphazard format, and with often-unwieldy prose. If Cobb himself is unleashed in these pages, the book's author needed to be reined in by a steady copy editor.

While Leerhsen insisted that tales of Cobb's on-field violence were exaggerations, Rosenberg cites no fewer than seven sources recalling his sharpening his spikes (quoting ex-teammate Ossie Vitt as saying, "I'll never forget how Ty Cobb used to sit on the bench, file his spikes, and shout: 'I'll get you in the third inning!' to some infielder") and several contemporary accounts of Cobb deliberately spiking infielders. Regarding race, Rosenberg reports notes that Cobb was fond of playing the popular "African Dodger" carnival game in the early twentieth century (where an African American man would stick his head in an opening as white fairgoers aimed baseballs at his head). Also, Rosenberg finds evidence that Cobb was approached to appear in a popular

Base Ball 12, pp. 256–258
ISSN 1934-2802 (Print) / ISSN 1934-3167 (Online)
978-1-4766-7473-5 (Print) / 978-1-4766-4112-6 (ebook)

blackface minstrel troupe after the 1912 season and that Cobb resisted blacks entering major league baseball until the early 1950s.

Unleashed is marred by Rosenberg's unwieldy writing style. He routinely refers to Leerhsen's *Ty Cobb: A Terrible Beauty* as "the Simon & Schuster book" and Tim Hornbaker's *War on the Basepaths* (2015) as "the Sports Publishing book," which would irritate readers unfamiliar with either biography (or who were simply indifferent to their publishing houses). Rosenberg's prose also lacks the conciseness of William R. Cobb's "Stumped by the Georgia Peach," a 2010 SABR article with systematic refutations of the more lurid Cobb stories. "Odds and Ends," an *Unleashed* chapter summarizing newspaper articles and correspondence from 1904 until Cobb's 1961 death, takes up almost 300 pages of a 544-page book. While Rosenberg inevitably unearths some intriguing tidbits here—one brief newspaper description of Cobb is succinctly head-lined "Who's Ty Cobb—And Why?" and a 1913 account describes Cobb vis-iting an Atlanta prison accompanied by Enrico Caruso—this chapter has the feel of a junk drawer, with only chronology linking the anecdotes. To see how such an approach can be presented successfully to an audience, one needs to study how Jane Leavy looked through decades of articles about Babe Ruth in *The Big Fella* (2018) but wisely kept the information within the narrative confines of a 1927 postseason barnstorming tour.

Ty Cobb Unleashed examines Cobb's previous biographers almost as thoroughly as it discusses the ballplayer himself. Rosenberg partially redeems much-maligned Cobb biographer Al Stump by establishing that Stump had interviewed Cobb several times for Elks publications as early as 1955, six years before Cobb's 1961 autobiography. "They used to say that pitching was 75 per-cent of the game," Cobb tells Stump in that piece. "Well, I'd call it 25 per cent *[sic]*! Baseball's lost all its science and gone fence-ball crazy!" Rosenberg also backs up one of Stump's most controversial claims in his infamous "Ty Cobb's Wild Ten-Month Fight to Live" article—namely that a hospitalized Cobb placed a revolver atop his securities. And Rosenberg implies, perhaps unfairly, that Leerhsen is less than honest by noting his collaboration on a book with Donald J. Trump.

To give the author his due, Rosenberg refuses to reduce Cobb to a ste-reotype. He unearths a 1915 quote where Cobb declares that his native Geor-gia "never suffered a heavier blow than when that mob stole Leo Frank from the prison guards and lynched him [...] Georgia has courts, and they are fully capable of administering justice and punishment." For all of Cobb's doc-umented racist comments, Rosenberg has Cobb counseling a young Henry Aaron and adds that Cobb eagerly requested to pose for a photograph with Willie Mays in 1960. And the many photos throughout the book of an elderly

Cobb joking with old teammates gives the lie to today's conventional wisdom that Cobb was the least beloved man in the game.

Howard Rosenberg, the author of *Ty Cobb Unleashed*, is to be commended for taking the time to sift through thousands of newspaper articles to present a more nuanced portrait of Cobb, even if he is, ultimately, a better aggregator than a writer. The task now is for a first-rate biographer to synthesize all the new information in the books by Rosenberg, Leerhsen, Hornbaker, and others and craft a thorough and objective one- or two-volume Cobb biography from scratch.

—**Andrew Milner** has written for *The Cooperstown Review* and *The National Pastime*. A SABR member since 1984, he lives in suburban Philadelphia.

THE RULES OF THE GAME

Strike Four: The Evolution of Baseball. Richard Hershberger. Foreword by John Thorn. Rowman & Littlefield, 2019, illus., 295 pages.

The September 11, 1867, edition of the *Owensboro Monitor* reported a baseball game in Owensboro, Kentucky, between a local club and the Resolute club of Evansville, Indiana. The box score included information which would be familiar today. For instance, each side had nine players who were assigned to positions with familiar designations, and the game lasted nine innings. But it also included information related to "foul bound catches," an aspect of the game at which the losing Owensboro side outshone its opponent. The August 6, 1868, edition of the *Louisville Daily Journal* printed a lengthy description of a game in Frankfort, Kentucky, between the Eagle Club of Louisville and the Valley Club of Frankfort. Again, the box score reflected that each side fielded a team of nine players who filled positions identified like those of today. The teams played for nine innings. However, the account of the game noted that in the first inning a Louisville batter by the name of Harry Truman "after waiting for some time was sent to his base on three balls..." (4).

Richard Hershberger's *Strike Four: The Evolution of Baseball* navigates the origins and transformation of rules surrounding the game lauded as America's national pastime. The book primarily focuses on baseball's early years, although the author does not overlook changes in the twentieth and twenty-first centuries.

Hershberger has mined relevant sources and included contemporaneous commentary regarding the problems and issues that a rule or rule change was intended to address. This approach, coupled with the author's lively prose, results in a fascinating discussion which gives the reader insights into the game and its growing pains, from its early days to the present. *Strike Four* is an engaging history of regulations which originally provided order to baseball, issues regarding play which arose and why, the various

Base Ball 12, pp. 259–262
ISSN 1934-2802 (Print) / ISSN 1934-3167 (Online)
978-1-4766-7473-5 (Print) / 978-1-4766-4112-6 (ebook)

remedies proposed, and the resulting rules which have governed a game that continues to evolve.

The author begins his discussions with the 1845 rules of the Knicker-bocker Base Ball Club, the game's oldest existing set of regulations. Hershberger provides detailed discussions of such early provisions as those regarding a dropped third strike and foul territory. Along the way, the reader is treated to early German descriptions of *Englische Base-Ball* and to assertions that the striker had the right to "knock the ball with his bat in any direction he chose…." (18). Of course, the Knickerbocker rules did not remain static and the impetus for change within the realm of baseball came early and in several guises.

Pressures came from the "competitive cauldron that was New York baseball, with clubs looking for any angle they could find" (xvii). This was reflected, for example, in the play of pitchers and batters. Pitchers strained to move away from merely feeding the ball to strikers/batters so they could put it in play and experimented with increased velocity, curveballs, and more effective deliveries. Batters, on the other hand, were not shy about refusing to swing at good pitches in the hopes that passed balls would provide opportunities for runners on base to advance.

These developments gave rise to concerns over other matters, including that games were "dragged out," and resulted in various changes to the governing provisions. However, the catalyst for rules review arose from several places. According to Hershberger, "the most contentious rules argument in the history of the game" (57) surrounded the efforts to replace the regulation allowing a fielder to put a batter out by catching a fair ball on the fly or the first bounce with the requirement that the ball be caught on the fly. This may have had its genesis from the concerns in some quarters that the game was not sufficiently "manly" and needed to be more difficult.

The topics covered range from the nine-inning game to video replay and from the foul pole to tagging up and many more in between. The reader may certainly conclude, especially from a twenty-first century perspective, that efforts to arrive at suitable regulations were on occasion unduly prolonged and difficult. For instance, batters reluctant to swing were introduced to called strikes. Inasmuch as swift pitching did not necessarily equate to accurate pitching, amendments to the rules provided for called balls. Umpires initially were reluctant to call either. Hershberger states, "The rules campaign took the form of gradually strengthening the language to make it imperative for the umpire to call balls and strikes" (87). Pages 87–88 address these efforts against the backdrop of rules which at different times provided for a warning to the batter or pitcher for his conduct, no call on the first ball pitched, "fair balls," and "unfair balls," and that certain behavior by the batter or pitcher occur "repeatedly" before a ball or strike could be called. The author states on page 88 that the 1872 rules "cleaned up some of the mess by removing the 'repeatedly' language entirely." It is further indicated the calling of pitches was affected by the presence of high and low strike zones as "only unfair balls, meaning pitches not in either the high or low strike zones, were called balls, and only balls in the zone the batter requested were called strikes." Balls pitched to the wrong strike zone "were neither fair nor unfair, and they were not called either way."

Readers may agree with the author that some early efforts related to calling balls and strikes were a "mess." In addition, it must be noted the 1872 rules in fact still required that the pitcher repeatedly fail to deliver fair balls to the striker before a ball would be called. Too, there were newspapers in the same year which advocated that pitches repeatedly delivered to the wrong strike zone should be called as balls.[1]

Hershberger has written various articles on early baseball although this is his first book. His writing style is generally clear and effective, and his occasionally acknowledging a statement as "a guess" or "an educated guess" is helpful. He tells his story through short chapters which provide for a brisk pace.

An outstanding feature of the book is his inclusion of numerous quotations from publications of the day regarding issues, actions, or behaviors surrounding the baseball fraternity. Various accounts are given of innovative and sharp play by men who well understood and took advantage of the rules of the game. Other passages relate to basic questions regarding play. The range of topics on which quotations are supplied is quite impressive and, as noted, reflects an immense amount of research from various publications. This aspect of the book as much as any provides the reader with the ability to share, at least to some small degree, the experiences of a fan at the time and brings life to what might otherwise be a dry reckoning of rules and regulations.

A few additional comments are warranted. The footnote for Chapter Seven references the newspaper from which a quote is taken but does not include the issue date; the reviewer believes the proper date is March 2, 1857. From this reviewer's perspective, various assertions, such as that of the fielder cutting a ball on a third out so his team would get a new ball for its at bat, would benefit from a citation to source material. There are also a few misspellings which could be addressed in subsequent editions. Finally, the images on the front cover provide a powerful contrast between the settings for an early and present-day game. It is believed the top sketch is from the July 2,

1870, edition of *Harper's Weekly*, as stated on page 111 of the text, and not the October 15, 1859, edition as noted on the back cover.

Strike Four is recommended for anyone interested in the development of the rules of baseball and should be of especial interest to students of the early game. The book discusses numerous issues and should be considered as a supplement to, not a substitute for, accessing and reading the rules addressed. Because *Strike Four* addresses the origin and progression of various rules from baseball's early days, it provides a context and meaning to games played long ago, including those in Kentucky, and informs fans of the varied experiences which have resulted in the rules of the game.

—**John P. Rall** is a retired attorney living in Murray, Kentucky. He is a member of the Society for American Baseball Research whose primary research interest is nineteenth century baseball in the far western portion of the Bluegrass State.

NOTE

1. *See* Rule Second, Sec. 8, "The Rules for Base-Ball for 1872," *The Dime Base-Ball Player* (Beadle and Company Publishers 1872) (*Nickels and Dimes*, Northern Illinois University Libraries, dimenovels.lib.niu.edu); "Calling Balls," *New York Clipper,* April 6, 1872, 5. (Illinois Digital Newspaper Collections. University of Illinois. https://idnc.library.illinois.edu/?a=d&d=NYC18720406&e=). *Brooklyn Daily Eagle,* April 8, 1872, 2.

LITTLE NAPOLEON

Manager of Giants: The Tactics, Temper, and True Record of John McGraw.
Lou Hernandez. McFarland, 2018, illus., 247 pp.

This reviewer has reviewed books for forty-plus years in a variety of disciplines. Reviews have appeared in such publications as *Library Journal* and several Civil War publications along with two in *Base Ball: A Journal of the Early Game*. Never, however, have I had such a difficult time with a review as I have had with this book. It is not because of the content, the difficulty of the text, or issues of accuracy. It has to do with the subject of the biography, John J. McGraw. In my mind, a reviewer of a biography in any field should have some affinity for the subject, even those individuals who have huge negative legacies. In this case, I cannot find much in John McGraw that would make him a likeable character—okay, he didn't beat his wife and he helped some of his old teammates and players. But this is far outweighed by his undesirable traits. Here I have tried to put aside my personal feelings and tried to balance the good and the bad in John McGraw.

There have been several biographies of McGraw written since his own autobiography, *My Thirty Years in Baseball*, originally published in 1923. Before writing *The New York Giants: An Informal History* for the Putnam series of histories of major league teams, Frank Graham wrote *McGraw of the Giants: An Informal Biography* in 1944. This stood alone until Charles Alexander's *John McGraw*, published in 1988 which has passed the test of time as the standard biography of McGraw. Hernandez's book will not replace Alexander's, but it amplifies and does provide more data than Alexander's as the advent of the Internet and electronic sources have made research substantially easier. In addition, McGraw is featured elsewhere. Frank Deford's 2005 book *The Old Ball Game: How John McGraw, Christy Mathewson, and the New York Giants Created Modern Baseball* addresses McGraw's role in the creation of modern baseball and Maury Klein's book *Stealing Games* described

Base Ball 12, pp. 263–267
ISSN 1934-2802 (Print) / ISSN 1934-3167 (Online)
978-1-4766-7473-5 (Print) / 978-1-4766-4112-6 (ebook)

how McGraw's 1911 Giants who stole 347 bases changed modern baseball. Klein's book was written in 2016. Although the role of the stolen base was already important, it was the game McGraw espoused with the players he had.

The Hernandez book covers McGraw's life in chronological fashion and contains ten chapters. Each chapter takes McGraw through his career. The author emphasizes the fine player that McGraw was during his major league career but also emphasizes how well McGraw fit into the Orioles rough method of play. Three chapters focus on the negative aspects of McGraw's life and career. These are: chapter three, "The Most Hated Man in Baseball"; chapter five, "The Irresponsible John McGraw"; and chapter seven, "Sidestepping More Scandal." The other seven chapters present the positives of John McGraw.

What makes Hernandez's book stand out is the detail of his research, particularly in two areas. First, he was able to determine with a great deal of accuracy the games McGraw missed while he was manager of the American League Baltimore Orioles and the New York Giants. The author seems to advocate not counting these games either as wins or losses for McGraw, correcting his winning percentage to reflect these absences. This reviewer is of two minds about this late-date correction. First, I am not certain that the list of individuals actually managing these teams during McGraw's absences is necessarily complete. Second, during these absences John McGraw was by title and salary still the manager. This follows the analogy that a military commander is responsible for all things his command does or does not do. A baseball manager in name is responsible for the team whether he is present or not.

The more valuable bit of research is contained in Appendix B, which is a detailed listing of the ejections and suspensions of John McGraw, both as a player and as a manager. This is the type of research that would have been nearly impossible for Charles Alexander to do before the proliferation of the Internet. Two comments: first, showing McGraw as a player-manager in the years 1903–1907 is a bit of a stretch as he played in a total of 25 games during those five years. Second, it is amazing to me that Booby Cox managed to be ejected more times (158) in 33 years of managing than McGraw, 131 ejections over 33 years.

Hernandez's book attempts to be evenhanded when dealing with McGraw. This is a balanced account. He has described the good qualities that McGraw exhibited, along with his less likeable tendencies. The Giants manager won more games—2,784—than any other save Connie Mack, who had the advantage of owning the team he managed and therefore could not fire himself even when his decisions resulted in the destruction of the team (twice!) Further, Mack himself acknowledged McGraw's success, claiming that there was only one real manager, McGraw, not himself. Mack felt that McGraw's approach to managing the Giants changed the essence of baseball, a claim that was probably true—at least until the advent of the lively ball, which McGraw was a bit slow to adopt.

However, while McGraw won ten National League pennants, he captured the World Series only three times. Some critics said that McGraw managed differently in the World Series than he did during the regular season. The debate about his lack of postseason success is an outgrowth of one of the main criticisms of McGraw as a manager. He was said to control everything his teams did both offensively and defensively and woe to the player who did not follow his explicit directions. While many current MLB managers call the pitches—witness the common practice of catcher turning his head to the dugout between every pitch—McGraw was the manager who began this practice. After the 1922 World Series between the Giants and Yankees, during which the Giants contained Babe Ruth, McGraw stated that he called every pitch made to Ruth. This control did not, however, always work. After the 1913 World Series his good friend Christy Mathewson said the Giants were a "team of puppets being manipulated from the bench on a string."

The author also points out that McGraw was an innovator as both a player and as a manger. During his entire managerial career, he advocated a running type of ball and the use of the strategically placed bunt as opposed to the type of play dominated by the "big hitter" It is interesting to note that while Ned Hanlon was the manager of the Orioles in the 1890s, where McGraw starred, many of the players felt they knew the game better than Hanlon did and used plays they devised themselves. As a player with the 1890s Baltimore Orioles, McGraw is said to have devised the hit-and-run in conjunction with Willie Keeler. Two other John McGraw innovations were the more frequent use of relief pitchers (although I think McGraw would not be in favor of the modern La Russa model of pitcher use that often calls for one pitcher an inning after the fifth inning). Another McGraw innovation was the extensive use of the platoon system, where left-handed batters were used against right-handed pitchers and vice versa. One of McGraw's students, Casey Stengel, carried platooning with the Yankees to ten pennants in 12 years. McGraw was one of the first managers to make frequent trades to strengthen his team. Sometimes he would misjudge talent but often he was able to help the Giants with these moves. McGraw also was flexible. With the advent of the lively ball in 1920, McGraw was able to adopt a style of play that relied more on the long ball. When analyzing his ten National League pennants, it is interesting to note that he had relatively few Hall of Fame–caliber players, a fact that may demonstrate his successful managerial skills.

Hernandez also presents the negatives of John McGraw, and they are many. TheDeadballEra.com website places John McGraw in the "Bad to the Bone" category. One of the criticisms by a reviewer of Alexander's book pointed out was that there was a lack of in-depth analysis of the character of John McGraw. It is a little late in the game to attempt to analyze someone born 146 years ago, but I think it is obvious that his early home life was a huge influence in the life of John McGraw. His father was a drinker who lost his wife and four of his children in an epidemic. Apparently he beat young John frequently and severely. Perhaps today McGraw's father would have been charged with child abuse, but this was a different time and place.

During his playing days and extending into his managerial career, Mc-Graw always was an "1890's" ball player. He was aggressive to the point of being a dirty player. He took advantage of every opportunity, legal or not, to win games. Two of the best known, possibly apocryphal, tales of McGraw's aggressiveness claimed that he held a runner's belt to prevent him leaving third base or cut across the diamond on his way around the bases, taking advantage of the one-umpire system in effect then. The first anecdote was completed with the baserunner loosening his belt and leaving it with McGraw holding in his hands; cutting across the diamond was common practice with one umpire on the diamond. Certainly McGraw was not the only person who did that. As he became a more experienced manager with the Giants, he had the reputation of being close to the edge on rules but perhaps not as blatantly as during his playing days.

The examples of McGraw's less admirable personal traits are numerous. McGraw was certainly an umpire baiter and foul-mouthed. He attacked anyone he thought was a threat to the Giants. McGraw was particularly cruel to Barney Dreyfuss, owner of the Pirates, because of his heavy German accent. His attacks on Dreyfuss occurred frequently but became more numerous after the Merkle incident in 1908. Throughout his career McGraw was quick to blame others when thing did not go right for the Giants. (This megalomania was the cause of the rupture with his long-time friend Wilbert Robinson.) McGraw was prone to forgive physical errors but was death on those who either made mental errors or did not carry out his explicit directions.

John McGraw was an even more questionable character off the field. In January 1919, a majority interest in the New York Giants was acquired by Charles A. Stoneham, who had a somewhat unsavory reputation in New York for possibly illegal financial transactions. McGraw was a social acquaintance of Stoneham and held a small stake in club ownership. During the Florida land rush in the early 1920s McGraw lent his name to a shady land deal. After a 1926 hurricane his investments in the Sunshine State were lost. To his credit, McGraw tried to repay investors.

As McGraw aged, he became more of a drinker, leading to an incident at the Lambs Club in New York in 1920, when he probably engaged in a drunken fight with several other men that resulted in the serious injury of an actor-club member. The details of this incident are murky to this day but did not reflect well on the Giants manager.

The issues that seem to stand out most negatively in his career were his indiscriminate association with gamblers and his employment of players suspected of game-fixing. Late in the 1908 season, the Giants team physician was accused of attempting to bribe the umpires prior to a crucial game, and it was widely suspected that McGraw had instigated the plot. Chase was almost certainly involved in the Black Sox scandal and was widely assumed to have fixed games his entire career. Months before the Black Sox scandal erupted, McGraw quietly released Chase and teammate Heinie Zimmerman, their corrupt play having become too blatant to ignore. No reason was ever given for the suspensions but the widespread assumption was that both Chase and Zimmerman were involved in game throwing and gambling.

This is the career (and life) balance for John McGraw. It is up to the readers of Hernandez's book to draw their own conclusions. No matter what they decide, the book is a great addition to the literature about John McGraw. It does not supplant Charles Alexander's earlier work but is an important supplement to it because of the additional facts it provides.

It seems that perhaps Hernandez had some of the same ambivalent feelings about John McGraw that this reviewer did. He has presented, however, a balanced picture of the man many baseball pundits, then and now, consider the greatest manager of all time. While there are only 17 pictures in the book, there are several that I had not seen before.

I highly recommend this book but feel there is still fertile ground about the life and career of John McGraw to afford him the type of biography that Norman L. Macht created for Connie Mack. The level of detail provided by Macht about Connie Mack would be appropriate for McGraw. A much more detailed examination of McGraw's early life, and a thorough detailing of his entire personal life would be of value and interest.

—**Bill Scheeren** holds a Ph.D. from the University of Pittsburgh in information science. He is a retired educator, having spent 32 years with the Hempfield Area School District, and a Vietnam veteran. He is the author of three college textbooks that deal with educational technology and is an adjunct instructor at both the University of Phoenix and St. Vincent College in Latrobe, Pennsylvania.

Walking Around the Babe's Field

When Boston Still Had the Babe. Bill Nowlin, editor. Rounder Books, 2008, illus., 213 pp.

With major recent works on Babe Ruth by Jane Leavy and Glenn Stout under fans' belts, the latest edition of *When Boston Still Had the Babe: The 1918 World Champion Red Sox,* edited by Bill Nowlin, should serve as a sort of *prequel* to the events in those other volumes. Leavy's *The Big Fella: Babe Ruth and the World He Created* and Stout's *The Selling of the Babe* contain entire eras within their covers. However, the third, edited by Bill Nowlin, captures a slice of Ruth's most pivotal season—1918. It demonstrates that that year was, at its worst, a most fascinating season for every player on the Boston Red Sox roster. This book's unique structure and focus on that one season earns it a spot on everyone's Babe Ruth bookshelf

When Boston Still Had the Babe, first published in 2008, was reissued late in 2018 for the 100-year anniversary of that Red Sox World Series win. The book has each chapter appearing as a standalone story of the 1918 season written by one of the 28 members of the Society for American Baseball Research. Through Bill Nowlin's skillful editing—and his authorship of some of the chapters—the book flows pleasingly through each player on the Red Sox that season. You get some of the same atmosphere in *When Boston Still Had the Babe,* as in the Leavy and Stout two works—for example, where Stout mentions that pitcher Ruth "took the mound as if the world was on his shoulders...."

But the Nowlin-edited book in some ways is not even committed to focusing on Ruth. Instead, *When Boston Still Had the Babe* presents detailed reports on all 32 players for the 1918 Red Sox, written by 28 Society for American Baseball Research members. Several of the players had their only major league appearances during this wartime season.

One, infielder Red Bluhm, got one pinch-hit appearance the entire sea-

Base Ball 12, pp. 268–270
ISSN 1934-2802 (Print) / ISSN 1934-3167 (Online)
978-1-4766-7473-5 (Print) / 978-1-4766-4112-6 (ebook)

son, a popup. After that, he never appeared in the majors and eventually went to work for Buick. It was the Babe who convinced the manager to keep Bluhm on the bench for what would prove his only chance ever to start in the major leagues.

When manager Ed Barrow explained that Stuffy McGinnis, the regular first baseman, was out for medical reasons, Ruth insisted he should play first base. Barrow agreed.

Another odd roster spot went to switch-hitting second baseman Frank Truesdale. He made the starting roster in a *Baseball Magazine* article naming the worst fielding team. Contributing author Jim Elfers writes that Truesdale's .914 fielding percentage of the 1918 season remains the lowest fielding percentage for a major league second baseman appearing in more the 100 games. He led the league in 1918 with 56 errors.

These unlikely bench players and forgotten journeymen found their small entry into the story of the Boston Red Sox 1918 World Series. But the heroes of the season get their stories told, as well. One of those heroes, utility infielder Fred Thomas, appeared in 44 games. He hit only one home run, but his successful pursuit of a foul flyout in one game ensured a no-hitter for Dutch Leonard. Craig Lammers reports that Thomas followed baseball religiously after retirement, although he never fell in love with the modern game. He described today's gloves as *bushel baskets* and declared that because of the gloves' size no fielder should have a ball get by them. Among other Red Sox heroes of 1918 is first baseman Stuffy McGinnis. In Game One of the World Series it was McGinnis who singled in the only run of a shutout win for pitcher Babe Ruth. He scored the deciding run of World Series Game Three on a squeeze bunt. As for fielding, McGinnis was a factor in three double plays in Game Four.

With its unique profiling of each player on the roster, *When Boston Still Had the Babe* brings readers to a dimension well beyond its claim as a work of history. It brings team members to life and raises readers to a new plateau of understanding.

When descendants of those players answered a Boston Red Sox invitation in 1993 for the 75th anniversary celebration of the 1918 World Series win, Fred Thomas' son, Warren, took the field on behalf of his dad. (Fred had passed away in 1986, the last survivor of the team.) The younger Thomas described the experience as "quite a thrill to walk around third base where my father played in 1918."

This book allows the readers a dimension of the same thrill.

—**Chuck Wharton** worked as a sports and news reporter in both radio and news services before settling into a 32-year career in corporate communications. He continues reporting play-by-play in baseball and other sports. He also writes about soccer for MLSMultiplex.com, one of the family of FanSided.com sites. He works as a district government property appraiser near Houston, Texas.

About the Contributors

Art **Ahrens**, a long-time baseball historian and a SABR member, lives in Chicago. He is the author or co-author of several books, including *The Cubs: The Complete Record of Chicago Cubs Baseball*. His articles have appeared in the *Baseball Research Journal*, *The National Pastime*, *Baseball Digest*, and *Chicago History*, among other publications.

Jack **Bales** is the author of *Before They Were the Cubs: The Early Years of Chicago's First Professional Baseball Team* and has published articles in *NINE* and the *Baseball Research Journal*. He has been the reference and humanities librarian at the University of Mary Washington in Fredericksburg, Virginia, since 1980.

James E. **Brunson** III is an art historian who specializes in American modernism. He is author of the three-volume work *Black Baseball, 1858–1900* as well as *The Early Image of Black Baseball: Race and Representation in the Popular Press, 1871–1890*. His essays and articles have appeared in *The Negro Leagues Were Major Leagues* and in the journals *NINE*, *Base Ball*, and *Black Ball*. A practicing artist who specializes in watercolor painting, he taught at Northern Illinois University.

Thomas W. **Gilbert** is the author of many baseball books, including *Baseball and the Color Line*, *Roberto Clemente*, and *Playing First*. Living in Brooklyn, New York, baseball's birthplace as a modern sport, he plays pickup softball, goes target shooting, socializes with firefighters, and is active in local politics. He aspires to be buried in Green-Wood Cemetery.

Craig **G. Greenham** is an assistant professor in the Department of Kinesiology at the University of Windsor (Canada). His writing appears in such publications as the *International Journal of the History of Sport*, the *Journal of Sport History*, and *Sport History Review*. He also writes essays for *The Allrounder* and is a frequent media source, nationally and internationally, on matters of sport. His interest in baseball stems from his childhood watching the Toronto Blue Jays and Montreal Expos of the 1980s.

Base Ball 12, pp. 271–273
ISSN 1934-2802 (Print) / ISSN 1934-3167 (Online)
978-1-4766-7473-5 (Print) / 978-1-4766-4112-6 (ebook)

About the Contributors

Brock E. **Helander** is the author of four books on the history of rock 'n' roll, most notably *The Rock Who's Who*. He has researched 19th-century baseball since joining SABR in 2002, and his articles have appeared in the *Baseball Research Journal*, *The National Pastime*, SABR's BioProject, and *Base Ball: A Journal of the Early Game*.

Don **Jensen**, editor of *Base Ball* and a longtime SABR member, is the author of *Timeline History of Baseball* and a contributing author to numerous other publications, including SABR's *Deadball Stars of the National League* and *Deadball Stars of the American League*. His research focuses on the sporting life in the Gilded Age and the histories of the Giants (in New York and San Francisco) and San Francisco Seals. A former U.S. diplomat, he is a senior fellow and editor in chief at the Center for European Policy Analysis and an adjunct professor at Johns Hopkins University. He lives in Alexandria, Virginia.

David **Kathman** lives in Chicago, Illinois, where he works for Morningstar as a mutual fund analyst. He has written many scholarly articles on linguistics, Shakespeare, and Elizabethan theater history over the past 30 years. He has a longtime interest in early baseball history.

Bill **Lamb** is the editor of *The Inside Game*, the quarterly newsletter for the SABR Deadball Era Committee, and the author of *Black Sox in the Courtroom*. A retired New Jersey prosecutor, he lives with his wife Barbara in Meredith, New Hampshire.

Eric **Miklich** is a member of SABR's Nineteenth Century Committee and the historian for the Vintage Base Ball Association (VBBA). He is the owner of 19cbaseball.com and coauthored, with David Nemec, *Forfeits and Successfully Protested Games in Major League Baseball*. He has appeared in more than 900 vintage base ball matches since 1998 and as a pitcher has won over 400 games. He plays for the Brooklyn Eckfords and lives in Islip, New York.

David **Nemec** is the author of *The Great Encyclopedia of Nineteenth Century Major League Baseball*, *The Beer and Whisky League*, *The Great Baseball Team Book*, *Mad Blood*, *The Official Rules of Baseball Illustrated*, *Early Dreams*, *The Picture Maker*, *Major League Baseball Profiles: 1871–1900*, and many other novels and works on baseball. He has won numerous baseball research awards and SABR national baseball trivia contests. He lives in Laguna Woods, California.

Bill **Scheeren** holds a Ph.D. from the University of Pittsburgh in information science. He is a retired educator, having spent 32 years with the Hempfield Area School District, and a Vietnam veteran. He is the author of three college textbooks that deal with educational technology and is an adjunct instructor at both the University of Phoenix and St. Vincent College in Latrobe, Pennsylvania.

John **Thorn** is the official historian of Major League Baseball, as well as the founding editor of *Base Ball: A Journal of the Early Game*. He has written *The Hidden Game of Baseball* (with Pete Palmer), *Baseball in the Garden of Eden*, and, since 1974, many other books.

Peter **Weil** is an emeritus associate professor of anthropology at the University of

Delaware. His research focus has always been material culture, and he spent much of his career working on African art, ritual, and political power in Gambia and Senegal. About 20 years ago, he became interested in typewriters and their role in the creation of industrial societies in the 19th and 20th centuries. He began a quarterly column in the *ETCetera* magazine in 2006 and co-authored a book on the history of typewriters that was published in 2016.

Index

Numbers in **bold italics** indicate pages with photographs

Base Ball 12, pp. 275–285
ISSN 1934-2802 (Print) / ISSN 1934-3167 (Online)
978-1-4766-7473-5 (Print) / 978-1-4766-4112-6 (ebook)